What Works
on Wall Street

Other Books by James P. O'Shaughnessy

Invest Like the Best: Using Your Computer to Unlock the
Secrets of the Top Money Managers

What Works on Wall Street

A Guide to the Best-Performing Investment Strategies of All Time

James P. O'Shaughnessy

McGraw-Hill

New York   San Francisco   Washington, D.C.   Auckland   Bogotá
Caracas   Lisbon   London   Madrid   Mexico City   Milan
Montreal   New Delhi   San Juan   Singapore
Sydney   Tokyo   Toronto

Library of Congress Cataloging-in-Publication Data

O'Shaughnessy, James P.
    What works on Wall Street : a guide to the best-performing investment strategies
    of all time / James P. O'Shaughnessy.
       p.   cm.
    Includes bibliographical references and index.
    ISBN 0-07-047985-2
    1. Investments—United States. 2. Investment analysis—United States. I. Title.
HG4910.0828 1996
332.6—dc20   96-20365
                                                                CIP

McGraw-Hill

A Division of The McGraw·Hill Companies

Copyright © 1997 by James P. O'Shaughnessy. All rights reserved.
Printed in the United States of America. Except as permitted under the
United States Copyright Act of 1976, no part of this publication may be
reproduced or distributed in any form or by any means, or stored in a
data base or retrieval system, without the prior written permission of the
publisher.

    4 5 6 7 8 9 0 DOC/DOC 9 0 1 0 9 8 7 6

ISBN 0-07-047985-2

*The sponsoring editor for this book was David Conti, the editing supervisor was
Patricia V. Amoroso, and the production supervisor was Suzanne Rapcavage. It
was set in Palatino by Renee Lipton of McGraw-Hill's Professional Book Group
composition unit.*

Printed and bound by R. R. Donnelley & Sons Company.

This publication is designed to provide accurate and authoritative information
in regard to the subject matter covered. It is sold with the understanding that the
publisher is not engaged in rendering legal, accounting, or other professional
service. If legal advice or other expert assistance is required, the services of a
competent professional person should be sought.
                     *—From a declaration of principles jointly adopted by a committee
                        of the American Bar Association and a committee of publishers.*

 This book is printed on recycled, acid-free paper containing a
minimum of 50% recycled de-inked fiber.

McGraw-Hill books are available at special quantity discounts to use as
premiums and sales promotions, or for use in corporate training pro-
grams. For more information, please write to the Director of Special Sales,
McGraw-Hill, 11 West 19th Street, New York, NY 10011. Or contact your
local bookstore.

To Lael, Kathryn, Patrick, and Melissa

Wait for the wisest of all counselors, Time.

—Pericles

Contents

Preface

The more original a discovery, the more obvious it seems afterward. —ARTHUR KOESTLER

Patrick Henry was right when he proclaimed that the only way to judge the future was by the past. To make the best investment plans for the future, investors need access to unbiased, long-term performance results. It doesn't matter if they are aggressive investors seeking fast growth or conservative investors seeking low-risk, high-yielding stocks for their retirement account. Knowing how a particular investment strategy performed historically gives you the vital information you need on its risk, variability, and persistence of returns. Access to long-term performance results lets you make informed choices, based on facts, not hype.

This book offers readers the first long-term studies of Wall Street's most popular investment strategies. To date, there is no widely available, comprehensive guide to which strategies are long-term winners and which are not. While there *are* many studies covering short periods of time, *What Works on Wall Street* is the first all-inclusive, definitive guide to the long-term efficacy of Wall Street's favorite investment strategies.

All the tests in this book use Standard & Poor's Compustat database, the largest, most comprehensive database of United States stock market information available. This is the *first* time the historical S&P Compustat data have been released in their entirety to an outside researcher. *What Works on Wall Street* includes 43 years of results for Wall Street's most popular investment strategies.

Origins

It took the combination of fast computers and huge databases like Compustat to prove that a portfolio's returns are essentially determined by the factors that define the portfolio. Before computers, it was almost impossible to determine what strategy guided the development of a portfolio. The number of underlying factors (characteristics that define a portfolio, like PE ratio and dividend yield) that an investor could consider seemed endless. The best you could do was look at portfolios in the most general ways. Sometimes even a *professional manager* didn't know what particular factors best characterized the stocks in his or her portfolio, relying more often on general descriptions and other qualitative measures.

The computer changed this. We can now analyze a portfolio and see which factors, if any, separate the best-performing strategies from the mediocre. With computers, we can also test combinations of factors over long periods of time, showing us what to expect in the future from any given investment strategy.

Most Strategies Are Mediocre

What Works on Wall Street shows that most investment strategies are mediocre and that the majority, *particularly those most appealing to investors over the short term*, fail to beat the simple strategy of indexing to the S&P 500. The book also provides evidence which disproves the academic theory that stock prices follow a "random walk."

Rather than moving about without rhyme or reason, the stock market methodically rewards certain investment strategies while punishing others. *What Works on Wall Street*'s 43 years of returns show there's nothing random about long-term stock market returns. Investors can do *much better* than the market if they consistently use time-tested strategies that are based on sensible, rational methods for selecting stocks.

Discipline Is Key

What Works on Wall Street shows that the only way to beat the market over the long term is to use sensible investment strategies consistently.

Eighty percent of the mutual funds covered by Morningstar fail to beat the S&P 500 because their managers lack the discipline to stick with one strategy through thick and thin. This lack of discipline devastates long-term performance.

Highlights

After reading *What Works on Wall Street*, investors will know the following:

- Most small-capitalization strategies owe their superior returns to micro-cap stocks with market capitalizations below $25 million. These stocks are too small for virtually any investor to buy.
- Buying low price-to-earnings ratio stocks is very profitable *only* if you stick to larger, better-known issues.
- Price-to-sales ratio is the best value ratio to use for buying market-beating stocks.
- Last year's biggest losers are the *worst* stocks you can buy.
- Last year's earnings gains alone are *worthless* when determining if a stock is a good investment.
- Using several factors dramatically improves long-term performance.
- You can do four times as well as the S&P 500 by concentrating on large, well-known stocks with high dividend yields.
- Relative strength is the only growth variable that consistently beats the market.
- Buying Wall Street's current darlings with the highest price-to-earnings ratios is one of the *worst* things you can do.
- A strategy's risk is one of the most important elements to consider.
- Uniting growth and value strategies is the best way to improve your investment performance.

Acknowledgments

This book would not have been possible without the help of many people. When I started the project several years ago, Jim Branscome, then head of S&P Compustat, was a champion of the project at every turn. His successor, Paul Cleckner, has also been extraordinarily supportive and is an outstanding example of a businessman who understands that the best way to help the bottom line of your business is to help the bottom line of thousands of ordinary investors. Thanks also to Bill Griffis, who did all the programming that allowed our computers to use data from Compustat's mainframe.

This book would not have been finished without the continual help, support, and encouragement of two people. The first is my wife, Melissa. I am extremely indebted to her for editing every line in this book. Her many talents came in especially handy in editing and rewriting the manuscript. Without her expert hand, this book might never have been finished. In addition to loving her dearly, I owe any success I have as an author to her.

The second is Steven Johansen, a specialist in the Compustat PC Plus product used for these tests. Going above and beyond his duty, Steve gave many hours of his personal time to ensure that the tests in this book had the highest integrity possible. He was always ready with wit, help, and advice to ensure that every test was designed in the most thorough, intelligent fashion. Steve has become a good friend, and I owe him the greatest gratitude for seeing the project through to the end.

Thanks also to the staff at my office—Cheryl Clifford, Jennifer Donofrio, and Susan Rizzi—for putting up with me while writing this book.

James P. O'Shaughnessy

What Works
on Wall Street

1

Stock Investment Strategies: Different Methods, Similar Goals

Good intelligence is nine-tenths of any battle.
—NAPOLEON

There are two main approaches to equity investing: active and passive. The active approach is most common. Here, managers attempt to maximize their returns at various levels of risk by buying stocks they believe are superior to others. Usually the managers follow similar routes to investigating a stock. They analyze the company, interview management, talk to customers and competitors, review historical trends and current forecasts, and then decide if the stock is worth buying.

Active investors are guided by styles, broadly called *growth* and *value*. What type of stock they buy depends largely on their underlying philosophy. Growth investors buy stocks that have higher-than-average growth in sales and earnings with expectations for more of the same. A classic growth stock's earnings just keep getting better and better. Growth investors believe in a company's potential and think a stock's price will follow its earnings higher.

Value investors seek stocks with current market values substantially below true or liquidating value. They use factors like price-to-earnings ratios and price-to-sales ratios to identify when a stock is selling below its intrinsic value. They bargain-hunt, looking for companies whose assets they can buy for 70 cents on the dollar. Value investors believe in a company's balance sheet, thinking a stock's price will eventually rise to meet its intrinsic value.

Many times actively managed funds use a hodgepodge of techniques from both schools of investing, but the most successful have strongly articulated strategies. The majority of mutual funds, professionally managed pension funds, and individual accounts are managed with an active approach.

Traditional Active Management Doesn't Work

This makes perfect sense until you review the record of traditional, actively managed funds. The majority do not beat the S&P 500. This is true over both short and long time periods. Figure 1-1 shows the percentage of actively managed mutual funds in Morningstar's database that beat the Vanguard Index 500, Vanguard's S&P 500 index fund. The *best* 10 years, ending December 31, 1994, saw only 26 percent of the traditionally managed active mutual funds beating the index. When you dig deeper and look at the percentage by which they beat the index, the news gets worse. As Figure 1-2 shows, of the 121 funds beating the Vanguard Index for the 10 years ending September 30, 1995, only 38 percent of the winning funds managed to beat the index by more than 2 percent a year on a compound basis.

What's more, this record *overstates* traditionally managed active funds' performances, since it doesn't include all the funds that failed to survive the 10 years.

Passive indexing has exploded in the past decade as a result. Here, investors buy an index they think broadly represents the market, such as the S&P 500, and let it go at that. Their objective is to match the market, not outperform it. They are willing to give up their shot at outperforming the market for the security of not underperforming it. Driven by the disappointing results of traditionally managed portfolios, index fund managers have seen their assets soar, from $10 billion in 1980 to over $250 billion in 1990, with estimates that index funds will account for more than half of all pension plan holdings by the end of the century. The pension plans lead the way, but retail investors are right on their heels.

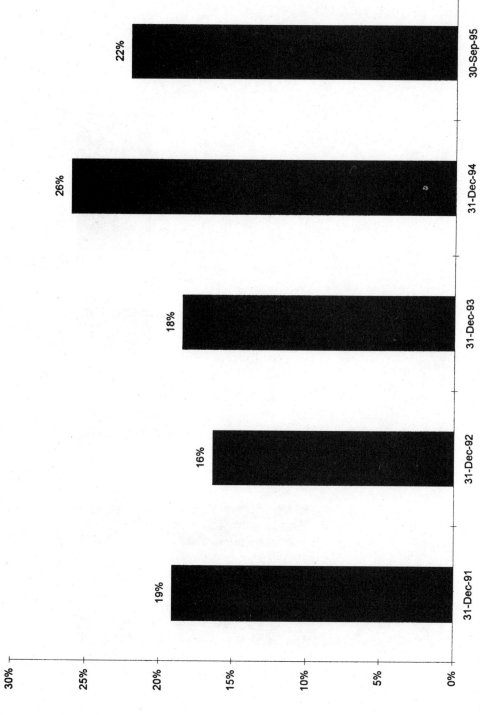

Figure 1-1. Percent of all equity funds with 10-year track records beating the Vanguard Index 500 for the 10 years ending each date. (Source: *Morningstar OnDisc*)

Figure 1-2. Relative performance of the 121 equity mutual funds beating the Vanguard Index 500 for the 10 years ending September 30, 1995. (Source: *Morningstar OnDisc*)

4

What's the Problem?

Academics aren't surprised that traditionally managed funds fail to beat the market. Most have long held that markets are efficient and that current security prices reflect all available information. They argue that prices follow a "random walk" and move without rhyme or reason. According to their theories, you might as well have a monkey throw darts at a stock page as attempt analysis, since stock prices are random and cannot be predicted.

The long-term evidence in this book contradicts the random walk theory. Far from stocks following a random walk, the evidence reveals a purposeful stride. The 43 years of data found in this book prove strong return predictability. The market clearly and consistently rewards certain attributes (e.g., stocks with low price-to-sales ratios) and clearly and consistently punishes others (e.g., stocks with high price-to-sales ratios) over long periods of time. Yet the paradox remains: If the tests show such high return predictability, why do 80 percent of traditionally managed mutual funds fail to beat the S&P 500?

Finding exploitable investment opportunities does not mean it's easy to make money, however. To do so requires an ability to consistently, patiently, and slavishly stick with a strategy, even when it's performing poorly relative to other methods. Few are capable of such action. Successful investors do not comply with nature; they defy it. In the next chapter I argue that the reason traditional management doesn't work well is that human decision making is *systematically flawed and unreliable.* The door is open to those who use a rational, disciplined method to buy and sell stocks on the basis of time-tested methods.

Studying the Wrong Things

It's no surprise that academics find traditionally managed stock portfolios following a "random walk." Most traditional managers' past records cannot predict future returns because their behavior is inconsistent. You cannot make forecasts on the basis of inconsistent behavior, because when you behave inconsistently, you are unpredictable. Even if a manager is a perfectly consistent investor—a hallmark of the best money managers—if *that* manager leaves the fund, all predictive ability from past performance is lost. Moreover, if a manager changes his or her style, all predictive ability from past performance is also lost. Academics, therefore, have been measuring the *wrong* things. They assume perfect, rational behavior in a capricious environment ruled by greed, hope, and fear. They have been contrasting the returns of a passively held portfolio—the S&P 500—with the returns of portfolios managed in an inconsistent, shoot-from-the-hip style. Track records are worthless unless you know what strategy the manager uses and if it is *still* being used. When you study a traditionally managed fund, you're really looking at two things: first, the strategy used and second, the ability of the manager to implement it successfully. It makes much more sense to contrast the one-factor S&P 500 portfolio with *other* one or multifactor portfolios.

Why Indexing Works

Indexing to the S&P 500 works because it sidesteps flawed decision making and automates the simple strategy of buying the big stocks that make up the S&P 500. The mighty S&P 500 consistently beats 80 percent of traditionally managed funds by doing nothing more than making a disciplined bet on large-capitalization stocks. Figure 1-3 compares the returns on the S&P 500 with those for our Large Stocks universe, which consists of all the stocks in the Compustat database with market capitalizations greater than the database mean in any given year. This effectively limits us to the top 16 percent of the Compustat database by market capitalization. Stocks are then bought in equal dollar amounts. The returns are virtually identical: $10,000 invested in the S&P 500 on December 31, 1951, was worth $1,027,828 on December 31, 1994. The same $10,000 invested in our Large Stock universe was worth $1,042,859, a mere $15,000 difference. (Both include the reinvestment of all dividends.) And it's not just the absolute returns that are similar—risk, as measured by the standard deviation of return, is also virtually identical for the two strategies. The S&P 500 had an annual standard deviation of return of 16.56 percent, whereas the deviation for the Large Stocks universe was 16.18 percent.

Indexing to the S&P 500 is just *one* form of passive implementation of a strategy. Buying the 10 highest-yielding stocks in the Dow Jones Industrial Average each year is another strategy that works consistently. I tested that strategy back to 1928 (when the Dow was expanded to 30 stocks) and found that it beat the S&P 500 in every decade, from the depressionary 1930s through the restructuring 1990s, and had only two 10-year rolling periods where it failed to beat the S&P 500. You'll find a number of other winning strategies in this book.

Pinpointing Performance

It took the combination of fast computers and huge databases like Compustat to prove that a portfolio's returns are essentially deter-

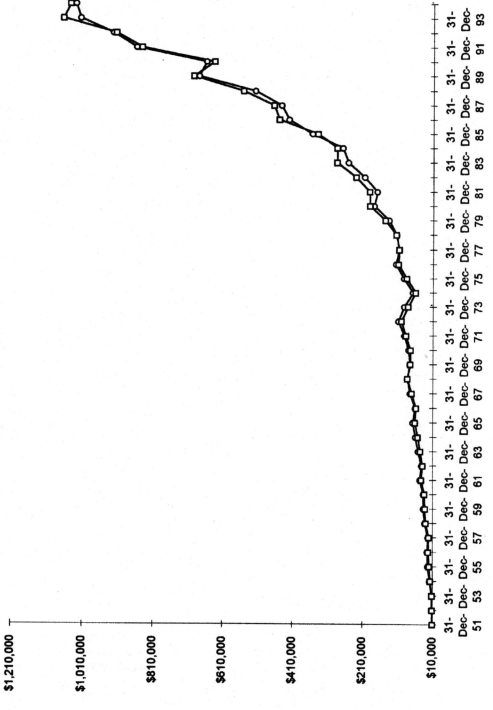

Figure 1-3. Comparative returns, December 31, 1951–December 31, 1994.
December 31, 1951 = $10,000.

mined by the factors that define the portfolio. Before computers, it was virtually impossible to determine what strategy guided the development of a portfolio. The number of underlying factors (characteristics that define a portfolio, like PE ratio and dividend yield) that an investor could consider seemed endless. The best you could do was look at portfolios in the most general ways. Sometimes even a *professional manager* didn't know what particular factors best characterized the stocks in his or her portfolio, relying more often on general descriptions and other qualitative measures. The computer changed this. We can now quickly analyze the factors that define any portfolio and see which, if any, separate the best-performing funds and strategies from the mediocre. With computers, we can also test combinations of factors over long periods of time, showing us what to expect in the future from any given investment strategy.

Discipline Is the Key

If you use a one-factor model based on market capitalization—like the two mentioned above—you get the same results. If, however, you change a portfolio's underlying factors so that they deviate significantly from the S&P 500, say by keeping price-to-sales ratios below 1 or dividend yields above a certain number, you can expect that portfolio to perform differently than the market. S&P 500 index funds are nothing more than *structured portfolios* that make disciplined bets on a large capitalization factor. *Many other factors perform much better.* Structured investing is a hybrid of active and passive management that automates buy and sell decisions. If a stock meets the criteria, it's bought. If not, not. No personal, emotional judgments enter the process. Disciplined implementation of active strategies is the key to performance. Traditional managers usually follow a hit-and-miss approach to investing. Their lack of discipline accounts for their inability to beat simple approaches that *never vary* from their methods.

Consistency Wins

In a study for my book *Invest Like the Best*, I found the *one* thing uniting the best managers is consistency. I'm not alone. In the 1970s, AT&T did a study of its pension fund managers and found that successful investing required, at a minimum, a structured decision-making process that can be easily defined and a stated investment philosophy that is consistently applied. John Neff of the Windsor fund and Peter Lynch of Magellan became legends because their success was the result of slavish devotion to their investment strategies.

A Structured Portfolio in Action

Very few funds or managers stick with their strategies for long periods of time. One that did, the Lexington Corporate Leaders Trust, is most unusual because it's a structured portfolio in action. Formed in 1935, the trust was designed to hold 30 stocks that were leaders in their industries. The fund's portfolio is *share-weighted,* holding the same number of shares in each company regardless of price. Since 1935, 7 companies have been eliminated, so the fund currently holds 23 stocks. Yet this single-factor portfolio is a market slayer—between January 1, 1976, and September 30, 1995, $10,000 invested in the fund grew to $149,863, a compound return of 14.62 percent a year. That beat both the S&P 500's return of 14.32 percent and all but 15 percent of traditionally managed funds. More, the trust's charter prevents rebalancing the portfolio, which would allow it to reflect changes in corporate leaders. Imagine how it would have performed if it bought today's leaders like Microsoft and Intel! Indeed, a structured strategy like the high-yielding Dow approach mentioned earlier, where you are allowed to refresh the stocks every year, posted *much better* returns. There, $10,000 invested on January 1, 1976, was worth $230,412, a compound return of 16.98 percent.

Overwhelmed by Our Nature

Knowing and doing are two very different things. As Goethe said, "In the realm of ideas, everything depends on enthusiasm; in the real world, all rests on perseverance." While we may *understand* what we should do, we usually are overwhelmed by our nature, allowing the intensely emotional present to overpower our better judgment. When someone questioned Gorbachev about actions he had taken against his better judgment, he replied, "Your question is academic because it is abstract. People don't have the luxury of living in the abstract. They live in the real, emotional, full-blooded world of reality."

It is in the full-blooded world of reality that our problems begin, for both investors and other professions. Let's see why this is so.

2

The Unreliable Experts: Getting in the Way of Outstanding Performance

What ails the truth is that it is mainly uncomfortable, and often dull. The human mind seeks something more amusing, and more caressing.　　　　　　—H. L. MENCKEN

Everyone is guilty of faulty decision making, not just the scions of Wall Street. An accountant must offer an opinion on the creditworthiness of a firm. A university administrator must decide which students to accept into a graduate program. A psychologist must decide if a patient's ills are neurosis or psychosis. A doctor must decide if it's liver cancer or not. More prosaically, a bookie tries to handicap the next horse race.

All these are activities for which an expert predicts an outcome. They occur every day and make up the fabric of our lives. Generally, there are two ways to make predictions. Most common is for a person to run through a variety of possible outcomes in his or her head, essentially relying on knowledge, experience, and common sense to reach a decision. This is known as a "clinical" or intuitive approach, and is the way traditional active money managers make choices. The stock analyst may pore over a company's financial statements; interview management; talk to customers and competitors; and finally try to make an overall forecast. The graduate school administrator might use a host of data, from college grade point average to interviews with applicants, to determine if students should be accepted. This type of judgment relies on the perceptiveness of the forecaster.

The other way to reach a decision is the actuarial, or quantitative, approach. Here, the forecaster makes no subjective judgments. Empirical relationships between the data and the desired outcome are used to reach conclusions. This method relies solely on proven relationships using large samples of data. It's similar to the structured process I described in Chapter 1. The graduate school administrator might use a model that finds college grade point average highly correlated to graduate school success and admit only those who have made a certain grade. In almost every instance, from stock analysts to doctors, we naturally prefer qualitative, intuitive methods. In most instances, we're wrong.

Human Judgment Is Limited

David Faust writes in his revolutionary book *The Limits of Scientific Reasoning:* "Human judgment is far more limited than we think. We have a surprisingly restricted capacity to manage or interpret complex information." Studying a wide range of professionals, from medical doctors making diagnoses to experts making predictions of job success in academic or military training, Faust found that *human judges were consistently outperformed by simple actuarial models.* Like traditional money managers, most professionals cannot beat the passive implementation of time-tested formulas.

Another researcher, Paul Meehl, offered the first comprehensive review of statistical prediction (similar to a structured approach) and clinical prediction (similar to an intuitive, traditional approach) in his 1954 study *Clinical Versus Statistical Prediction: A Theoretical Analysis and Review of the Literature.* He reviewed 20 studies that compared clinical and statistical predictions for academic success, response to electroshock therapy, and criminal recidivism. In almost every instance, Meehl found that simple actuarial models outperformed the human judges. In predicting academic success in college, for example, a model using just high school grade point average and the level attained on an aptitude test outperformed the judgments of admissions officers at several colleges.

Robyn Dawes, in his book *House of Cards: Psychology and Psychotherapy Built on Myth*, tells us more. He refers to Jack Sawyer, a researcher who published a review of 45 studies comparing the two forecasting techniques: In *none* was the clinical, intuitive method—the one favored by most people—found to be superior. What's more, Sawyer included instances where the human judges had more information than the model *and* were given the results of the quantitative models *before* being asked for a prediction. *The human judges still failed to beat the actuarial models!*

Psychology researcher L. R. Goldberg went further. He devised a simple model based on the results of the Minnesota Multiphasic Personality Inventory (MMPI), a personality test commonly used to distinguish between neurosis and psychosis, to determine into which category a patient falls. His test achieved a success rate of 70 percent. He found that no human experts could match his model's results. The *best* judge achieved an overall success ratio of 67 percent. Reasoning that his human judges might do better with practice, he gave training packets consisting of 300 additional MMPI profiles to his judges along with immediate feedback on their accuracy. Even after the practice sessions, *none* of the human judges matched the model's success ratio of 70 percent.

What's the Problem?

The problem doesn't seem to be lack of insight on the part of human judges. One study of pathologists predicting survival time following the initial diagnosis of Hodgkin's disease, a form of cancer, found that the human judges were vastly outperformed by a simple actuarial formula. Oddly, the model used criteria that the judges *said* were predictive to outperform them. *The judges were largely unable to use their own ideas properly.* They used perceptive, intelligent criteria, but were unable to take advantage of the predictive ability of their ideas. The judges themselves, not the value of their insights, accounted for their dismal predictive performance.

Why Models Beat Humans

In a famous cartoon, Pogo says: "We've met the enemy, and he is us." This illustrates our dilemma. Models beat human forecasters because they reliably and consistently apply the same criteria time after time. In almost every instance, *it is the total reliability of application of the model that accounts for its superior performance.* Models never vary. They are always consistent. They are never moody, never fight with their spouse, are *never* hung over from a night on the town, and *never get bored.* They don't favor vivid, interesting stories over reams of statistical data. They never take anything personally. They don't have egos. They're not out to prove anything. If they were people, they'd be the death of any party.

People, on the other hand, are far more interesting. It's more natural to react emotionally or personalize a problem than it is to dispassionately review broad statistical occurrences—and so much more fun! We are a bundle of inconsistencies, and while that may make us interesting, it plays havoc with our ability to invest our money successfully. In most instances, money managers, like the college administrators, doctors, and accountants mentioned above, favor the intuitive method of forecasting. They all follow the same path: Analyze the company, interview the management, talk to customers and competitors, and so on. *All* of them think they have superior insights, intelligence, and ability to pick winning stocks, yet 80 percent of them are routinely outperformed by the S&P 500.

Base Rates Are Boring

The majority of investors, as well as *anyone else using traditional, intuitive forecasting methods,* are overwhelmed by their human nature. They use information unreliably, one time including a stock in a portfolio and another time excluding it, even though in each instance the information is the same. Our decision making is systematically flawed because we prefer gut reactions and individual, colorful stories to boring base rates. Base rates are among the most illuminating statistics that exist. They're just like batting averages. For example, if a town of 100,000 people has 70,000 lawyers and 30,000 librarians, the base rate for lawyers in that town is 70 percent. When used in the stock market, base rates tell you what to expect from a certain *class* of stocks (e.g., all stocks with high dividend yields) and what that variable *generally* predicts for the future. But base rates tell you *nothing* about how each *individual* member of that class will behave.

Most statistical prediction techniques use base rates. Some 75 percent of students with grade point averages above 3.5 go on to do well in graduate school. Smokers are twice as likely to get cancer. Stocks with low price-to-earnings ratios outperform the market 65 percent of the time. The best way to predict the future is to bet with the base rate that is derived from a large sample. Yet numerous studies have found that people make full use of base rate information *only* when there is a lack of descriptive data. In one example, people are told that out of a sample of 100 people, 70 are lawyers and 30 are engineers. When provided with no additional information and asked to guess the occupation of a randomly selected 10, people use the base rate information, saying 7 are lawyers and 3 are engineers.

However, when worthless yet descriptive data are added, such as "Dick is a highly motivated 30-year-old married man who is well liked by his colleagues," people largely *ignore* the base rate information in favor of their "feel" for the person. They are *certain* that their unique insights will help them make a better forecast, even when the additional information is meaningless. We prefer descriptive data to impersonal statistics because the data better represent our individual experience. When stereotypical information is added, such as "Dick is 30 years old, is married, shows no interest in politics or social issues, and likes to spend free time on his many hobbies, which include carpentry and mathematical puzzles," people *totally* ignore the base rate and bet Dick is an engineer, despite the 70 percent chance that he is a lawyer.

It's difficult to blame people. Base rates are boring; experience is vivid and fun. The only way anyone will pay 100 times a company's earnings for a stock is if it's got a tremendous story. Never mind that stocks with high price-to-earnings ratios beat the market just 35 percent of the time over the last 43 years—the story is so compelling you're happy to throw the base rates out the window.

The Individual Versus the Group

Human nature makes it virtually impossible to forgo the specific information of an individual case in favor of the results of a great number of cases. We're interested in *this stock* and *this company*, not in this class of stocks or this class of companies. Large numbers mean nothing to us. As Stalin chillingly said: "One death is a tragedy, a million, a statistic." When making an investment, we almost always do so on a stock-by-stock basis, rarely thinking about an overall strategy. If a story about *one* stock is compelling enough, we're willing to ignore what the base rate tells us about an entire class of stocks.

Imagine if the insurance industry made decisions on a case-by-case basis. An agent visits you at home, interviews you, and checks out your spouse and children, finally making a judgment on the basis of his or her *gut feelings*. How many people who *should* get coverage would be denied and how many millions of dollars in premiums would be lost? The reverse is also true. Someone who should be denied might be extended coverage because the agent's gut feeling was that *this* individual is different, despite what actuarial tests say. The company would lose millions in additional payouts.

The same thing happens when we think in terms of individual stocks, rather than strategies. A case-by-case approach wreaks havoc with returns, since it virtually guarantees that we will base many of our choices on emotions. This is a highly unreliable, unsystematic way to buy stocks, yet it's the most natural and the most common.

Personal Experience Preferred

We always place more reliance on personal experience than impersonal base rates. An excellent example is the 1972 presidential campaign. The reporters on the campaign trail with George McGovern unanimously agreed that he could not lose by more than 10 percent, even though they knew that he lagged 20 percent in the polls and that no major poll had been wrong by more than 3 percent in 24 years. These tough, intelligent people bet against the base rate because the concrete evidence of their personal experience overwhelmed them. They saw huge crowds of supporters, felt their enthusiasm, and trusted their feelings. In much the same way, a market analyst who has visited a company and knows the president may ignore the statistical information that indicates a company is a poor investment. In social science terms, the analyst is overweighting the vivid and underweighting the pallid statistics.

Simple Versus Complex

We also prefer the complex and artificial to the simple and unadorned. We are certain that investment success requires an incredibly complex ability to judge a host of variables correctly and then act upon that knowledge.

Professor Alex Bavelas designed a fascinating experiment in which two subjects, Smith and Jones, face individual projection screens. They cannot see or communicate with each other. They're told that the purpose of the experiment is to learn to recognize the difference between healthy and sick cells. They must learn to distinguish between the two using trial and error. In front of each are two buttons marked Healthy and Sick, along with two signal lights marked Right and Wrong. Every time a slide is projected they guess if it's healthy or sick by pressing the button so marked. After they guess, their signal light will flash Right or Wrong, informing them if they have guessed correctly.

Here's the hitch. Smith gets true feedback. If he's correct, his light flashes Right; if he's wrong, it flashes Wrong. Since he's getting true feedback, Smith soon gets around 80 percent correct, since it's a matter of simple discrimination.

Jones's situation is entirely different. He doesn't get true feedback on his guesses. Rather, the feedback he gets is based on Smith's guesses! It doesn't matter if he's right or wrong about a particular slide, he's told he's right if Smith guessed right and wrong if Smith guessed wrong. Of course, Jones doesn't know this. He's been told there is a true order that he can discover from the feedback. He ends up searching for order when there is no way to find it.

The moderator then asks Smith and Jones to discuss the rules they use for judging healthy and sick cells. Smith, who got true feedback, offers rules that are simple, concrete, and to the point. Jones, on the other hand, uses rules that are, out of necessity, subtle, complex, and highly adorned. After all, he had to base his opinions on contradictory guesses and hunches.

The amazing thing is that Smith doesn't think Jones's explanations are absurd, crazy, or unnecessarily complicated. He's impressed by the "brilliance" of Jones's method and feels inferior and vulnerable because of the pedestrian simplicity of his own rules. The more complicated and ornate Jones's explanations, *the more likely they are to convince Smith.*

Before the next test with new slides, the two are asked to guess who will do better than the first time around. All Joneses and most Smiths say that Jones will. In fact, Jones shows no improvement at all. Smith, on the other hand, does significantly worse than he did the first time around, since he's now making guesses on the basis of the complicated rules he learned from Jones.

A Simple Solution

William of Ockham, a fourteenth-century Franciscan monk from the village of Ockham in Surrey, England, developed the "principle of parsimony," now called Ockham's Razor. For centuries it has been a guiding principle of modern science. Its axioms—such as "What can be done with fewer assumptions is done in vain with more," and "Entities are not to be multiplied without necessity"—boil down to this: Keep it simple, stupid. Ockham's Razor shows that most often, the simplest theory is the best.

This is also the key to successful investing. However, successful investing runs contrary to human nature. We make the simple complex, follow the crowd, fall in love with the story, let our emotions dictate decisions, buy and sell on tips and hunches, and approach each investment decision on a case-by-case basis, with no underlying consistency or strategy. When making decisions, we view everything in the present tense. And, since we time-weight information, we give the most recent the greatest import. It's extremely difficult *not* to make decisions this way. Think about the last time you really goofed. Time passes and you see: *What was I thinking! It's so obvious that I was wrong, why didn't I see it?* The mistake becomes obvious when you see the situation historically, drained of emotion and feeling. When the mistake was made, you had to contend with emotion. Emotion often wins, since as John Junor says, "An ounce of emotion is equal to a ton of facts."

This isn't a phenomenon reserved for the unsophisticated. Pension sponsors have access to the best research and talent that money can buy, yet are notorious for investing heavily in stocks just as bear markets begin, and for firing managers at the absolute bottom of their cycle. Institutional investors *say* they make decisions objectively and unemotionally, but they don't. The authors of the book *Fortune & Folly* found that while institutional investors' desks are cluttered with in-depth, analytical reports, the majority of pension executives select outside managers using gut feelings and keep managers with consistently poor performance simply because they have good personal relationships with them.

The path to achieving investment success is to study long-term results and find a strategy or group of strategies that make sense. Remember to consider risk (the standard deviation of return) and choose a level that is acceptable. *Then stay on the path.*

To succeed, let history guide you. Successful investors look at history. They understand and react to the present in terms of the past. Yesterday and tomorrow, as well as today, make up their *now.* Something as simple as looking at a strategy's best and worst years is a good example. Knowing the potential parameters of a strategy gives investors a tremendous advantage over the uninformed. If the maximum expected loss is 35 percent, and the strategy is down 15 percent, instead of panicking, an informed investor can feel happy that things aren't as bad as they could be. This knowledge tempers expectations and emotions, giving informed investors a *perspective* that acts as an emotional pressure valve. Thinking historically, they let what they *know* transcend what they *feel.* This is the only way to perform well.

This book gives perspective. It helps you understand that hills and valleys are part of every investment scheme and are to be expected, not feared. They tell you what to expect from various classes of stocks. Don't second-guess. Don't change your mind. Don't reject an individual stock—if it meets the criteria of your strategy—because you think *it* will do poorly. Don't try to outsmart. Looking over 43 years, you see that many strategies had periods in which they didn't do as well as the S&P 500, but also had many in which they did much better. Understand. See the long term and let it work. If you do, you're chance of succeeding is very high. If you don't, no amount of knowledge will save you and you'll find yourself with the 80 percent of underperformers and thinking: "What went wrong?"

3

Rules of the Game

It is amazing to reflect how little systematic knowledge Wall Street has to draw upon as regards the historical behavior of securities with defined characteristics. We do, of course, have charts showing the long-term price movements of stock groups and individual stocks. But there is no real classification here, except by type of business. Where is the continuous, ever-growing body of knowledge and technique handed down by the analysts of the past to those of the present and future? When we contrast the annals of medicine with those of finance, the paucity of our recorded and digested experience becomes a reproach. We lack the codified experience which will tell us whether codified experience is valuable or valueless. In the years to come we analysts must go to school to the older established disciplines. We must study their ways of amassing and scrutinizing facts and from this study develop methods of research suited to the peculiarities of our own field of work. —BEN GRAHAM
The father of securities analysis, 1946

We've made little progress since 1946. Many studies *have* found that smaller stocks (based on total market capitalization) do better than larger stocks; that stocks with low price-to-earnings ratios do better than stocks with high price-to-earnings ratios; that high-yielding stocks perform well; and so forth. Yet the time periods covered by most studies *remain* a reproach to the money management industry. Many tests are flawlessly designed, especially after criticism of early studies sent

researchers back to the drawing board to design more rigorous proce-
dures. In almost every instance, researchers seem to have followed
carefully thought out, reasonable plans. However, the time covered in
most studies is far too short to reach reasonable conclusions. Many
studies cover as little as 3 to 5 years, and many researchers believe a 5-
year track record is sufficient to judge a manager's abilities. But like
Alexander Pope's maxim that a little learning is a dangerous thing, too
little time gives investors extremely misleading information. One
respected researcher estimated that to make reasonable assumptions
about a strategy's validity (i.e., to assume it was 95 percent likely to be
statistically relevant), you would need more than 25 years of data.

Short Periods Are Valueless

Consider the "Soaring Sixties." The go-go growth managers of the era
switched stocks so fast they were called gunslingers. Performance was
the name of the game, and buying stocks with outstanding earnings
growth was the way to achieve it.

Now, look at how misleading a 5-year period can be. Between
December 31, 1963, and December 31, 1968, $10,000 invested in a port-
folio which annually bought the 50 stocks in the Compustat database
with the best 1-year earnings-per-share percentage gains soared to
almost $35,000 in value, a compound return of more than 28 percent a
year. That more than doubled the S&P 500's 10.16 percent annual
return, which saw $10,000 grow to just over $16,000. Unfortunately, the
strategy didn't fare so well over the next 5 years. It went on to *lose* over
half its value between 1968 and 1973, compared with a gain of 2 percent
for the S&P 500.

It's Different This Time

People want to believe the present is different from the past. Markets
are now computerized and block traders dominate. The individual
investors are gone and in their place sit huge mutual funds to which
they have given their money. Some people think these masters of
money make decisions differently, and believe that looking at how a
strategy performed in the 1950s or 1960s offers little insight into how it
will perform in the future.

But not much has really changed since Isaac Newton—a brilliant man
indeed—lost a fortune in the South Sea Trading Company bubble of
1720. Newton lamented that he could "calculate the motions of heav-

enly bodies but not the madness of men." Here lies the key to why basing investment decisions on long-term results is vital: The price of a stock is still determined by *people*. And as long as people let fear, greed, hope, and ignorance cloud their judgment, they will continue to misprice stocks and provide opportunities to those who rigorously use simple, time-tested strategies to pick stocks. Names change. Industries change. Styles come in and out of fashion, but the underlying characteristics that identify a good investment remain the same. A long view of returns is essential, because only the fullness of time uncovers basic relationships that short-term gyrations conceal. It also lets us analyze how the market responds to a large number of events, such as inflation, stock market crashes, stagflation, recessions, wars, and new discoveries. From the past the future flows. History never repeats *exactly*, but the same *types* of events continue to occur.

Anecdotal Evidence Is Not Enough

Investment advice bombards us from many directions with little to support it but anecdotal accounts. Many managers will give a handful of stocks as examples, demonstrating how well they went on to perform. Unfortunately, these managers conveniently ignore the many *other stocks* that also possessed the preferred characteristics but *failed*. We must look at how well *strategies*, not stocks, perform. There's often a chasm of difference between what we *think* might work and what *really* works. This book's goal is to bring a more methodical, scientific method to stock market decisions and portfolio construction. To do this, I have tried to stay true to those scientific rules which distinguish a method from a less rigorous model. Among these rules:

An Explicit Method. All models must use explicitly stated rules. There must be no ambiguity in the statement of the rule to be tested. There is no allowance for a private or unique interpretation of the rule.

A Public Rule. The rule must be stated explicitly and publicly so anyone with the time, money, data, equipment, and inclination can reproduce the results. The rule must make sense and must not be derived from the data.

A Reliable Method. Someone using the same rules and the same database must get the same results. Also, the results must be consistent over time. Long-term results cannot owe all their benefit to a few years.

An Objective Rule.   I have attempted to use only rules that are intuitive and logical and that appeal to sensibility, but in all cases the rules are objective. They are independent of the social position, financial status, and cultural background of the investigator and do not require superior insight, information, or interpretation.

A Reliable Database.   There are many problems with backtesting, and the quality of data is the top concern. *All* large collections of historical data contain many errors. A review of Standard & Poor's Compustat Active and Research Database reveals that the data are remarkably clean. Nevertheless, problems remain. Undoubtedly, the database contains stocks where a split was unaccounted for, where a bad book value persisted for several years, where earnings were misstated and went uncorrected, where a price was inverted from 31 to 13, and more. These problems will be present for *any* test of stock market methods and must not be discounted, especially when a method shows just a slight advantage over the market in general.

Potential Pitfalls

Many studies of Wall Street's favorite investment methods have been seriously flawed. Among their problems:

Data Mining.   It takes approximately 40 minutes for an express train to go from Greenwich, Connecticut, to Grand Central Station in Manhattan. In that time, you could look around your car and find all sorts of statistically relevant characteristics about your fellow passengers. Perhaps there are a huge number of blonds, or 75 percent have blue eyes, or the majority were born in May. These relationships, however, are most likely the result of chance occurrences and probably wouldn't be true for the car in front of or behind you. When you went looking for these relationships, you went data mining. You've found a statistical relationship that fits *one set of data very well, but will not translate to another.* If there is no sound theoretical or commonsense reason for the relationship, it's most likely a chance occurrence. Thus, if you see strategies that require you buy stocks only on a Wednesday and hold them for 16½ months, you're looking at the results of data mining.

A Limited Time Period.   *Anything* can look good for 5 to 10 years. There are innumerable strategies that look great during some time periods but perform horribly over the long term. Even zany strategies can work in any given year. For example, a portfolio of stocks with ticker symbols that are vowels—A, E, I, O, U, and Y—beat the market in 1988, but that doesn't make it a good strategy. The *more* time studied, the greater the chance a strategy will continue to work in the future. Statistically, you will always have greater confidence in results derived from large samples than in those derived from small ones.

Micro-Capitalization Stocks Allowed.   Many studies are deeply flawed because they include tiny stocks that are nearly impossible to buy. Take stocks with a market capitalization below $25 million. During the 43 years of our study, $10,000 invested in all the stocks in the Compustat database with a market capitalization below $25 million would have grown to over $29 million! Unfortunately, no professional money manager can realistically *buy* these stocks. They possess virtually no trading liquidity and a large order would send their prices skyrocketing. Moreover, the trading costs incurred, even if the stocks could be bought, would be enormous.

Most academic studies define small capitalization stocks as those making up the fifth (smallest) market capitalization quintile of the New York Stock Exchange. Yet many of these stocks are *impossible* to trade. Indeed, on September 30, 1995, the median market cap of the 350 mutual funds in Morningstar's all-equity, small-cap category was $632 million! Only eight had median market caps below $100 million, and of these, only one managed more than $50 million. Thus, while many small-cap funds use academic studies to support their methods, no fund can manage to buy the stocks that fuel their superior performance.

Look at how a strategy's performance is affected by different levels of market capitalization. Consider 1967, a time of "go-go" growth stock investing. Had you bought the 50 stocks with the best 1-year earnings-per-share gains for the previous year, the returns by market capitalization would be as follows:

- Capitalization greater than $ 1 million (almost all stocks in the database): +121.3 percent
- Capitalization greater than database median (the upper half of stocks in the database): +83.9 percent
- Capitalization greater than database average (largest 16 percent): +29.6 percent

Survivorship Bias, or Then It Was There, Now It's Thin Air.
Many studies don't include stocks that fail, producing an upward bias to their results. Numerous companies disappear from the database

because of bankruptcy or, more brightly, takeover. While most newer studies include a research file made up of delisted stocks, many early ones did not.

Look-Ahead Bias, or Hindsight Better Than 20/20.   Many studies assumed that fundamental information was available when it was not. For example, researchers often assumed you had annual earnings data in January; in reality, the data might not be available until March. This upwardly biases results.

Rules of the Game

I have attempted to correct these problems by using the following methodology:

Universe.   Our universe is the Standard & Poor's Compustat Active and Research Database from 1950 through 1994. This 44 years of data is, to my knowledge, the longest period ever used to study a variety of popular investment strategies. I cannot overstate the importance of this. Any study from the early 1970s to the early 1980s will find strong results for value investing, just as any study from the 1960s will favor growth stocks. Styles come in and out of fashion on Wall Street, so the longer the time period studied, the more illuminating the results. From a statistical viewpoint, the strangest results come from the smallest samples. Large samples always provide better conclusions than small ones. Some pension consultants use a branch of statistics called *reliability mathematics* that uses past returns to predict future performance. They've found that you need a *minimum* of 14 periods to even *begin* to make accurate predictions about the future.

Compustat's research file includes stocks originally listed in the database but removed because of merger, bankruptcy, or other reason. This avoids *survivorship bias.* Most of the models tested were developed by my firm, O'Shaughnessy Capital Management, Inc., between 1994 and 1995. Thus, the period 1950–1993 serves as the time when no modifications were made on any of the strategies. This is what other studies call the *out-of-sample* holdout period.

Market Capitalization.   Except for specific small capitalization tests, I review stocks from two distinct groups. The first includes only stocks with market capitalizations in excess of $150 million (adjusted for inflation), called All Stocks throughout the book. Table 3-1 shows how I created the deflated minimums. The second includes larger, better-known

Table 3-1. Inflation-adjusted value of $150 million in each year, with the 5-year averages used as minimums.

Year ending	Inflation-adjustment factor	Value of $150 million	Average from previous 5 years
31-Dec-52	5.60	$26,763,261.88	
31-Dec-53	5.57	$26,924,919.17	
31-Dec-54	5.60	$26,799,185.73	$26,829,122.26
31-Dec-55	5.58	$26,888,995.33	
31-Dec-56	5.42	$27,661,357.92	
31-Dec-57	5.26	$28,505,568.20	
31-Dec-58	5.17	$29,008,501.98	
31-Dec-59	5.10	$29,439,588.07	$28,300,802.30
31-Dec-60	5.02	$29,870,674.17	
31-Dec-61	4.99	$30,068,255.30	
31-Dec-62	4.93	$30,445,455.63	
31-Dec-63	4.85	$30,948,389.41	
31-Dec-64	4.79	$31,307,627.83	$30,528,080.47
31-Dec-65	4.70	$31,918,333.13	
31-Dec-66	4.55	$32,978,086.46	
31-Dec-67	4.41	$33,983,954.02	
31-Dec-68	4.22	$35,582,564.96	
31-Dec-69	3.97	$37,755,957.37	$34,443,779.19
31-Dec-70	3.77	$39,839,540.17	
31-Dec-71	3.64	$41,168,722.31	
31-Dec-72	3.52	$42,587,714.05	
31-Dec-73	3.24	$46,323,793.56	
31-Dec-74	2.89	$51,981,798.59	$44,380,313.73
31-Dec-75	2.70	$55,628,068.49	
31-Dec-76	2.57	$58,304,394.68	
31-Dec-77	2.41	$62,256,017.24	
31-Dec-78	2.21	$67,860,136.51	
31-Dec-79	1.95	$76,894,982.64	$64,188,719.91
31-Dec-80	1.74	$86,432,762.54	
31-Dec-81	1.59	$94,156,388.46	
31-Dec-82	1.53	$97,802,658.36	
31-Dec-83	1.48	$101,520,775.95	
31-Dec-84	1.42	$105,526,284.28	$97,087,773.92
31-Dec-85	1.37	$109,513,830.68	
31-Dec-86	1.35	$110,753,203.21	
31-Dec-87	1.30	$115,638,845.65	
31-Dec-88	1.24	$120,740,031.13	
31-Dec-89	1.19	$126,344,150.40	$116,598,012.21
31-Dec-90	1.12	$134,067,776.31	
31-Dec-91	1.09	$138,181,056.16	
31-Dec-92	1.05	$142,186,564.48	
31-Dec-93	1.03	$146,084,301.28	
31-Dec-94	1.00	$150,000,000.00	$150,000,000.00

stocks with market capitalizations greater than the database average (usually the top 16 percent of the database by market capitalization). These larger stocks are called Large Stocks throughout the book. Table 3-2 shows the number of stocks with market capitalizations above the database mean. In all cases, I remove the smallest stocks in the database from consideration. For example, at the end of 1993 more than 4000 stocks were jettisoned because their market capitalization fell below an inflation-adjusted minimum of $150 million. In the same year, only 990 stocks had market capitalizations exceeding the database average.

I chose the $150 million value after consulting a trader at a large Wall Street brokerage who felt it was the minimum necessary if he was investing $100 million in 50 stocks in 1995. I use this figure to avoid tiny stocks and focus only on those stocks that a professional investor could buy without running into liquidity problems. Inflation has taken its toll: A stock with a market capitalization of $27 million in 1950 is the equivalent of a $150 million stock at the end of 1994.

Avoiding Look-Ahead Bias. I use only publicly available, annual information. I also time-lag the data by a minimum of 11 months so only data available at the time the portfolio was constructed are used. While 11 months may seem excessive, it conforms to what you would find using the current database on an annual basis.

One potential problem is the changing nature of the Compustat database. As Figure 3-1 shows, Standard & Poor's has continually expanded the database. Many smaller stocks have been added, including up to 5 years of retroactive data. And since these firms were usually added *because* they were successful, the likelihood of a look-ahead bias becomes a real concern. Though *What Works on Wall Street* may suffer from this bias, I think because I eliminate the smallest stocks from consideration the problem is greatly diminished.

Annual Rebalance with Risk-Adjusted Figures. I construct and rebalance portfolios annually. Stocks are equally weighted with no adjustments for beta, industry, or other variables. Foreign stocks included in the Compustat universe are allowed. Because of data limitations, I was forced to add dividend returns to capital appreciation to arrive at a total return for the year. The result is a slight understatement of the compounding effect of dividend reinvestment.

I assume no trades are made throughout the year. This may bias my results slightly, as it rewards trade-averse strategies, but I believe many excellent strategies that require numerous trades turn mediocre once trading costs are included. I also examined annual returns and removed stocks with extreme returns or data that were inconsistent with outside information.

Table 3-2. Large Stocks as percentage of Compustat, 1952–1994.

Year ending	Number of stocks with a market capitalization above the database mean	Number of stocks in the database	Percent
31-Dec-52	110	560	20%
31-Dec-53	137	581	24%
31-Dec-54	153	629	24%
31-Dec-55	147	657	22%
31-Dec-56	136	682	20%
31-Dec-57	141	692	20%
31-Dec-58	148	797	19%
31-Dec-59	160	860	19%
31-Dec-60	177	1447	12%
31-Dec-61	220	1622	14%
31-Dec-62	300	1792	17%
31-Dec-63	272	1986	14%
31-Dec-64	342	2136	16%
31-Dec-65	377	2351	16%
31-Dec-66	402	2487	16%
31-Dec-67	430	2698	16%
31-Dec-68	479	2969	16%
31-Dec-69	525	3132	17%
31-Dec-70	539	3155	17%
31-Dec-71	541	3414	16%
31-Dec-72	580	3684	16%
31-Dec-73	589	3639	16%
31-Dec-74	584	3644	16%
31-Dec-75	544	3695	15%
31-Dec-76	599	3832	16%
31-Dec-77	635	3852	16%
31-Dec-78	667	3980	17%
31-Dec-79	670	4262	16%
31-Dec-80	739	4478	17%
31-Dec-81	712	4917	14%
31-Dec-82	814	5030	16%
31-Dec-83	830	5531	15%
31-Dec-84	868	5476	16%
31-Dec-85	833	5537	15%
31-Dec-86	860	5992	14%
31-Dec-87	842	6130	14%
31-Dec-88	830	6009	14%
31-Dec-89	842	5877	14%
31-Dec-90	833	5457	15%
31-Dec-91	806	5891	14%
31-Dec-92	845	6554	13%
31-Dec-93	947	7312	13%
31-Dec-94	1008	7919	13%
Average	540	3566	16%

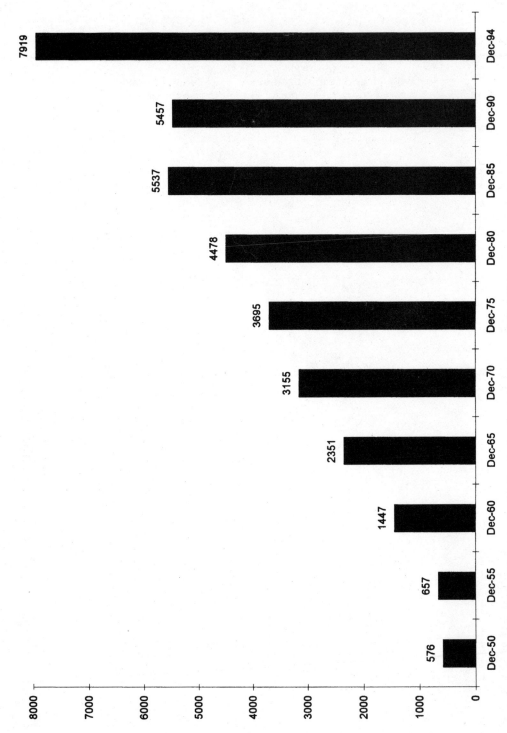

Figure 3-1. Number of stocks in Standard & Poor's Compustat universe, 1950–1994.

I also compare absolute and risk-adjusted returns. Risk-adjusted returns take the volatility of a portfolio—as measured by the standard deviation of return—into account when considering absolute returns. Generally, investors prefer a portfolio earning 15 percent a year with a standard deviation of 20 percent to one earning 16 percent a year with a standard deviation of 30 percent. A 1 percent absolute advantage doesn't compensate for the terror of the wild ride. I use the well-known Sharpe ratio of reward to risk for my calculations, with higher numbers indicating better risk-adjusted returns. To arrive at the Sharpe ratio, simply take the average return from a strategy, subtract the risk-free rate of interest, and then divide that number by the standard deviation of return. The ratio is important because it reflects risk. The strategy in Table 3-3, for example, had a higher *absolute* return than the S&P 500 but a *lower* risk-adjusted return because it was much more volatile.

Minimum and Maximum Expected Returns. Also, in all summary information about a strategy, I provide the maximum and minimum projected returns, as well as the actual maximum and minimum over the past 43 years. This is *extremely* useful information, since investors can glance at the worst loss and decide if they can stomach the volatility of any particular strategy.

Table 3-3. Determining a strategy's risk-adjusted return.

Year ending	S&P 500	Strategy	T-bills	S&P 500 T-bills	Strategy T-bills
31-Dec-84	6.27%	−10.10%	9.85%	−3.58%	−19.95%
31-Dec-85	32.16%	45.20%	7.72%	24.44%	37.48%
31-Dec-86	18.47%	27.00%	6.16%	12.31%	20.84%
31-Dec-87	5.23%	10.50%	5.47%	−0.24%	5.03%
31-Dec-88	16.81%	7.00%	6.35%	10.46%	0.65%
31-Dec-89	31.49%	36.50%	8.37%	23.12%	28.13%
31-Dec-90	−3.17%	−10.90%	7.81%	−10.98%	−18.71%
31-Dec-91	30.55%	63.90%	5.60%	24.95%	58.30%
31-Dec-92	7.67%	0.70%	3.51%	4.16%	−2.81%
31-Dec-93	9.99%	44.10%	2.90%	7.09%	41.20%
31-Dec-94	1.31%	−4.20%	3.90%	−2.59%	−8.10%
Average	14.25%	19.06%	6.15%	8.10%	12.91%
Standard deviation	12.01%	24.37%	2.07%	11.68%	24.75%

Risk-adjusted return for the S&P 500 equals 8.10% divided by 12.01%, or 67.44.
Risk-adjusted return for the strategy equals 12.91% divided by 24.37%, or 52.97.

50 Stock Portfolios.   Except for Chapter 4, which reviews returns by market capitalization, all portfolios contain 50 stocks. A cursory review of private and institutional money managers reveals that 50 stocks are a common portfolio minimum. Many of the popular averages, such as the S&P 500, use more, yet many, such as the Dow Jones Industrial Average and *Barron's* 50 stock average, use the same or less. Next, I considered the benefits of diversification. Researchers J. L. Evans and S. H. Archer found most of the benefits of diversification come from as few as 16 stocks. Subsequent research confirms their findings. You also want to avoid holding too many stocks. This can lead to *deworsification*.

Discipline.   I test investment disciplines, not trading strategies. My results show that United States equity markets are not perfectly efficient. Investors *can* outperform the market by sticking with superior strategies over long periods. Simple, disciplined strategies—such as buying the top 10 yielding stocks in the Dow Jones Industrial Average, for example—have worked over the last 67 years because they are immune to the emotions of the market and *force* investors to buy industrial stocks when they are under distress. No one *wants* to buy Union Carbide after Bophal or Exxon after the Valdez oil spill, yet it is precisely these times that offer the best buys.

Costs.   Transaction costs are not included. Each reader faces different transaction costs. Institutional investors trading in million-dollar lots face substantially different costs from an individual, odd-lot trader. Thus, each will be able to review raw data and remove whatever costs fit the situation.

Now let's look at the tests. We'll start with a review of return by market capitalization and then look at returns by single and multifactor combinations.

Ranking Stocks by Market Capitalization: Size Matters

Order and simplification are the first steps toward the mastery of a subject. —THOMAS MANN

First, we'll look at the returns from our two universes of stocks ranked by market capitalization. This will establish a base rate to which we'll compare all other strategies. All Stocks are those with market capitalizations in excess of a deflated $150 million. Large Stocks are those with a market capitalization greater than the Compustat database average (usually the top 16 percent of the database by market capitalization). In each case we start with a $10,000 investment on December 31, 1951, and rebalance the portfolio annually. As with all my tests, the stocks are equally weighted, all dividends are reinvested, and all variables such as common shares outstanding are time-lagged to avoid look-ahead bias. Figure 4-1 shows the results. As mentioned in Chapter 1, there is virtually no difference between stocks with market capitalizations above the Compustat mean (Large Stocks) and the S&P 500: $10,000 invested in the S&P 500 on December 31, 1951, was worth $1,027,828 on December 31, 1994, and $1,042,859 if invested in the Large Stocks group. This is

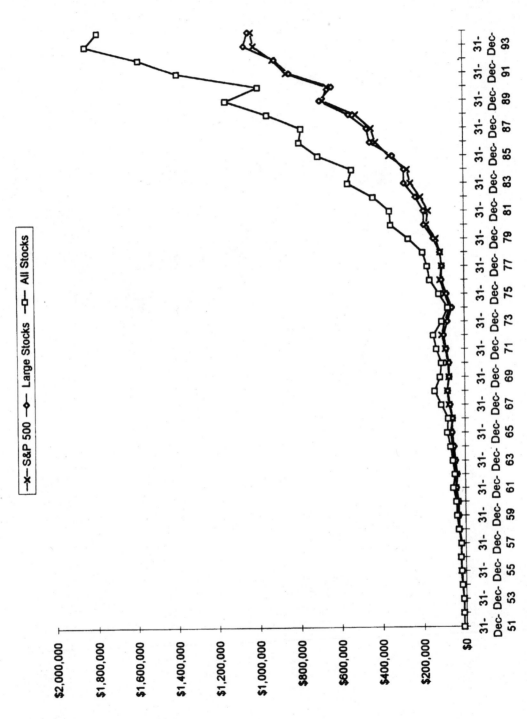

Figure 4-1. Total return by universe, 1951–1994. Year-end 1951 = $10,000.

not surprising, since investing in the S&P 500 is nothing more than a bet on big, well-known stocks. Table 4-1 shows the annual returns for each universe.

An investment in the All Stocks group did considerably better: $10,000 grew to $1,782,174. The performance was not without bumps, however, as Table 4-2 shows. There were several periods when All Stocks significantly outperformed Large Stocks and other times when the reverse was true. Large Stocks did quite a bit worse than All Stocks between December 31, 1975, and December 31, 1983, only to turn around and do somewhat better between December 31, 1984, and December 31, 1990. The All Stocks universe also had a higher standard deviation of return than the Large Stocks universe.

Looking at returns for rolling 5- and 10-year periods to establish a base rate, we see that All Stocks outperformed Large Stocks in 28 of the 39 rolling 5-year periods, or 71 percent of the time. All Stocks also outperformed Large Stocks in 27 of the 34 rolling 10-year periods, or 79 percent of the time.

The returns show you're better off fishing in the larger pond of All Stocks than exclusively buying large, well-known stocks. Table 4-3 summarizes the results and Table 4-4 shows returns by decade.

How Much Better?

Most academic studies of market capitalization sort stocks by deciles (10 percent) and review how an investment in each fares over time. The studies are nearly unanimous in their findings that small stocks (those in the lowest four deciles) do significantly better than large ones. We too have found tremendous returns from tiny stocks.

The glaring problem with this method is that it's virtually impossible to *buy* the stocks that account for the performance advantage of small capitalization strategies. Table 4-5 illustrates the problem. On December 31, 1994, there were approximately 7700 stocks in the active Compustat database that had both year-end prices and a number for common shares outstanding. If we sorted the database by decile, each decile would be made up of 770 stocks. As Table 4-5 shows, market capitalization doesn't get past $150 million until you get to decile 7! The top market capitalization in the *fourth* decile is $40 million, a number far too small to allow widespread buying of those stocks. This presents an interesting paradox: Small-cap mutual funds justify their investments with academic research showing that small stocks outperform large ones, yet the funds themselves *cannot buy the stocks that provide the lion's share of performance because of a lack of trading liquidity.*

Table 4-1. Annual returns for stocks with market capitalizations above the Compustat mean (Large Stocks) and those with capitalizations above a deflated $150 million (All Stocks).

Year ending	S&P 500	Capitalization>mean Large Stocks	Capitalization>deflated $150M All Stocks
31-Dec-52	18.37%	9.30%	7.90%
31-Dec-53	−0.99%	2.30%	2.90%
31-Dec-54	52.62%	44.90%	47.00%
31-Dec-55	31.56%	21.20%	20.70%
31-Dec-56	6.56%	9.60%	17.00%
31-Dec-57	−10.78%	−6.90%	−7.10%
31-Dec-58	43.36%	42.10%	55.00%
31-Dec-59	11.96%	9.90%	23.00%
31-Dec-60	0.47%	4.80%	6.10%
31-Dec-61	26.89%	27.50%	31.20%
31-Dec-62	−8.73%	−8.90%	−12.00%
31-Dec-63	22.80%	19.50%	18.00%
31-Dec-64	16.48%	15.30%	16.30%
31-Dec-65	12.45%	16.20%	22.60%
31-Dec-66	−10.06%	−4.90%	−5.20%
31-Dec-67	23.98%	21.30%	41.10%
31-Dec-68	11.06%	16.80%	27.40%
31-Dec-69	−8.50%	−9.90%	−18.50%
31-Dec-70	4.01%	−0.20%	−5.80%
31-Dec-71	14.31%	17.30%	21.30%
31-Dec-72	18.98%	14.90%	11.00%
31-Dec-73	−14.66%	−18.90%	−27.20%
31-Dec-74	−26.47%	−26.70%	−27.90%
31-Dec-75	37.20%	43.10%	55.90%
31-Dec-76	23.84%	28.00%	35.60%
31-Dec-77	−7.18%	−2.50%	6.90%
31-Dec-78	6.56%	8.10%	12.20%
31-Dec-79	18.44%	27.30%	34.30%
31-Dec-80	32.42%	30.80%	31.50%
31-Dec-81	−4.91%	0.60%	1.70%
31-Dec-82	21.41%	19.90%	22.50%
31-Dec-83	22.51%	23.80%	28.10%
31-Dec-84	6.27%	−0.40%	−3.40%
31-Dec-85	32.16%%	19.50%	30.80%
31-Dec-86	18.47%	32.20%	13.10%
31-Dec-87	5.23%	3.30%	−1.30%
31-Dec-88	16.81%	19.00%	21.20%
31-Dec-89	31.49%	26.00%	21.40%
31-Dec-90	−3.17%	−8.70%	−13.80%
31-Dec-91	30.55%	33.00%	39.80%
31-Dec-92	7.67%	8.70%	13.80%
31-Dec-93	9.99%	16.30%	16.60%
31-Dec-94	1.31%	−1.90%	−3.40%
Arithmetic average	12.62%	12.62%	14.61%
Standard deviation	16.56%	16.18%	19.86%

Table 4-2. Annual performance of All Stocks versus Large Stocks.

Year ending	Large Stocks Cap>mean	All Stocks Cap>deflated 150M	All Stocks Relative performance
31-Dec-52	9.30%	7.90%	−1.40%
31-Dec-53	2.30%	2.90%	0.60%
31-Dec-54	44.90%	47.00%	2.10%
31-Dec-55	21.20%	20.70%	−0.50%
31-Dec-56	9.60%	17.00%	7.40%
31-Dec-57	−6.90%	−7.10%	−0.20%
31-Dec-58	42.10%	55.00%	12.90%
31-Dec-59	9.90%	23.00%	13.10%
31-Dec-60	4.80%	6.10%	1.30%
31-Dec-61	27.50%	31.20%	3.70%
31-Dec-62	−8.90%	−12.00%	−3.10%
31-Dec-63	19.50%	18.00%	−1.50%
31-Dec-64	15.30%	16.30%	1.00%
31-Dec-65	16.20%	22.60%	6.40%
31-Dec-66	−4.90%	−5.20%	−0.30%
31-Dec-67	21.30%	41.10%	19.80%
31-Dec-68	16.80%	27.40%	10.60%
31-Dec-69	−9.90%	−18.50%	−8.60%
31-Dec-70	−0.20%	−5.80%	−5.60%
31-Dec-71	17.30%	21.30%	4.00%
31-Dec-72	14.90%	11.00%	−3.90%
31-Dec-73	−18.90%	−27.20%	−8.30%
31-Dec-74	−26.70%	−27.90%	−1.20%
31-Dec-75	43.10%	55.90%	12.80%
31-Dec-76	28.00%	35.60%	7.60%
31-Dec-77	−2.50%	6.90%	9.40%
31-Dec-78	8.10%	12.20%	4.10%
31-Dec-79	27.30%	34.30%	7.00%
31-Dec-80	30.80%	31.50%	0.70%
31-Dec-81	0.60%	1.70%	1.10%
31-Dec-82	19.90%	22.50%	2.60%
31-Dec-83	23.80%	28.10%	4.30%
31-Dec-84	−0.40%	−3.40%	−3.00%
31-Dec-85	19.50%	30.80%	11.30%
31-Dec-86	32.20%	13.10%	−19.10%
31-Dec-87	3.30%	−1.30%	−4.60%
31-Dec-88	19.00%	21.20%	2.20%
31-Dec-89	26.00%	21.40%	−4.60%
31-Dec-90	−8.70%	−13.80%	−5.10%
31-Dec-91	33.00%	39.80%	6.80%
31-Dec-92	8.70%	13.80%	5.10%
31-Dec-93	16.30%	16.60%	0.30%
31-Dec-94	−1.90%	−3.40%	−1.50%
Arithmetic average	12.62%	14.61%	1.99%
Standard deviation	16.18%	19.86%	3.69%

Table 4-3. Summary return results, Large Stocks, All Stocks, and Standard and Poor's 500, December 31, 1951–December 31, 1994.

	S&P 500	Large Stocks Capitalization>mean	All Stocks Capitalization>deflated $150M
Arithmetic average	12.62%	12.62%	14.61%
Standard deviation of return	16.56%	16.18%	19.86%
Sharpe risk-adjusted ratio	44.00	45.00	47.00
3-yr compounded	6.26%	7.44%	8.63%
5-yr compounded	8.69%	8.53%	9.09%
10-yr compounded	14.40%	13.93%	12.74%
15-yr compounded	14.52%	14.03%	13.55%
20-yr compounded	14.58%	15.42%	16.95%
25-yr compounded	10.97%	11.16%	11.51%
30-yr compounded	9.95%	10.48%	11.47%
35-yr compounded	10.06%	10.54%	11.39%
40-yr compounded	10.66%	10.97%	12.45%
Compound annual return	11.38%	11.41%	12.81%
$10,000 becomes	$1,027,827.56	$1,042,858.62	$1,782,174.48
Maximum return	52.62%	44.90%	55.90%
Minimum return	−26.47%	−26.70%	−27.90%
Maximum expected return*	45.75%	44.97%	54.33%
Minimum expected return**	−20.50%	−19.73%	−25.11%

*Maximum expected return is average return plus 2 times the standard deviation.

**Minimum expected return is average return minus 2 times the standard deviation.

Table 4-4. Compound annual rates of return by decade.

Universe	1950s*	1960s	1970s	1980s	1990s**
S&P 500	17.33%	7.81%	5.86%	17.55%	8.69%
Large Stocks	15.33%	8.99%	6.99%	16.89%	8.53%
All Stocks	19.22%	11.09%	8.53%	15.85%	9.09%

*Returns for 1952–1959.

**Returns for 1990–1994.

Table 4-5. Compustat database sorted by market capitalization decile on December 31, 1994.

Decile	Largest market capitalization of top stock
1	$6 million
2	$13 million
3	$23 million
4	$40 million
5	$66 million
6	$107 million
7	$189 million
8	$391 million
9	$1.7 billion
10	$87 billion

A review of the Morningstar Mutual Fund database proves this. On September 30, 1995, the median market capitalization of the 350 mutual funds in Morningstar's all-equity, small-cap category was $632 million! That's right between decile 8 and 9 from the Compustat universe—hardly small. Only eight of these had median market capitalizations below $100 million, and of these, only one managed more than $50 million.

Reviewing Stocks by Size

Rather than review stocks by decile, it's illuminating to review performance by grouping stocks in absolute size categories. This doesn't take inflation into account, as in our All Stocks universe, but it conforms to the practices of money managers and investors. They don't think about a stock being in the sixth decile; they think of it as a mid-cap stock.

Thus, I split up the universe by absolute market:

Micro-cap stocks

- Capitalization less than $25 million

Small-cap stocks

- Capitalization between $25 million and $100 million
- Capitalization between $100 million and $250 million
- Capitalization between $250 million and $500 million

Mid-cap stocks

■ Capitalization between $500 million and $1 billion

Large Stocks

■ Capitalization above $1 billion

The returns, shown in Figures 4-2 and 4-3, are stunning. Almost all the superior returns offered by small stocks come from micro-cap stocks with market capitalizations below $25 million: $10,000 invested in that group on December 31, 1951, soared to over $29 million in value, achieving a compound growth rate of over 20 percent for the 43 years reviewed! The micro-cap returns absolutely dwarf their nearest competitor, the All Stocks group. They even manage to overcome their breathtaking risk—an annual standard deviation of return of 34.65 percent—and land at the top of the risk-adjusted return index featured in Figure 4-4.

But the micro-cap stock's returns are a chimera. The only way to achieve these stellar returns is to invest only a few million dollars in over 2000 stocks. Precious few investors can do that. The stocks are far too small for a mutual fund to buy and far too numerous for an individual to tackle. So there they sit, tantalizingly out of reach of nearly everyone.

All Stocks Is the Winner

Figure 4-5 shows returns by market capitalization with the micro-cap stocks removed. These results show that investors are best off buying *all* the stocks in the Compustat database with market caps above $150 million rather than concentrating on *just* small stocks. The returns for All Stocks beat all the others on both an absolute and risk-adjusted basis. Note that these findings still confirm the studies showing smaller stocks beating large stocks, since most of the stocks in the Compustat database *are* small stocks. It's interesting that the smallest stocks, those with market caps between $25 million and $100 million, don't beat the All Stocks group on either an absolute or a risk-adjusted basis. What's really fascinating is the performance of the mid-cap stocks, with capitalizations between $500 million and $1 billion. They perform *worse* than Large Stocks and stocks with capitalizations above $1 billion. This contradicts the belief that mid-cap stocks offer the greatest potential to investors. Tables 4-6 through 4-9 summarize the findings for each market capitalization group.

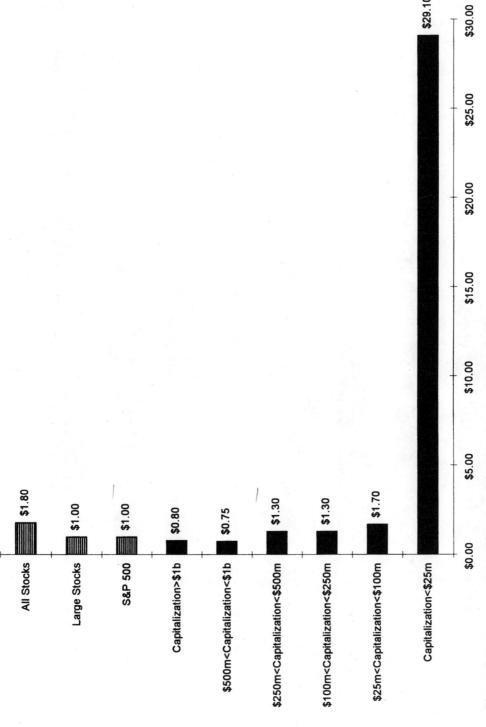

Figure 4-2. December 31, 1994, value of $10,000 invested on December 31, 1951, and annually rebalanced by market capitalization (in millions).

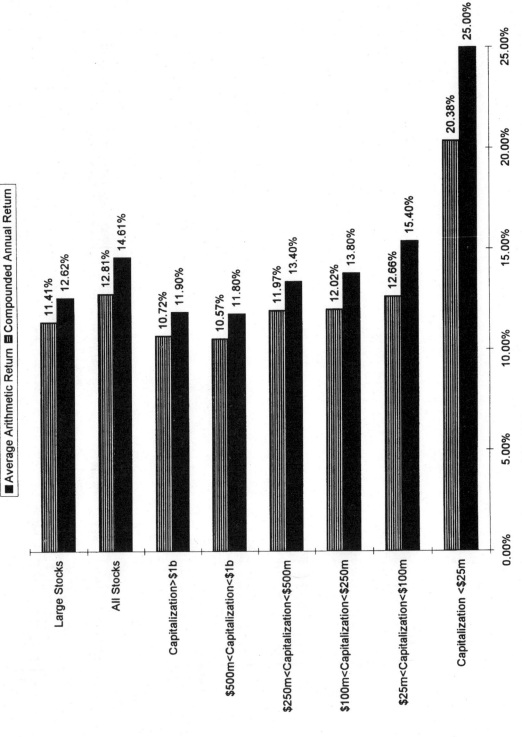

Figure 4-3. Market returns by capitalization, 1951–1994.

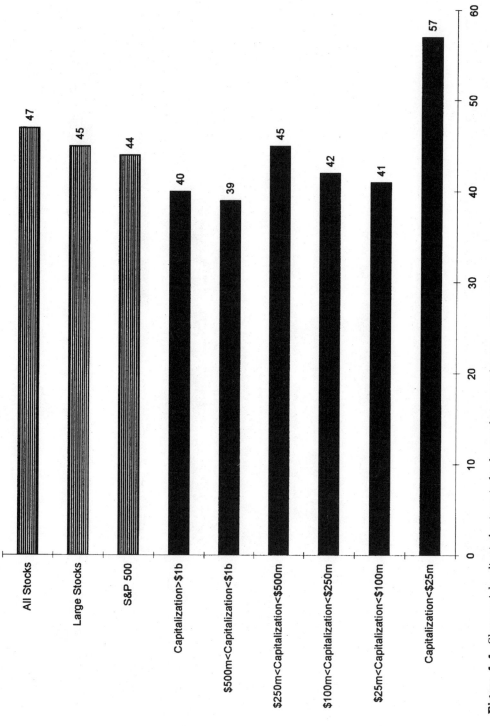

Figure 4-4. Sharpe risk-adjusted return index by market capitalization, 1951–1994. (Higher is better.)

Figure 4-5. December 31, 1994, value of $10,000 invested on December 31, 1951, and annually rebalanced; excludes micro-cap stocks (in millions).

Table 4-6. Annual returns for stocks by market capitalization—portfolios rebalanced annually.

Year ending	Capitalization<$25m	$25m<capitalization<$100m	$100m<capitalization<$250m
31-Dec-52	11.40%	7.50%	6.70%
31-Dec-53	4.80%	3.10%	4.80%
31-Dec-54	57.30%	50.50%	41.20%
31-Dec-55	31.60%	20.30%	18.10%
31-Dec-56	19.50%	13.91%	10.28%
31-Dec-57	−5.90%	−9.50%	−3.70%
31-Dec-58	73.61%	66.53%	49.00%
31-Dec-59	64.10%	25.28%	3.50%
31-Dec-60	8.80%	6.00%	7.90%
31-Dec-61	46.31%	32.50%	32.30%
31-Dec-62	−16.20%	−13.84%	−13.20%
31-Dec-63	18.40%	21.80%	16.20%
31-Dec-64	26.90%	16.90%	17.40%
31-Dec-65	67.61%	30.70%	19.90%
31-Dec-66	3.50%	−4.60%	−6.60%
31-Dec-67	134.18%	61.00%	37.90%
31-Dec-68	75.00%	35.30%	28.80%
31-Dec-69	−31.30%	−26.00%	−15.70%
31-Dec-70	−18.90%	−12.60%	−4.10%
31-Dec-71	33.40%	21.80%	25.80%
31-Dec-72	8.60%	7.70%	10.60%
31-Dec-73	−35.80%	−35.00%	−26.60%
31-Dec-74	−23.02%	−27.30%	−29.90%
31-Dec-75	78.43%	55.52%	57.54%
31-Dec-76	50.40%	46.00%	39.40%
31-Dec-77	31.44%	17.70%	8.00%
31-Dec-78	31.50%	17.80%	13.30%
31-Dec-79	44.82%	45.00%	37.40%
31-Dec-80	46.46%	36.80%	30.50%
31-Dec-81	2.50%	−0.02%	3.80%
31-Dec-82	28.43%	26.60%	24.00%
31-Dec-83	48.38%	32.40%	30.20%
31-Dec-84	−13.31%	−11.70%	−3.50%
31-Dec-85	19.80%	28.80%	29.90%
31-Dec-86	7.10%	2.90%	7.70%
31-Dec-87	−7.30%	−13.20%	−6.70%
31-Dec-88	18.41%	19.10%	24.00%
31-Dec-89	8.12%	9.55%	16.20%
31-Dec-90	−23.83%	−25.80%	−17.40%
31-Dec-91	67.08%	46.70%	43.10%
31-Dec-92	46.93%	21.50%	15.10%
31-Dec-93	44.11%	21.35%	18.20%
31-Dec-94	−3.20%	−6.50%	−6.00%
Arithmetic average	25.12%	15.41%	13.84%
Standard deviation	34.65%	24.52%	19.95%

Table 4-7. Annual returns for stocks by market capitalization—portfolios rebalanced annually.

Year ending	$250m<capitalization<$500m	$500m<capitalization<$1b	Capitalization>$1b
31-Dec-52	8.60%	12.40%	13.50%
31-Dec-53	3.10%	−2.70%	1.20%
31-Dec-54	45.40%	45.60%	56.70%
31-Dec-55	19.70%	25.20%	28.70%
31-Dec-56	8.30%	4.20%	17.90%
31-Dec-57	−1.10%	−8.00%	−15.70%
31-Dec-58	42.40%	40.30%	40.50%
31-Dec-59	8.10%	12.60%	12.00%
31-Dec-60	10.40%	5.50%	−2.80%
31-Dec-61	32.80%	24.80%	22.50%
31-Dec-62	−7.00%	−11.60%	−8.90%
31-Dec-63	17.30%	21.10%	19.50%
31-Dec-64	15.30%	12.80%	15.70%
31-Dec-65	21.00%	13.60%	9.30%
31-Dec-66	−4.40%	−3.20%	−7.90%
31-Dec-67	24.90%	14.70%	19.20%
31-Dec-68	17.60%	19.00%	12.50%
31-Dec-69	−10.70%	−10.90%	−9.80%
31-Dec-70	1.50%	0.40%	−1.40%
31-Dec-71	17.80%	15.30%	15.30%
31-Dec-72	13.20%	10.90%	22.90%
31-Dec-73	−23.30%	−21.60%	−11.70%
31-Dec-74	−26.60%	−26.50%	−27.00%
31-Dec-75	52.20%	40.90%	32.90%
31-Dec-76	30.20%	28.10%	20.00%
31-Dec-77	1.90%	−3.60%	−7.60%
31-Dec-78	9.20%	5.70%	8.20%
31-Dec-79	30.60%	29.00%	18.70%
31-Dec-80	31.10%	30.00%	29.10%
31-Dec-81	3.50%	1.90%	−2.90%
31-Dec-82	21.30%	21.90%	16.60%
31-Dec-83	26.20%	23.20%	21.60%
31-Dec-84	−2.30%	−3.40%	3.10%
31-Dec-85	29.20%	31.60%	32.60%
31-Dec-86	10.10%	16.20%	21.80%
31-Dec-87	−2.20%	0.07%	6.10%
31-Dec-88	20.80%	21.70%	18.10%
31-Dec-89	20.50%	23.20%	27.10%
31-Dec-90	−17.90%	−12.00%	−8.70%
31-Dec-91	46.30%	32.60%	33.90%
31-Dec-92	18.80%	14.50%	8.10%
31-Dec-93	16.00%	16.30%	16.20%
31-Dec-94	−3.70%	−2.60%	−2.40%
Arithmetic average	13.40%	11.84%	11.97%
Standard deviation	17.69%	16.53%	16.56%

Table 4-8. Summary return results based on market capitalization: December 31, 1951–December 31, 1994.

	Capitalization<$25m	$25m<capitalization<$100m	$100m<capitalization<$250m
Arithmetic average	25.12%	15.41%	13.84%
Standard deviation of return	34.65%	24.52%	19.95%
Sharpe risk-adjusted ratio	57.00	41.00	42.00
3-yr compounded	27.03%	11.30%	8.54%
5-yr compounded	21.14%	8.46%	8.61%
10-yr compounded	14.79%	8.46%	11.01%
15-yr compounded	16.47%	10.64%	12.69%
20-yr compounded	23.32%	16.39%	16.75%
25-yr compounded	15.71%	10.18%	11.50%
30-yr compounded	19.06%	10.96%	11.40%
35-yr compounded	18.46%	11.04%	11.35%
40-yr compounded	20.23%	12.23%	11.69%
Compound annual return	20.38%	12.66%	12.02%
$10,000 becomes	$29,120,351.39	$1,685,357.24	$1,316.478.96
Maximum return	134.18%	66.53%	57.54%
Minimum return	−35.80%	−35.00%	−29.90%
Maximum expected return*	94.43%	64.46%	53.75%
Minimum expected return**	−44.19%	−33.64%	−26.06%

*Maximum expected return is average return plus 2 times the standard deviation.
**Minimum expected return is average return minus 2 times the standard deviation.

Table 4-9. Summary return results based on market capitalization: December 31, 1951–December 31, 1994.

	$250m<capitalization<$500m	$500m<capitalization<$1b	Capitalization>$1b
Arithmetic average	13.40%	11.84%	11.97%
Standard deviation of return	17.69%	16.53%	16.56%
Sharpe risk-adjusted ratio	45.00	39.00	40.00
3-yr compounded	9.89%	9.06%	7.03%
5-yr compounded	9.77%	8.64%	8.43%
10-yr compounded	12.43%	13.26%	14.45%
15-yr compounded	13.35%	13.49%	13.92%
20-yr compounded	15.82%	14.81%	13.84%
25-yr compounded	11.25%	10.34%	10.47%
30-yr compounded	10.82%	9.60%	9.36%
35-yr compounded	11.13%	9.62%	9.23%
40-yr compounded	11.56%	10.12%	9.94%
Compounded annual return	11.97%	10.57%	10.72%
$10,000 becomes	$1,292,268.70	$751,895.08	$796,646.21
Maximum return	52.20%	45.60%	56.70%
Minimum return	−26.60%	−26.50%	−27.00%
Maximum expected return*	48.77%	44.91%	45.09%
Minimum expected return**	−21.97%	−21.23%	−21.15%

*Maximum expected return is average return plus 2 times the standard deviation.
**Minimum expected return is average return minus 2 times the standard deviation.

Implications for Investors

Investors should be wary of small-stock strategies that promise high returns *simply* because they invest in smaller issues. The numbers show that the smallest stocks—those with market capitalizations below $25 million—account for almost all the difference between small and large stock returns. They're virtually impossible to buy and are therefore shunned by mutual funds.

Stocks with market capitalizations between $25 million and $100 million, as well as those with market capitalizations between $100 million and $250 million, *do* outperform large stocks on an absolute basis but fail to do so when risk is taken into account. The Sharpe ratio for each is 41 and 42 respectively, compared with ratios of 47 for All Stocks and 45 for Large Stocks. (Remember, higher Sharpe ratios are better.)

The big surprise is the performance of stocks with market capitalizations between $500 million and $1 billion. They posted the *lowest* returns on both an absolute and risk-adjusted basis, with a compound return of 10.57 percent and a Sharpe ratio of 39. The cause is a mystery, but should caution investors looking at a mid-capitalization indexing strategy. It should also caution those in small-cap mutual funds, for, as previously noted, on September 30, 1995, the median market capitalization of the 350 mutual funds in Morningstar's all-equity, small-capitalization category was $632 million.

As Table 4-10 shows, investors who want to beat the S&P 500 and are willing to take more risk should concentrate on all reasonably sized stocks—those in the All Stocks group with market capitalizations above $150 million—instead of focusing exclusively on small stocks. The All Stocks universe was both the absolute and risk-adjusted winner, with a compound return of 12.81 percent and a Sharpe ratio of 47. That's a premium of 1.4 percent over the Large Stocks universe and well worth the extra risk. As of December 31, 1994, the All Stocks group included 2800 stocks, ranging from General Electric at the top to ROC Communities,

Table 4-10. Base rates for All Stocks universe and Large Stocks universe, 1951–1994.

Item	All Stocks beat Large Stocks	Percent
Single-year return	26 out of 43	60%
Rolling 5-year compound return	28 out of 39	72%
Rolling 10-year compound return	27 out of 34	79%

Inc. at the bottom. Their average market capitalization of $2.2 billion was considerably smaller than in the Large Stocks universe, which had an average market capitalization of $5.4 billion.

Our Two Benchmarks

In each chapter to follow, we'll use the All Stocks and Large Stocks groups as benchmarks for all the strategies we study. Each provides an excellent indication of what you can achieve in each capitalization class.

5

Price-to-Earnings Ratios: Separating the Winners and Losers

When it comes to making money, everyone is of the same religion. —VOLTAIRE

For many on Wall Street, buying stocks with low price-to-earnings (PE) ratios is the one true faith. You find a stock's current PE ratio by dividing the price by the current earnings per share. The higher the PE, the more investors are paying for earnings, and the larger the implied expectations for future earnings growth. A stock's PE ratio is the most common measurement of how cheap or expensive it is relative to other stocks.

Investors who buy stocks with low PE ratios think they're getting a bargain. Generally, they believe that when a stock's PE ratio is high, investors have unrealistic expectations for the earnings growth of that stock. High hopes, the low PE investors reason, are usually dashed, along with the price of the stock. Conversely, they believe the prices of low PE stocks are unduly discounted and when earnings recover, the price of the stock will follow.

The Results

Remember that we look at two distinct groups—those with high and low PE ratios drawn from the All Stocks universe (all stocks with market capitalizations greater than a deflated $150 million) and those with high and low PE ratios drawn from the Large Stocks universe (those stocks with market capitalizations greater than the Compustat mean, usually the upper 16 percent of the database).

Let's look at low PE stocks first. We start with $10,000 on December 31, 1951, and buy the 50 stocks with the highest earnings-to-price ratios from the All Stocks and Large Stocks universes. Because of Compustat's internal math, we must rank stocks by the 50 with the *highest* earnings-to-price ratio, which is the reciprocal of the PE ratio. Remember that stocks with high earnings-to-price ratios are low PE stocks. We rebalance the portfolios annually to hold the 50 stocks with the lowest PE ratios in any given year. As with all the tests, the stocks are equally weighted and the earnings variable is time-lagged to avoid look-ahead bias.

Figure 5-1 shows the growth of $10,000 invested on December 31, 1951, and Tables 5-1 through 5-6 summarize the results for low PE investing.

Forty-three years of data show that low PE ratios are not nearly as important for smaller stocks as they are for larger stocks. The 50 lowest PE stocks from the All Stocks universe turned $10,000 into $1,230,992, a compound rate of return of 11.84 percent a year. While that beat the return for the Large Stocks universe, it failed to beat the All Stocks universe's overall return of 12.81 percent a year. The 50 stocks with the lowest PEs also did worse than All Stocks on a risk-adjusted basis: the Sharpe ratio for the 50 low PE stocks was 37, 10 points behind the All Stocks universe score of 47. Analyzing the base rate information in Table 5-5, we see little more than chance at work in the number of years the strategy beats the universe.

Large Stocks Are Different

Large Stocks are entirely different. Here, an investment in the 50 stocks with the lowest PE ratios turned $10,000 into $2,287,003, more than double the Large Stock universe's $1,042,859 return. The compound return of the 50 low PE stocks was 13.47 percent, 2.06 percent better than the Large Stock's return of 11.41 percent a year. Moreover, the 50 low PE stocks from Large Stocks had a better risk-adjusted return—sporting a Sharpe ratio of 47, compared with the Large Stocks group's

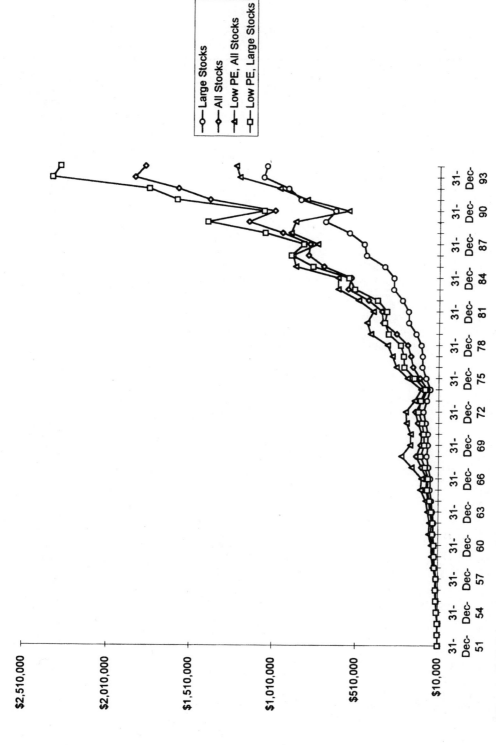

Figure 5-1. Returns on low PE strategies versus All Stocks and Large Stocks, 1951–1994. Year-end 1951 = $10,000.

Table 5-1. Annual performance of All Stocks versus 50 stocks with high earnings-to-price (low PE) ratios drawn from All Stocks universe.

Year ending	All Stocks	Universe = All Stocks Top 50 EPS/price	Top 50 EPS/price Relative performance
31-Dec-52	7.90%	11.10%	3.20%
31-Dec-53	2.90%	−5.60%	−8.50%
31-Dec-54	47.00%	69.20%	22.20%
31-Dec-55	20.70%	29.50%	8.80%
31-Dec-56	17.00%	18.90%	1.90%
31-Dec-57	−7.10%	−16.80%	−9.70%
31-Dec-58	55.00%	75.30%	20.30%
31-Dec-59	23.00%	21.90%	−1.10%
31-Dec-60	6.10%	6.70%	0.60%
31-Dec-61	31.20%	28.90%	−2.30%
31-Dec-62	−12.00%	−5.30%	6.70%
31-Dec-63	18.00%	19.90%	1.90%
31-Dec-64	16.30%	14.00%	−2.30%
31-Dec-65	22.60%	34.90%	12.30%
31-Dec-66	−5.20%	−4.10%	1.10%
31-Dec-67	41.10%	52.80%	11.70%
31-Dec-68	27.40%	36.30%	8.90%
31-Dec-69	−18.50%	−23.00%	−4.50%
31-Dec-70	−5.80%	−1.80%	4.00%
31-Dec-71	21.30%	14.10%	−7.20%
31-Dec-72	11.00%	2.50%	−8.50%
31-Dec-73	−27.20%	−25.50%	1.70%
31-Dec-74	−27.90%	−25.10%	2.80%
31-Dec-75	55.90%	71.60%	15.70%
31-Dec-76	35.60%	34.60%	−1.00%
31-Dec-77	6.90%	9.40%	2.50%
31-Dec-78	12.20%	10.10%	−2.10%
31-Dec-79	34.30%	31.50%	−2.80%
31-Dec-80	31.50%	5.30%	−26.20%
31-Dec-81	1.70%	−8.70%	−10.40%
31-Dec-82	22.50%	22.10%	−0.40%
31-Dec-83	28.10%	25.00%	−3.10%
31-Dec-84	−3.40%	−0.10%	3.30%
31-Dec-85	30.80%	41.10%	10.30%
31-Dec-86	13.10%	2.00%	−11.10%
31-Dec-87	−1.30%	−16.70%	−15.40%
31-Dec-88	21.20%	21.80%	0.60%
31-Dec-89	21.40%	−3.20%	−24.60%
31-Dec-90	−13.80%	−36.30%	−22.50%
31-Dec-91	39.80%	44.60%	4.80%
31-Dec-92	13.80%	20.40%	6.60%
31-Dec-93	16.60%	25.10%	8.50%
31-Dec-94	−3.40%	1.80%	5.20%
Arithmetic average	14.61%	14.66%	0.04%
Standard deviation	19.86%	25.41%	5.55%

Table 5-2. Annual performance of Large Stocks versus 50 stocks with high earnings-to-price (low PE) ratios drawn from Large Stocks universe.

Year ending	Large Stocks	Universe = Large Stocks Top 50 EPS/price	Top 50 EPS/price Relative performance
31-Dec-52	9.30%	14.60%	5.30%
31-Dec-53	2.30%	−5.10%	−7.40%
31-Dec-54	44.90%	64.10%	19.20%
31-Dec-55	21.20%	23.20%	2.00%
31-Dec-56	9.60%	11.10%	1.50%
31-Dec-57	−6.90%	−13.80%	−6.90%
31-Dec-58	42.10%	48.70%	6.60%
31-Dec-59	9.90%	5.60%	−4.30%
31-Dec-60	4.80%	5.30%	0.50%
31-Dec-61	27.50%	28.10%	0.60%
31-Dec-62	−8.90%	−2.90%	6.00%
31-Dec-63	19.50%	19.50%	0.00%
31-Dec-64	15.30%	20.50%	5.20%
31-Dec-65	16.20%	23.60%	7.04%
31-Dec-66	−4.90%	−6.60%	−1.70%
31-Dec-67	21.30%	25.90%	4.60%
31-Dec-68	16.80%	30.30%	13.50%
31-Dec-69	−9.90%	−19.50%	−9.60%
31-Dec-70	−0.20%	3.70%	3.90%
31-Dec-71	17.30%	10.30%	−7.00%
31-Dec-72	14.90%	19.40%	4.50%
31-Dec-73	−18.90%	−11.10%	7.80%
31-Dec-74	−26.70%	−22.20%	4.50%
31-Dec-75	43.10%	72.90%	29.80%
31-Dec-76	28.00%	39.80%	11.80%
31-Dec-77	−2.50%	1.50%	4.00%
31-Dec-78	8.10%	8.60%	0.50%
31-Dec-79	27.30%	30.70%	3.40%
31-Dec-80	30.80%	7.90%	−22.90%
31-Dec-81	0.60%	−4.00%	−4.60%
31-Dec-82	19.90%	17.60%	−2.30%
31-Dec-83	23.80%	35.50%	11.70%
31-Dec-84	−0.40%	6.90%	7.30%
31-Dec-85	19.50%	38.70%	19.20%
31-Dec-86	32.20%	17.20%	−15.00%
31-Dec-87	3.30%	−8.30%	−11.60%
31-Dec-88	19.00%	28.10%	9.10%
31-Dec-89	26.00%	33.10%	7.10%
31-Dec-90	−8.70%	−24.40%	−15.70%
31-Dec-91	33.00%	49.90%	16.90%
31-Dec-92	8.70%	10.60%	1.90%
31-Dec-93	16.30%	32.90%	16.60%
31-Dec-94	−1.90%	−2.10%	−0.20%
Arithmetic average	12.62%	15.48%	2.87%
Standard deviation	16.18%	21.70%	5.52%

Table 5-3. Summary return results for All Stocks and 50 highest earnings-to-price (low PE) stocks from All Stocks universe: December 31, 1951–December 31, 1994.

	All Stocks	Universe = All Stocks Top 50 EPS/price (low PE)
Arithmetic average	14.61%	14.66%
Standard deviation of return	19.86%	25.41%
Sharpe risk-adjusted ratio	47.00	37.00
3-yr compounded	8.63%	15.31%
5-yr compounded	9.09%	7.15%
10-yr compounded	12.74%	7.16%
15-yr compounded	13.55%	7.42%
20-yr compounded	16.95%	12.59%
25-yr compounded	11.51%	8.01%
30-yr compounded	11.47%	9.26%
35-yr compounded	11.39%	9.68%
40-yr compounded	12.45%	11.18%
Compound annual return	12.81%	11.84%
$10,000 becomes	$1,782,174.48	$1,230.991.62
Maximum return	55.90%	75.30%
Minimum return	−27.90%	−36.30%
Maximum expected return*	54.33%	65.47%
Minimum expected return**	−25.11%	−36.16%

*Maximum expected return is average return plus 2 times the standard deviation.

**Minimum expected return is average return minus 2 times the standard deviation.

45. Here, as Table 5-6 shows, base rates are not random. When looking at rolling 10-year rates of return for the 50 low PE stocks, we see that they beat the Large Stocks group 88 percent of the time.

While both the Large and All Stocks versions of the strategy had higher standard deviations of return than their universes, only the Large Stocks with low PE ratios compensated for the higher risk. The difference in returns for the large- and small-stock sections of the data-

Table 5-4. Summary return results for Large Stocks and 50 highest earnings-to-price (low PE) stocks from Large Stocks universe: December 31, 1951–December 31, 1994.

	Large Stocks	Universe = Large Stocks Top 50 EPS/price (low PE)
Arithmetic average	12.62%	15.48%
Standard deviation of return	16.18%	21.70%
Sharpe risk-adjusted ratio	45.00	47.00
3-yr compounded	7.44%	12.90%
5-yr compounded	8.53%	10.28%
10-yr compounded	13.93%	15.28%
15-yr compounded	14.03%	14.18%
20-yr compounded	15.42%	17.57%
25-yr compounded	11.16%	13.57%
30-yr compounded	10.48%	12.76%
35-yr compounded	10.54%	12.87%
40-yr compounded	10.97%	12.90%
Compound annual return	11.41%	13.47%
$10,000 becomes	$1,042,858.62	$2,287,003.25
Maximum return	44.90%	72.90%
Minimum return	−26.70%	−24.40%
Maximum expected return*	44.97%	58.88%
Minimum expected return**	−19.73%	−27.92%

*Maximum expected return is average return plus 2 times the standard deviation.

**Minimum expected return is average return minus 2 times the standard deviation.

base is striking, but it makes sense. Small companies can have a string of spectacular earnings gains on their way to becoming large companies. It's sensible for investors to award them higher PE ratios. Indeed, while you would not want to buy small stocks with very high PE ratios, you might not want them too low, either. Since low PE ratios indicate lower investor expectations for earnings growth, a small company with a low PE ratio might have very limited prospects. As companies grow,

Table 5-5. Base rates for All Stocks and 50 highest earnings-
to-price (low PE) stocks from All Stocks universe: 1951–1994.

Item	50 low PE beat All Stocks	Percent
Single-year return	24 out of 43	56%
Rolling 5-year compound return	20 out of 39	51%
Rolling 10-year compound return	18 out of 34	53%

Table 5-6. Base rates for Large Stocks and 50 highest
earnings-to-price (low PE) stocks from Large Stocks universe:
1951–1994.

Item	50 low PE beat Large Stocks	Percent
Single-year return	30 out of 43	70%
Rolling 5-year compound return	28 out of 39	72%
Rolling 10-year compound return	30 out of 34	88%

their ability to produce dazzling earnings gains decreases, and so too should the expectations of investors. On the other hand, we see investors consistently rewarding large stocks with lower PE ratios, possibly because their prices are more realistic in relation to their prospective growth rates.

We'll see that low PE ratios become even more important when multifactor models are used to select stocks, but their importance now for larger stocks is obvious from the data.

High PE Ratios Are Dangerous

Buying high PE stocks, regardless of their market capitalization, is a dangerous endeavor. You shouldn't let the flash of the latest glamour stock draw you in to paying ridiculous prices for earnings, as some investors did when Polaroid's PE ratio soared to 164 in 1961. Figure 5-2 and Tables 5-7 through 5-12 catalog the damage.

Starting with the All Stocks universe, $10,000 invested in 1951 in the 50 stocks with the highest PE ratios and rebalanced annually grew to

Figure 5-2. Returns on high PE strategies versus All Stocks and Large Stocks, 1951–1994. Year-end 1951 = $10,000.

Table 5-7. Annual performance of All Stocks versus 50 stocks with high PE ratios from All Stocks.

Year ending	All Stocks	Universe = All Stocks Top 50 price/EPS	Top 50 price/EPS Relative performance
31-Dec-52	7.90%	0.30%	−7.60%
31-Dec-53	2.90%	5.60%	2.70%
31-Dec-54	47.00%	43.10%	−3.90%
31-Dec-55	20.70%	24.30%	3.60%
31-Dec-56	17.00%	10.10%	−6.90%
31-Dec-57	−7.10%	−2.00%	5.10%
31-Dec-58	55.00%	57.50%	2.50%
31-Dec-59	23.00%	27.90%	4.90%
31-Dec-60	6.10%	4.00%	−2.10%
31-Dec-61	31.20%	15.30%	−15.90%
31-Dec-62	−12.00%	−27.10%	−15.10%
31-Dec-63	18.00%	53.20%	35.20%
31-Dec-64	16.30%	6.80%	−9.50%
31-Dec-65	22.60%	42.00%	19.40%
31-Dec-66	−5.20%	−4.60%	0.60%
31-Dec-67	41.10%	84.80%	43.70%
31-Dec-68	27.40%	9.90%	−17.50%
31-Dec-69	−18.50%	−28.10%	−9.60%
31-Dec-70	−5.80%	−33.20%	−27.40%
31-Dec-71	21.30%	23.50%	2.20%
31-Dec-72	11.00%	9.80%	−1.20%
31-Dec-73	−27.20%	−27.50%	−0.30%
31-Dec-74	−27.90%	−36.10%	−8.20%
31-Dec-75	55.90%	22.20%	−33.70%
31-Dec-76	35.60%	21.10%	−14.50%
31-Dec-77	6.90%	0.06%	−6.84%
31-Dec-78	12.20%	24.30%	12.10%
31-Dec-79	34.30%	61.90%	27.60%
31-Dec-80	31.50%	53.90%	22.40%
31-Dec-81	1.70%	−30.30%	−32.00%
31-Dec-82	22.50%	9.70%	−12.80%
31-Dec-83	28.10%	20.60%	−7.50%
31-Dec-84	−3.40%	−23.60%	−20.20%
31-Dec-85	30.80%	20.80%	−10.00%
31-Dec-86	13.10%	8.80%	−4.30%
31-Dec-87	−1.30%	13.60%	14.90%
31-Dec-88	21.20%	9.80%	−11.40%
31-Dec-89	21.40%	21.40%	0.00%
31-Dec-90	−13.80%	−16.80%	−3.00%
31-Dec-91	39.80%	24.70%	−15.10%
31-Dec-92	13.80%	9.00%	−4.80%
31-Dec-93	16.60%	9.70%	−6.90%
31-Dec-94	−3.40%	−0.50%	2.90%
Arithmetic average	14.61%	12.09%	−2.52%
Standard deviation	19.86%	26.63%	6.77%

Table 5-8. Annual performance of Large Stocks versus 50 stocks with high PE ratios drawn from Large Stocks universe.

Year ending	Large Stocks	Universe = Large Stocks Top 50 price/EPS	Top 50 price/EPS Relative performance
31-Dec-52	9.30%	3.50%	−5.80%
31-Dec-53	2.30%	5.40%	3.10%
31-Dec-54	44.90%	38.00%	−6.90%
31-Dec-55	21.20%	23.60%	2.40%
31-Dec-56	9.60%	8.40%	−1.20%
31-Dec-57	−6.90%	−7.30%	−0.40%
31-Dec-58	42.10%	37.70%	−4.40%
31-Dec-59	9.90%	16.90%	7.00%
31-Dec-60	4.80%	−4.30%	−9.10%
31-Dec-61	27.50%	20.70%	−6.80%
31-Dec-62	−8.90%	−15.30%	−6.40%
31-Dec-63	19.50%	25.80%	6.30%
31-Dec-64	15.30%	7.80%	−7.50%
31-Dec-65	16.20%	27.00%	10.80%
31-Dec-66	−4.90%	3.00%	7.90%
31-Dec-67	21.30%	41.60%	20.30%
31-Dec-68	16.80%	4.20%	−12.60%
31-Dec-69	−9.90%	10.30%	20.20%
31-Dec-70	−0.20%	−22.20%	−22.00%
31-Dec-71	17.30%	33.40%	16.10%
31-Dec-72	14.90%	21.70%	6.80%
31-Dec-73	−18.90%	−25.30%	−6.40%
31-Dec-74	−26.70%	−33.40%	−6.70%
31-Dec-75	43.10%	19.20%	−23.90%
31-Dec-76	28.00%	9.90%	−18.10%
31-Dec-77	−2.50%	−12.70%	−10.20%
31-Dec-78	8.10%	13.60%	5.50%
31-Dec-79	27.30%	34.40%	7.10%
31-Dec-80	30.80%	60.90%	30.10%
31-Dec-81	0.60%	−20.00%	−20.60%
31-Dec-82	19.90%	9.90%	−10.00%
31-Dec-83	23.80%	24.90%	1.10%
31-Dec-84	−0.40%	−17.70%	−17.30%
31-Dec-85	19.50%	22.10%	2.60%
31-Dec-86	32.20%	25.40%	−6.80%
31-Dec-87	3.30%	15.80%	12.50%
31-Dec-88	19.00%	11.20%	−7.80%
31-Dec-89	26.00%	30.60%	4.60%
31-Dec-90	−8.70%	−18.00%	−9.30%
31-Dec-91	33.00%	32.60%	−0.40%
31-Dec-92	8.70%	−4.50%	−13.20%
31-Dec-93	16.30%	30.60%	14.30%
31-Dec-94	−1.90%	−1.40%	0.50%
Arithmetic average	12.62%	11.35%	−1.27%
Standard deviation	16.18%	20.51%	4.34%

Table 5-9. Summary return results for All Stocks and 50 highest PE stocks from All Stocks universe: December 31, 1951–December 31, 1994.

	All Stocks	Universe = All Stocks Top 50 high PE ratios
Arithmetic average	14.61%	12.09%
Standard deviation of return	19.86%	26.63%
Sharpe risk-adjusted ratio	47.00	25.00
3-yr compounded	8.63%	5.96%
5-yr compounded	9.09%	4.30%
10-yr compounded	12.74%	9.40%
15-yr compounded	13.55%	6.75%
20-yr compounded	16.95%	10.91%
25-yr compounded	11.51%	4.93%
30-yr compounded	11.47%	6.49%
35-yr compounded	11.39%	6.62%
40-yr compounded	12.45%	8.43%
Compound annual return	12.81%	8.87%
$10,000 becomes	$1,782,174.48	$385,890.32
Maximum return	55.90%	84.80%
Minimum return	−27.90%	−36.10%
Maximum expected return*	54.33%	65.35%
Minimum expected return**	−25.11%	−41.17%

*Maximum expected return is average return plus 2 times the standard deviation.

**Minimum expected return is average return minus 2 times the standard deviation.

$385,890 by the end of 1994—$1,396,284 less than if you bought the All Stocks universe itself! The compound return of 8.87 percent was well behind All Stocks' 12.81 percent annual return. When you adjust for risk the news gets even grimmer. The 50 high PE stocks' Sharpe ratio of 25 was nearly half that of the All Stocks universe. The high PE stocks beat the All Stocks group just 12 percent of the time in all rolling 10-year periods.

Table 5-10. Summary return results for Large Stocks and 50 highest PE stocks from Large Stocks universe: December 31, 1951–December 31, 1994.

	Large Stocks	Universe = Large Stocks Top 50 high PE ratios
Arithmetic average	12.62%	11.35%
Standard deviation of return	16.18%	20.51%
Sharpe risk-adjusted ratio	45.00	29.00
3-yr compounded	7.44%	7.14%
5-yr compounded	8.53%	5.98%
10-yr compounded	13.93%	13.16%
15-yr compounded	14.03%	11.34%
20-yr compounded	15.42%	11.45%
25-yr compounded	11.16%	7.05%
30-yr compounded	10.48%	8.54%
35-yr compounded	10.54%	8.15%
40-yr compounded	10.97%	8.97%
Compound annual return	11.41%	9.35%
$10,000 becomes	$1,042,858.62	$467,012.63
Maximum return	44.90%	60.90%
Minimum return	−26.70%	−33.40%
Maximum expected return*	44.97%	52.38%
Minimum expected return**	−19.73%	−29.68%

*Maximum expected return is average return plus 2 times the standard deviation.

**Minimum expected return is average return minus 2 times the standard deviation.

Large Stocks Fare No Better

The high PE damage is similar in the Large Stocks group: $10,000 invested in the 50 Large Stocks with the highest PE ratios grew to $467,013 at the end of 1994, half as much as you'd earn with an investment in Large Stocks. All the high PE stocks' compound returns, from the most recent to the long term, fall short of the Large Stocks universe

Table 5-11. Base rates for All Stocks and 50 highest PE stocks from All Stocks universe: 1951–1994.

Item	50 high PE beat All Stocks	Percent
Single-year return	15 out of 43	35%
Rolling 5-year compound return	11 out of 39	28%
Rolling 10-year compound return	4 out of 34	12%

Table 5-12. Base rates for Large Stocks and 50 highest PE stocks from Large Stocks universe: 1951–1994.

Item	50 high PE beat Large Stocks	Percent
Single-year return	19 out of 43	44%
Rolling 5-year compound return	11 out of 39	28%
Rolling 10-year compound return	8 out of 34	24%

with a Sharpe ratio of 29, 16 points lower than the Large Stocks universe.

Adding insult to injury, the 50 Large Stocks with the highest PE ratios beat the Large Stocks universe just 24 percent of the time over all rolling 10-year periods.

Implications

Figures 5-3 and 5-4, as well as Table 5-13, summarize what you can expect when buying stocks with low and high PE ratios. The results are striking. Both Large and All Stocks with high PE ratios do substantially worse than the market. Companies with low PE ratios from the Large Stocks universe do much better than the universe. In both groups, *stocks with low PE ratios do much better than stocks with high PE ratios.* More, there's not much difference in risk. In the All Stocks universe, the standard deviation of return on the 50 low PE stocks was 25.41 percent, whereas the 50 highest PE stocks had a standard deviation of 26.63 percent. In the Large Stocks universe, the low PE strategy had a standard

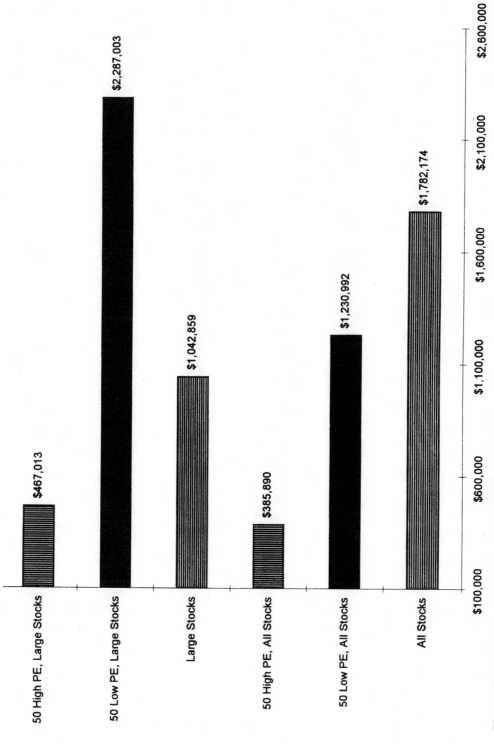

Figure 5-3. December 31, 1994, value of $10,000 invested on December 31, 1951, and annually rebalanced.

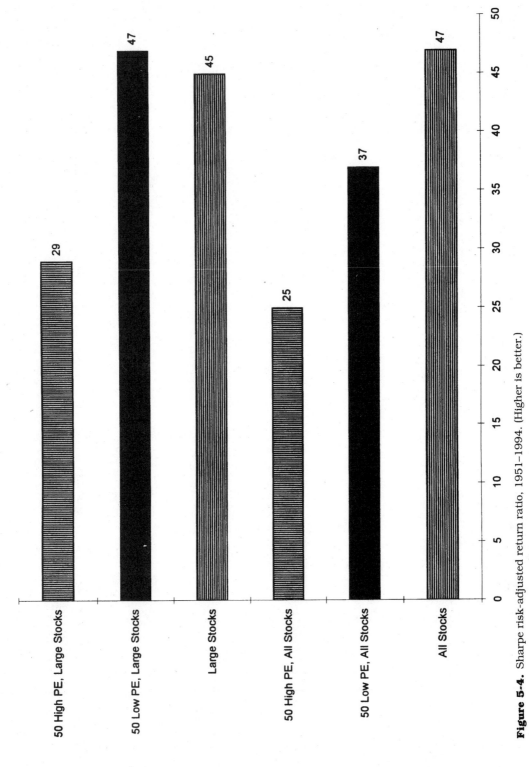

Figure 5-4. Sharpe risk-adjusted return ratio, 1951–1994. (Higher is better.)

Table 5-13. Compound annual rates of return by decade.

Portfolio	1950s*	1960s	1970s	1980s	1990s**
Large Stocks	15.33%	8.99%	6.99%	16.89%	8.53%
50 high PE from Large Stocks	14.77%	10.94%	0.93%	14.11%	5.98%
50 low PE from Large Stocks	16.12%	11.14%	12.64%	16.19%	10.28%
All Stocks	19.22%	11.09%	8.53%	15.85%	9.09%
50 high PE from All Stocks	19.27%	10.96%	2.26%	7.99%	4.30%
50 low PE from All Stocks	21.84%	13.96%	8.89%	7.56%	7.15%

*Returns for 1952–1959.
**Returns for 1990–1994.

deviation of 21.70 percent, whereas the high PE strategy's standard deviation was 20.51 percent.

Ben Graham and David Dodd were absolutely right in their 1940 book *Security Analysis: Principles and Technique.* They said: "People who habitually purchase common stocks at more than about 20 times their average earnings are likely to lose considerable money in the long run."

6

Price-to-Book Ratios:
A Better Gauge
of Value

*Life can only be understood backwards; but it
must be lived forwards.*

—SÖREN KIERKEGAARD

In this chapter, we'll review stocks' price-to-book ratios. Many investors believe this is a more important ratio when looking for a bargain. They argue that earnings can be easily manipulated by a clever chief financial officer, using an old joke as an example. A company wants to hire a new chief financial officer. Each candidate is asked just one question: "What does 2 plus 2 equal?" Each candidate answers 4, with the exception of the one they hire. Her answer is: "What number did you have in mind?"

You find the price-to-book ratio by dividing the current price of the stock by the book value per share. Here, we use the common equity liquidating value per share as a proxy for book value per share. Essentially, investors who buy stocks with low price-to-book ratios believe they are getting stocks at a price close to their liquidating value, and that they will be rewarded for not paying high prices for assets.

We'll look at both the high and low price-to-book ratio stocks from All Stocks and Large Stocks. We'll start on December 31, 1951, and buy the 50 stocks with the highest book-to-price ratios from the All Stocks universe. (Again, because of Compustat's ranking function, we must rank stocks by the 50 *highest* book-to-price ratios, the inverse of the price-to-book ratio.)

The Results

Over the long term, the market rewards stocks with low price-to-book ratios and punishes those with high ones. An investment of $10,000 on December 31, 1951, in the 50 stocks with the lowest price-to-book ratios from the All Stocks universe grew to $3,591,446 by December 31, 1994, a compound return of 14.66 percent a year. That's much better than the $1,782,174 you'd earn from an investment in All Stocks. Risk was fairly high. The standard deviation for the 50 low price-to-book stocks was 25.89 percent, considerably higher than the All Stocks universe's 19.86 percent. But, because of the higher returns, the Sharpe ratio for both the 50 low price-to-book stocks and the All Stocks universe was 47.

Large Stocks Are Less Volatile

The 50 low price-to-book stocks from the Large Stocks universe did much better on a risk-adjusted basis. Here, $10,000 invested in 1951 grew to $3,417,758 by the end of 1994, a compound return of 14.53 percent a year. That's almost three times the $1,042,859 you'd earn from $10,000 invested in the Large Stocks universe, but with a standard deviation of 20.34 percent. While higher than the Large Stocks' 16.18 percent, it's much less volatile than the low price-to-book stocks from All Stocks. The Sharpe ratio here was 54, a strong showing from a single variable.

Base rates here are mixed. While the 50 low price-to-book stocks from All Stocks beat the universe 61 percent of the time on a year-by-year basis and 68 percent of the time over all rolling 10-year periods, they beat the All Stocks group just 49 percent of the time on a rolling 5-year basis. This suggests the low price-to-book group saw some wild rides on the way to beating the All Stocks universe. Indeed, when you look at the annual performance comparisons in Table 6-1, you see 4 years where the low price-to-book group did 20 percent better than All Stocks. But there was also some rough sledding. The low price-to-book strategy underperformed the All Stocks universe 4 years in a row between 1976 and 1980, and had a devastating period between 1988 and

Table 6-1. Annual performance of All Stocks versus 50 stocks with high book-to-price (low price-to-book) ratios drawn from All Stocks universe.

Year ending	All Stocks	Universe = All Stocks Top 50 book/price	Top 50 book/price Relative performance
31-Dec-52	7.90%	5.40%	−2.50%
31-Dec-53	2.90%	−2.60%	−5.50%
31-Dec-54	47.00%	62.20%	15.20%
31-Dec-55	20.70%	19.30%	−1.40%
31-Dec-56	17.00%	8.20%	−8.80%
31-Dec-57	−7.10%	−14.50%	−7.40%
31-Dec-58	55.00%	77.49%	22.49%
31-Dec-59	23.00%	22.10%	−0.90%
31-Dec-60	6.10%	−8.50%	−14.60%
31-Dec-61	31.20%	32.60%	1.40%
31-Dec-62	−12.00%	−4.10%	7.90%
31-Dec-63	18.00%	23.50%	5.50%
31-Dec-64	16.30%	16.80%	0.50%
31-Dec-65	22.60%	39.20%	16.60%
31-Dec-66	−5.20%	−12.80%	−7.60%
31-Dec-67	41.10%	43.60%	2.50%
31-Dec-68	27.40%	37.40%	10.00%
31-Dec-69	−18.50%	−26.20%	−7.70%
31-Dec-70	−5.80%	0.07%	5.87%
31-Dec-71	21.30%	23.30%	2.00%
31-Dec-72	11.00%	13.80%	2.80%
31-Dec-73	−27.20%	−10.30%	16.90%
31-Dec-74	−27.90%	−8.50%	19.40%
31-Dec-75	55.90%	69.80%	13.90%
31-Dec-76	35.60%	62.40%	26.80%
31-Dec-77	6.90%	6.30%	−0.60%
31-Dec-78	12.20%	10.10%	−2.10%
31-Dec-79	34.30%	29.90%	−4.40%
31-Dec-80	31.50%	13.50%	−18.00%
31-Dec-81	1.70%	2.70%	1.00%
31-Dec-82	22.50%	36.70%	14.20%
31-Dec-83	28.10%	41.90%	13.80%
31-Dec-84	−3.40%	−19.40%	−16.00%
31-Dec-85	30.80%	33.60%	2.80%
31-Dec-86	13.10%	−5.80%	−18.90%
31-Dec-87	−1.30%	9.70%	11.00%
31-Dec-88	21.20%	34.40%	13.20%
31-Dec-89	21.40%	1.70%	−19.70%
31-Dec-90	−13.80%	−34.50%	−20.70%
31-Dec-91	39.80%	48.20%	8.40%
31-Dec-92	13.80%	40.40%	26.60%
31-Dec-93	16.60%	36.70%	20.10%
31-Dec-94	−3.40%	−1.80%	1.60%
Arithmetic average	14.61%	17.53%	2.92%
Standard deviation	19.86%	25.89%	6.03%

1990. These periods are important to keep in mind when thinking about using any strategy, as many investors would jettison the strategy after such a poor showing. For a strategy to be valuable, it must be consistent enough for investors to stick with it through rough patches.

Large Stocks Base Rates More Consistent

Base rates for the low price-to-book stocks from the Large Stocks universe are more consistent. Here, the low price-to-book stocks beat the Large Stocks universe a minimum of 65 percent of the time, with rolling 10-year returns showing the highest probability of beating the Large Stocks universe. Figure 6-1 and Tables 6-2 through 6-6 summarize the results.

High Price-to-Book Stocks Do Poorly

Like high price-to-earnings stocks, stocks with high price-to-book ratios are generally bad investments. Figure 6-2 and Tables 6-7 through 6-12 summarize the results. An investment of $10,000 in the 50 stocks with the highest price-to-book ratios drawn from the All Stocks universe grew to just $286,347 at the end of 1994, $1 million behind an investment in All Stocks and several million behind an investment in the 50 stocks with the lowest price-to-book ratios. The standard deviation of almost 29 percent signifies a wild ride, verified by the year-by-year returns. In 1973 through 1976 and 1981 through 1985, the group did 20 percent *worse* than the All Stocks universe annually. The years 1981 and 1984 are worthy of special mention. In 1981, the All Stocks universe had a gain of 1.7 percent. The 50 stocks with the highest price-to-book ratios *lost* over 31 percent. The year 1984 was more terrifying, with the All Stocks group losing 3.4 percent while high price-to-book stocks lost almost 40 percent.

The 50 stocks with high price-to-book ratios from the Large Stocks group didn't fare much better. An investment of $10,000 on December 31, 1951, grew to only $562,992 by the end of 1994, a compound return of 9.83 percent, about half the return of the Large Stocks group. The standard deviation was a bit lower—23.16 percent—but the Sharpe ratio of 30 was still dismal. Figures 6-3 and 6-4 summarize the results.

The base rates for the high price-to-book stocks are unusual. While the longer-term numbers are overwhelmingly negative, high price-to-

Figure 6-1. Returns on low price-to-book strategies versus All Stocks and Large Stocks, 1951–1994. Year-end 1951 = $10,000.

Table 6-2. Annual performance of Large Stocks versus 50 stocks with high book-to-price (low price-to-book) ratios drawn from Large Stocks universe.

Year ending	Large Stocks	Universe = Large Stocks Top 50 book/price	Top 50 book/price Relative performance
31-Dec-52	9.30%	11.90%	2.60%
31-Dec-53	2.30%	1.40%	−0.90%
31-Dec-54	44.90%	59.60%	14.70%
31-Dec-55	21.20%	17.20%	−4.00%
31-Dec-56	9.60%	10.90%	1.30%
31-Dec-57	−6.90%	−10.70%	−3.80%
31-Dec-58	42.10%	41.70%	−0.40%
31-Dec-59	9.90%	5.70%	−4.20%
31-Dec-60	4.80%	−1.10%	−5.90%
31-Dec-61	27.50%	28.20%	0.70%
31-Dec-62	−8.90%	−3.20%	5.70%
31-Dec-63	19.50%	24.60%	5.10%
31-Dec-64	15.30%	19.30%	4.00%
31-Dec-65	16.20%	17.90%	1.70%
31-Dec-66	−4.90%	−10.10%	−5.20%
31-Dec-67	21.30%	22.50%	1.20%
31-Dec-68	16.80%	30.80%	14.00%
31-Dec-69	−9.90%	−19.50%	−9.60%
31-Dec-70	−0.20%	1.80%	2.00%
31-Dec-71	17.30%	19.00%	1.70%
31-Dec-72	14.90%	12.00%	−2.90%
31-Dec-73	−18.90%	−2.90%	16.00%
31-Dec-74	−26.70%	−16.90%	9.80%
31-Dec-75	43.10%	66.60%	23.50%
31-Dec-76	28.00%	50.10%	22.10%
31-Dec-77	−2.50%	2.50%	5.00%
31-Dec-78	8.10%	5.50%	−2.60%
31-Dec-79	27.30%	24.70%	−2.60%
31-Dec-80	30.80%	18.50%	−12.30%
31-Dec-81	0.60%	10.20%	9.60%
31-Dec-82	19.90%	33.00%	13.10%
31-Dec-83	23.80%	46.60%	22.80%
31-Dec-84	−0.40%	1.80%	2.20%
31-Dec-85	19.50%	29.10%	9.60%
31-Dec-86	32.20%	4.40%	−27.80%
31-Dec-87	3.30%	5.50%	2.20%
31-Dec-88	19.00%	36.30%	17.30%
31-Dec-89	26.00%	23.20%	−2.80%
31-Dec-90	−8.70%	−21.90%	−13.20%
31-Dec-91	33.00%	49.00%	16.00%
31-Dec-92	8.70%	18.80%	10.10%
31-Dec-93	16.30%	32.50%	16.20%
31-Dec-94	−1.90%	4.00%	5.90%
Arithmetic average	12.62%	16.29%	3.67%
Standard deviation	16.18%	20.34%	4.16%

Table 6-3. Summary return results for All Stocks and 50 highest book-to-price (low price-to-book) stocks from All Stocks universe: December 31, 1951–December 31, 1994.

	All Stocks	Universe = All Stocks Top 50 book/price
Arithmetic average	14.61%	17.53%
Standard deviation of return	19.86%	25.89%
Sharpe risk-adjusted ratio	47.00	47.00
3-yr compounded	8.63%	23.52%
5-yr compounded	9.09%	12.84%
10-yr compounded	12.74%	13.19%
15-yr compounded	13.55%	13.05%
20-yr compounded	16.95%	17.78%
25-yr compounded	11.51%	14.63%
30-yr compounded	11.47%	14.20%
35-yr compounded	11.39%	13.73%
40-yr compounded	12.45%	14.38%
Compound annual return	12.81%	14.66%
$10,000 becomes	$1,782,174.48	$3,591,446.26
Maximum return	55.90%	77.49%
Minimum return	−27.90%	−34.50%
Maximum expected return*	54.33%	69.31%
Minimum expected return**	−25.11%	−34.24%

*Maximum expected return is average return plus 2 times the standard deviation.

**Minimum expected return is average return minus 2 times the standard deviation.

Table 6-4. Summary return results for Large Stocks and 50 highest book-to-price (low price-to-book) stocks from Large Stocks universe: December 31, 1951–December 31, 1994.

	Large Stocks	Universe = Large Stocks Top 50 book/price
Arithmetic average	12.62%	16.29%
Standard deviation of return	16.18%	20.34%
Sharpe risk-adjusted ratio	45.00	54.00
3-yr compounded	7.44%	17.86%
5-yr compounded	8.53%	13.76%
10-yr compounded	13.93%	16.36%
15-yr compounded	14.03%	17.88%
20-yr compounded	15.42%	20.22%
25-yr compounded	11.16%	16.29%
30-yr compounded	10.48%	14.59%
35-yr compounded	10.54%	14.33%
40-yr compounded	10.97%	14.00%
Compound annual return	11.41%	14.53%
$10,000 becomes	$1,042.858.62	$3,417,757.90
Maximum return	44.90%	66.60%
Minimum return	−26.70%	−21.90%
Maximum expected return*	44.97%	59.97%
Minimum expected return**	−19.73%	−24.39%

*Maximum expected return is average return plus 2 times the standard deviation.
**Minimum expected return is average return minus 2 times the standard deviation.

Table 6-5. Base rates for All Stocks and 50 highest book-to-price (low price-to-book) stocks from All Stocks universe: 1951–1994.

Item	50 low price-to-book beat All Stocks	Percent
Single-year return	26 out of 43	61%
Rolling 5-year compound return	19 out of 39	49%
Rolling 10-year compound return	23 out of 34	68%

Table 6-6. Base rates for Large Stocks and 50 highest book-to-price (low price-to-book) stocks from Large Stocks universe: 1951–1994.

Item	50 low price-to-book beat Large Stocks	Percent
Single-year return	28 out of 43	65%
Rolling 5-year compound return	30 out of 39	77%
Rolling 10-year compound return	30 out of 34	88%

Figure 6-2. Returns on high price-to-book strategies versus All Stocks and Large Stocks, 1951–1994. Year-end 1951 = $10,000.

Table 6-7. Annual performance of All Stocks versus 50 stocks with high price-to-book ratios from All Stocks universe.

Year ending	All Stocks	Universe = All Stocks Top 50 price/book	Top 50 price/book Relative performance
31-Dec-52	7.90%	3.90%	−4.00%
31-Dec-53	2.90%	3.40%	0.50%
31-Dec-54	47.00%	49.60%	2.60%
31-Dec-55	20.70%	19.00%	−1.70%
31-Dec-56	17.00%	21.50%	4.50%
31-Dec-57	−7.10%	−5.40%	1.70%
31-Dec-58	55.00%	61.80%	6.80%
31-Dec-59	23.00%	40.90%	17.90%
31-Dec-60	6.10%	19.20%	13.10%
31-Dec-61	31.20%	23.00%	−8.20%
31-Dec-62	−12.00%	−23.00%	−11.30%
31-Dec-63	18.00%	21.82%	3.82%
31-Dec-64	16.30%	3.20%	−13.10%
31-Dec-65	22.60%	20.20%	−2.40%
31-Dec-66	−5.20%	5.90%	11.10%
31-Dec-67	41.10%	87.60%	46.50%
31-Dec-68	27.40%	18.00%	−9.40%
31-Dec-69	−18.50%	−13.80%	4.70%
31-Dec-70	−5.80%	−22.20%	−16.40%
31-Dec-71	21.30%	45.10%	23.80%
31-Dec-72	11.00%	17.60%	6.60%
31-Dec-73	−27.20%	−38.10%	−10.90%
31-Dec-74	−27.90%	−44.80%	−16.90%
31-Dec-75	55.90%	21.90%	−34.00%
31-Dec-76	35.60%	7.30%	−28.30%
31-Dec-77	6.90%	7.90%	1.00%
31-Dec-78	12.20%	16.30%	4.10%
31-Dec-79	34.30%	45.70%	11.40%
31-Dec-80	31.50%	43.00%	11.50%
31-Dec-81	1.70%	−31.20%	−32.90%
31-Dec-82	22.50%	5.90%	−16.60%
31-Dec-83	28.10%	−6.30%	−34.40%
31-Dec-84	−3.40%	−38.60%	−35.20%
31-Dec-85	30.80%	34.60%	3.80%
31-Dec-86	13.10%	15.40%	2.30%
31-Dec-87	−1.30%	−7.10%	−5.80%
31-Dec-88	21.20%	7.60%	−13.60%
31-Dec-89	21.40%	30.60%	9.20%
31-Dec-90	−13.80%	−20.90%	−7.10%
31-Dec-91	39.80%	68.30%	28.50%
31-Dec-92	13.80%	−15.80%	−29.60%
31-Dec-93	16.60%	22.50%	5.90%
31-Dec-94	−3.40%	−8.10%	−4.70%
Arithmetic average	14.61%	11.93%	−2.68%
Standard deviation	19.86%	28.65%	8.79%

Table 6-8. Annual performance of Large Stocks versus 50 stocks with high price-to-book ratios drawn from Large Stocks universe.

Year ending	Large Stocks	Universe = Large Stocks Top 50 price/book	Top 50 price/book Relative performance
31-Dec-52	9.30%	6.00%	−3.30%
31-Dec-53	2.30%	0.60%	−1.70%
31-Dec-54	44.90%	43.50%	−1.40%
31-Dec-55	21.20%	31.90%	10.70%
31-Dec-56	9.60%	9.50%	−0.10%
31-Dec-57	−6.90%	−11.00%	−4.10%
31-Dec-58	42.10%	44.60%	2.50%
31-Dec-59	9.90%	19.70%	9.80%
31-Dec-60	4.80%	2.80%	−2.00%
31-Dec-61	27.50%	24.20%	−3.30%
31-Dec-62	−8.90%	−17.20%	−8.30%
31-Dec-63	19.50%	21.80%	2.30%
31-Dec-64	15.30%	8.40%	−6.90%
31-Dec-65	16.20%	20.00%	3.80%
31-Dec-66	−4.90%	8.40%	13.30%
31-Dec-67	21.30%	40.20%	18.90%
31-Dec-68	16.80%	2.30%	−14.50%
31-Dec-69	−9.90%	12.00%	21.90%
31-Dec-70	−0.20%	−19.90%	−19.70%
31-Dec-71	17.30%	34.60%	17.30%
31-Dec-72	14.90%	26.10%	11.20%
31-Dec-73	−18.90%	28.80%	−9.90%
31-Dec-74	−26.70%	−38.70%	−12.00%
31-Dec-75	43.10%	18.60%	−24.50%
31-Dec-76	28.00%	9.20%	−18.80%
31-Dec-77	−2.50%	−10.40%	−7.90%
31-Dec-78	8.10%	10.40%	2.30%
31-Dec-79	27.30%	23.90%	−3.40%
31-Dec-80	30.80%	67.80%	37.00%
31-Dec-81	0.60%	−18.80%	−19.40%
31-Dec-82	19.90%	15.80%	−4.10%
31-Dec-83	23.80%	13.80%	−10.00%
31-Dec-84	−0.40%	−18.40%	−18.00%
31-Dec-85	19.50%	29.80%	10.30%
31-Dec-86	32.20%	28.40%	−3.80%
31-Dec-87	3.30%	1.00%	−2.30%
31-Dec-88	19.00%	4.80%	−14.20%
31-Dec-89	26.00%	48.50%	22.50%
31-Dec-90	−8.70%	−7.00%	1.70%
31-Dec-91	33.00%	65.60%	32.60%
31-Dec-92	8.70%	−0.90%	−9.60%
31-Dec-93	16.30%	15.20%	−1.10%
31-Dec-94	−1.90%	−10.80%	−8.90%
Arithmetic average	12.62%	12.27%	−0.35%
Standard deviation	16.18%	23.16%	6.98%

Table 6-9. Summary return results for All Stocks and 50 highest price-to-book stocks from All Stocks universe: December 31, 1951–December 31, 1994.

	All Stocks	Universe = All Stocks Top 50 price/book
Arithmetic average	14.61%	11.93%
Standard deviation of return	19.86%	28.65%
Sharpe risk-adjusted ratio	47.00	23.00
3-yr compounded	8.63%	−1.77%
5-yr compounded	9.09%	4.76%
10-yr compounded	12.74%	9.85%
15-yr compounded	13.55%	2.89%
20-yr compounded	16.95%	6.71%
25-yr compounded	11.51%	2.06%
30-yr compounded	11.47%	4.77%
35-yr compounded	11.39%	5.11%
40-yr compounded	12.45%	7.47%
Compound annual return	12.81%	8.11%
$10,000 becomes	$1,782,174.48	$286,346.61
Maximum return	55.90%	87.60%
Minimum return	−27.90%	−44.80%
Maximum expected return*	54.33%	69.24%
Minimum expected return**	−25.11%	−45.37%

*Maximum expected return is average return plus 2 times the standard deviation.
**Minimum expected return is average return minus 2 times the standard deviation.

Table 6-10. Summary return results for Large Stocks and 50 highest price-to-book stocks from Large Stocks universe: December 31, 1951–December 31, 1994.

	Large Stocks	Universe = Large Stocks Top 50 price/book
Arithmetic average	12.62%	12.27%
Standard deviation of return	16.18%	23.16%
Sharpe risk-adjusted ratio	45.00	30.00
3-yr compounded	7.44%	0.61%
5-yr compounded	8.53%	9.42%
10-yr compounded	13.93%	15.18%
15-yr compounded	14.03%	12.71%
20-yr compounded	15.42%	11.95%
25-yr compounded	11.16%	7.19%
30-yr compounded	10.48%	8.59%
35-yr compounded	10.54%	8.35%
40-yr compounded	10.97%	9.43%
Compound annual return	11.41%	9.83%
$10,000 becomes	$1,042.858.62	$562,991.50
Maximum return	44.90%	67.80%
Minimum return	−26.70%	−38.70%
Maximum expected return*	44.97%	58.58%
Minimum expected return**	−19.73%	−34.04%

*Maximum expected return is average return plus 2 times the standard deviation.
**Minimum expected return is average return minus 2 times the standard deviation.

Table 6-11. Base rates for All Stocks and 50 highest price-to-book stocks from All Stocks universe: 1951–1994.

Item	50 high price-to-book beat All Stocks	Percent
Single-year return	22 out of 43	51%
Rolling 5-year compound return	14 out of 39	36%
Rolling 10-year compound return	12 out of 34	35%

Table 6-12. Base rates for Large Stocks and 50 highest price-to-book stocks from Large Stocks universe: 1951–1994.

Item	50 high price-to-book beat Large Stocks	Percent
Single-year return	16 out of 43	37%
Rolling 5-year compound return	20 out of 39	51%
Rolling 10-year compound return	13 out of 34	38%

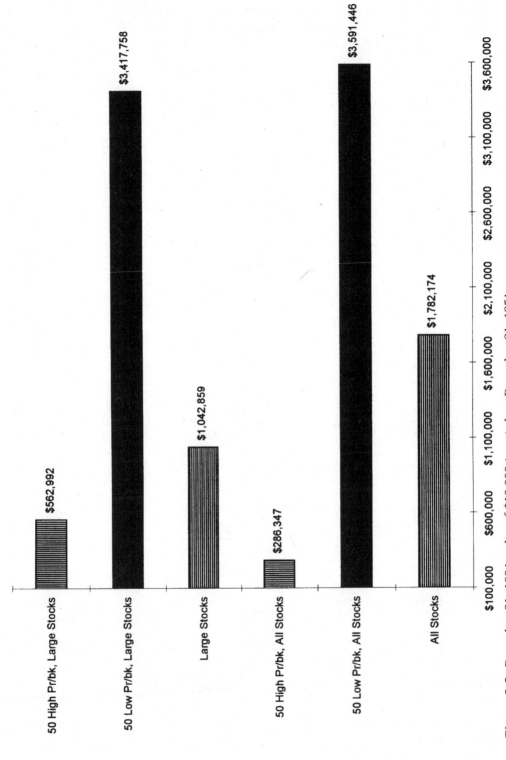

Figure 6-3. December 31, 1994, value of $10,000 invested on December 31, 1951, and annually rebalanced.

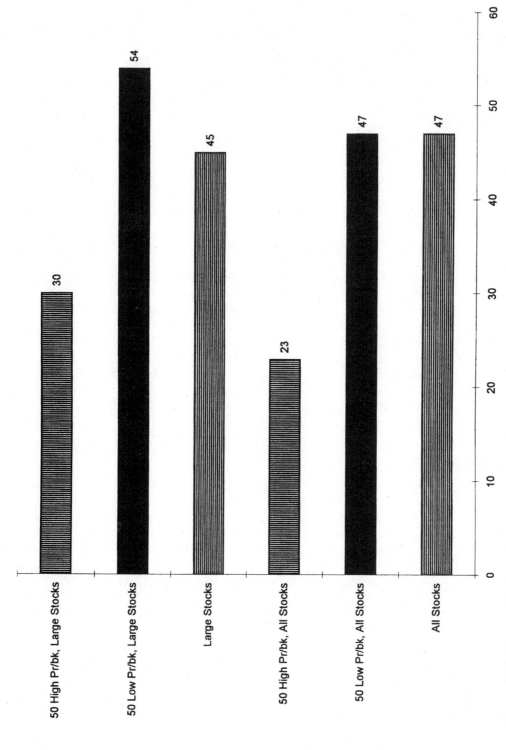

Figure 6-4. Sharpe risk-adjusted return ratio, 1951–1994. (Higher is better.)

Table 6-13. Compound annual rates of return by decade.

Portfolio	1950s*	1960s	1970s	1980s	1990s**
Large Stocks	15.33%	8.99%	6.99%	16.89%	8.53%
50 high price-to-book from Large Stocks	16.55%	11.30%	−0.60%	14.40%	9.42%
50 low price-to-book from Large Stocks	15.41%	9.57%	13.95%	19.99%	13.76%
All Stocks	19.22%	11.09%	8.53%	15.85%	9.09%
50 high price-to-book from All Stocks	22.32%	13.13%	0.82%	1.97%	4.76%
50 low price-to-book from All Stocks	18.86%	11.49%	17.06%	13.15%	12.84%

*Returns for 1952–1959.
**Returns for 1990–1994.

book stocks from the Large Stocks universe actually beat the group 51 percent of the time for rolling 5-year returns. What's more, the compound returns in Table 6-13 show that the 50 large stocks with the highest price-to-book ratios did better than Large Stocks in both the 1950s and 1960s! In contrast, large stocks with high PE ratios failed to beat the universe in any of the decades from the 1950s to the 1990s. This teaches you to be careful when reviewing returns by decade. As Table 6-14 shows, you're better off looking at rolling 10-year returns on a continuous basis.

Implications

Over the long term, the market rewards low price-to-book ratios and punishes high ones. Yet the data show why investors are willing to overlook high price-to-book ratios—for 20 years, large stocks with high price-to-book ratios did *better* than the Large Stocks universe. A high price-to-book ratio is one of the hallmarks of a growth stock, so high price-to-book ratios alone shouldn't keep you from buying a stock. But the long-term results should caution you against the highest price-to-book ratio stocks.

Table 6-14. Rolling compound 10-year returns for All Stocks and 50 highest price-to-book stocks from All Stocks universe: December 31, 1961– December 31, 1994.

For the 10 years ending	All Stocks	Universe = All Stocks Top 50 price/book	Top 50 price/book Relative performance
31-Dec-61	18.97%	22.07%	3.10%
31-Dec-62	16.57%	18.42%	1.85%
31-Dec-63	18.18%	20.38%	2.20%
31-Dec-64	15.44%	15.99%	0.55%
31-Dec-65	15.63%	16.11%	0.48%
31-Dec-66	13.22%	14.52%	1.31%
31-Dec-67	18.05%	22.64%	4.59%
31-Dec-68	15.76%	18.83%	3.07%
31-Dec-69	11.09%	13.13%	2.04%
31-Dec-70	9.78%	8.41%	−1.37%
31-Dec-71	8.92%	10.21%	1.29%
31-Dec-72	11.48%	15.02%	3.55%
31-Dec-73	6.22%	7.49%	1.27%
31-Dec-74	1.26%	0.97%	−0.29%
31-Dec-75	3.72%	1.12%	−2.61%
31-Dec-76	7.50%	1.25%	−6.26%
31-Dec-77	4.56%	−4.20%	−8.76%
31-Dec-78	3.24%	−4.34%	−7.58%
31-Dec-79	8.53%	0.82%	−7.71%
31-Dec-80	12.21%	7.14%	−5.07%
31-Dec-81	10.25%	−0.56%	−10.81%
31-Dec-82	11.34%	−1.60%	−12.94%
31-Dec-83	17.82%	2.57%	−15.25%
31-Dec-84	21.31%	3.67%	−17.65%
31-Dec-85	19.20%	4.70%	−14.50%
31-Dec-86	17.06%	5.46%	−11.59%
31-Dec-87	16.13%	3.90%	−12.23%
31-Dec-88	17.03%	3.09%	−13.93%
31-Dec-89	15.85%	1.97%	−13.88%
31-Dec-90	11.06%	−3.89%	−14.95%
31-Dec-91	14.65%	5.10%	−9.55%
31-Dec-92	13.81%	2.72%	−11.09%
31-Dec-93	12.74%	5.51%	−7.24%
31-Dec-94	12.74%	9.85%	−2.89%
Arithmetic average	12.69%	7.31%	−5.38%

7

Price-to-Cashflow
Ratios: Using Cash
to Determine Value

Losing an illusion makes you wiser than finding a truth.   —LUDWIG BORNE

The price-to-cashflow ratio is yet another measure of whether a stock is cheap or not. You find cashflow by adding income (before extraordinary items) to depreciation and amortization. The price-to-cashflow ratio is the market value of the stock divided by total cashflow. We'll look at it on a per share basis.

Some value investors prefer using price-to-cashflow ratios to find bargain-priced stocks because cashflow is more difficult to manipulate than earnings. We exclude utility stocks here, since utilities show up frequently and we want to avoid bias to one industry.

As usual, we look at both the low and high price-to-cashflow stocks from our All Stocks and Large Stocks universes. We start with $10,000 on December 31, 1951, and buy the 50 stocks with the highest cashflow-to-price ratios from the All Stocks universe. (Again, because of Compustat's ranking function, we must rank stocks by the 50 *highest* cashflow-to-price ratios, the inverse of the price-to-cashflow ratio.) We'll rebalance the portfolio annually. The stocks are equally weighted, and all variables except price are time-lagged to avoid look-ahead bias.

The Results

As with the other value criteria, investors reward stocks with low price-to-cashflow ratios and punish those with high ones. Figure 7-1 summarizes the results. Let's look at the returns of low price-to-cashflow stocks first. An investment of $10,000 on December 31, 1951, in the 50 stocks with the lowest price-to-cashflow ratios from the All Stocks universe was worth $2,947,183 on December 31,1994, a compound return of 14.14 percent a year—better than the $1,782,174 you'd earn from the same investment in the All Stocks universe. Risk was fairly high. The standard deviation of return for the 50 lowest price-to-cashflow stocks was 26.25 percent, considerably higher than the All Stocks universe's 19.86 percent. Indeed, because of the higher risk, the Sharpe ratio for the low price-to-cashflow stocks was lower than that for the All Stocks universe, indicating risk was not being fully rewarded. Tables 7-1 through 7-4 summarize the returns for the All Stocks group.

Large Stocks Are Less Volatile

As we've seen with the other value factors, the 50 low price-to-cashflow stocks from the Large Stocks universe did much better on both an absolute and a risk-adjusted basis. The original $10,000 invested in 1951 grew to $3,618,123 at the end of 1994, a compound return of 14.68 percent a year. That's 3 times better than the $1,042,859 you'd earn from $10,000 invested in the Large Stocks universe. The standard deviation of return of 20.91 percent is higher than the Large Stocks' 16.18 percent, but considerably lower than that of the low price-to-cashflow stocks from the All Stocks category. The Sharpe ratio for the low price-to-cashflow stocks from Large Stocks was 53. Reviewing Table 7-5, we see that the low price-to-cashflow stocks from the Large Stocks universe had 5 years in which they did at least 15 percent better than the Large Stocks universe and only 1 year in which they did more than 15 percent worse.

Table 7-6 summarizes the Large Stocks base rates. The base rates for the low price-to-cashflow stocks from the Large Stocks universe are uniformly high. Over all rolling 10-year periods, the 50 lowest price-to-cashflow stocks from the Large Stocks group beat the universe 91 percent of the time.

Figure 7-1. Returns on low price-to-cashflow strategies versus All Stocks and Large Stocks, 1951–1994. Year-end 1951 = $10,000.

Table 7-1. Annual performance of All Stocks versus 50 stocks with high cashflow-to-price (low price-to-cashflow) ratios drawn from All Stocks universe.

Year ending	All Stocks	Universe = All Stocks Top 50 cashflow/price	Top 50 cashflow/price Relative performance
31-Dec-52	7.90%	8.80%	0.90%
31-Dec-53	2.90%	−3.50%	−6.40%
31-Dec-54	47.00%	72.40%	25.40%
31-Dec-55	20.70%	26.70%	6.00%
31-Dec-56	17.00%	7.88%	−9.12%
31-Dec-57	−7.10%	−17.50%	−10.40%
31-Dec-58	55.00%	70.40%	15.40%
31-Dec-59	23.00%	13.40%	−9.60%
31-Dec-60	6.10%	−8.60%	−14.70%
31-Dec-61	31.20%	32.20%	1.00%
31-Dec-62	−12.00%	0.90%	12.90%
31-Dec-63	18.00%	31.30%	13.30%
31-Dec-64	16.30%	26.00%	9.70%
31-Dec-65	22.60%	40.60%	18.00%
31-Dec-66	−5.20%	−8.80%	−3.60%
31-Dec-67	41.10%	60.70%	19.60%
31-Dec-68	27.40%	36.50%	9.10%
31-Dec-69	−18.50%	−26.10%	−7.60%
31-Dec-70	−5.80%	−2.10%	3.70%
31-Dec-71	21.30%	28.30%	7.00%
31-Dec-72	11.00%	9.10%	−1.90%
31-Dec-73	−27.20%	−27.70%	−0.50%
31-Dec-74	−27.90%	−20.40%	7.50%
31-Dec-75	55.90%	77.70%	21.80%
31-Dec-76	35.60%	41.00%	5.40%
31-Dec-77	6.90%	15.10%	8.20%
31-Dec-78	12.20%	18.70%	6.50%
31-Dec-79	34.30%	32.20%	−2.10%
31-Dec-80	31.50%	18.90%	−12.60%
31-Dec-81	1.70%	−6.40%	−8.10%
31-Dec-82	22.50%	26.60%	4.10%
31-Dec-83	28.10%	28.70%	0.60%
31-Dec-84	−3.40%	−14.70%	−11.30%
31-Dec-85	30.80%	29.40%	−1.40%
31-Dec-86	13.10%	−2.60%	−15.70%
31-Dec-87	−1.30%	−0.60%	0.70%
31-Dec-88	21.20%	42.30%	21.10%
31-Dec-89	21.40%	18.10%	−3.30%
31-Dec-90	−13.80%	−31.60%	−17.80%
31-Dec-91	39.80%	36.30%	−3.50%
31-Dec-92	13.80%	31.20%	17.40%
31-Dec-93	16.60%	26.00%	9.40%
31-Dec-94	−3.40%	−0.50%	2.90%
Arithmetic average	14.61%	17.12%	2.51%
Standard deviation	19.86%	26.25%	6.39%

Table 7-2. Annual performance of Large Stocks versus 50 stocks with high cashflow-to-price (low price-to-cashflow) ratios drawn from Large Stocks universe.

Year ending	Large Stocks	Universe = Large Stocks Top 50 cashflow/price	Top 50 cashflow/price Relative performance
31-Dec-52	9.30%	14.10%	4.80%
31-Dec-53	2.30%	−0.09%	−2.39%
31-Dec-54	44.90%	64.60%	19.70%
31-Dec-55	21.20%	27.20%	6.00%
31-Dec-56	9.60%	16.50%	6.90%
31-Dec-57	−6.90%	−16.30%	−9.40%
31-Dec-58	42.10%	46.20%	4.10%
31-Dec-59	9.90%	5.20%	−4.70%
31-Dec-60	4.80%	−2.10%	−6.90%
31-Dec-61	27.50%	22.20%	−5.30%
31-Dec-62	−8.90%	0.01%	8.91%
31-Dec-63	19.50%	22.50%	3.00%
31-Dec-64	15.30%	22.90%	7.60%
31-Dec-65	16.20%	27.70%	11.50%
31-Dec-66	−4.90%	−7.30%	−2.40%
31-Dec-67	21.30%	25.70%	4.40%
31-Dec-68	16.80%	29.90%	13.10%
31-Dec-69	−9.90%	−23.00%	−13.10%
31-Dec-70	−0.20%	−0.30%	−0.10%
31-Dec-71	17.30%	18.20%	0.90%
31-Dec-72	14.90%	20.80%	5.90%
31-Dec-73	−18.90%	−5.60%	13.30%
31-Dec-74	−26.70%	−12.40%	14.30%
31-Dec-75	43.10%	75.70%	32.60%
31-Dec-76	28.00%	44.30%	16.30%
31-Dec-77	−2.50%	5.00%	7.50%
31-Dec-78	8.10%	10.90%	2.80%
31-Dec-79	27.30%	20.50%	−6.80%
31-Dec-80	30.80%	20.80%	−10.00%
31-Dec-81	0.60%	2.60%	2.00%
31-Dec-82	19.90%	19.40%	−0.50%
31-Dec-83	23.80%	45.80%	22.00%
31-Dec-84	−0.40%	−6.20%	−5.80%
31-Dec-85	19.50%	30.00%	10.50%
31-Dec-86	32.20%	10.00%	−22.20%
31-Dec-87	3.30%	6.70%	3.40%
31-Dec-88	19.00%	29.70%	10.70%
31-Dec-89	26.00%	23.20%	−2.80%
31-Dec-90	−8.70%	−21.00%	−12.30%
31-Dec-91	33.00%	43.80%	10.80%
31-Dec-92	8.70%	12.20%	3.50%
31-Dec-93	16.30%	33.40%	17.10%
31-Dec-94	−1.90%	7.30%	9.20%
Arithmetic average	12.62%	16.53%	3.91%
Standard deviation	16.81%	20.91%	4.73%

Table 7-3. Summary return results for All Stocks and 50 highest cashflow-to-price (low price-to-cashflow) stocks from All Stocks universe: December 31, 1951–December 31, 1994.

	All Stocks	Universe = All Stocks Top 50 cashflow/price
Arithmetic average	14.61%	17.12%
Standard deviation of return	19.86%	26.25%
Sharpe risk-adjusted ratio	47.00	45.00
3-yr compounded	8.63%	18.04%
5-yr compounded	9.09%	8.93%
10-yr compounded	12.74%	12.43%
15-yr compounded	13.55%	11.32%
20-yr compounded	16.95%	16.87%
25-yr compounded	11.51%	12.21%
30-yr compounded	11.47%	12.80%
35-yr compounded	11.39%	13.12%
40-yr compounded	12.45%	13.58%
Compound annual return	12.81%	14.14%
$10,000 becomes	$1,782,174.48	$2,947,183.34
Maximum return	55.90%	77.70%
Minimum return	−27.90%	−31.60%
Maximum expected return*	54.33%	69.63%
Minimum expected return**	−25.11%	−35.38%

*Maximum expected return is average return plus 2 times the standard deviation.
**Minimum expected return is average return minus 2 times the standard deviation.

Table 7-4. Base rates for All Stocks and 50 highest cashflow-to-price (low price-to-cashflow) stocks from All Stocks universe: 1951–1994.

Item	50 low price-to-cashflow beat All Stocks	Percent
Single-year return	25 out of 43	58%
Rolling 5-year compound return	21 out of 39	54%
Rolling 10-year compound return	22 out of 34	65%

Table 7-5. Summary return results for Large Stocks and 50 highest cashflow-to-price (low price-to-cashflow) stocks from Large Stocks universe: December 31, 1951–December 31, 1994.

	Large Stocks	Universe = Large Stocks Top 50 cashflow/price
Arithmetic average	12.62%	16.53%
Standard deviation of return	16.18%	20.91%
Sharpe risk-adjusted ratio	45.00	53.00
3-yr compounded	7.44%	17.11%
5-yr compounded	8.53%	12.78%
10-yr compounded	13.93%	16.10%
15-yr compounded	14.03%	15.78%
20-yr compounded	15.42%	18.93%
25-yr compounded	11.16%	15.63%
30-yr compounded	10.48%	14.37%
35-yr compounded	10.54%	14.10%
40-yr compounded	10.97%	14.06%
Compound annual return	11.41%	14.68%
$10,000 becomes	$1,042.858.62	$3,618,122.68
Maximum return	44.90%	75.70%
Minimum return	−26.70%	−23.00%
Maximum expected return*	44.97%	58.34%
Minimum expected return**	−19.73%	−25.29%

*Maximum expected return is average return plus 2 times the standard deviation.
**Minimum expected return is average return minus 2 times the standard deviation.

Table 7-6. Base rates for Large Stocks and 50 highest cashflow-to-price (low price-to-cashflow) stocks from Large Stocks universe: 1951–1994.

Item	50 low price-to-cashflow beat Large Stocks	Percent
Single-year return	28 out of 43	65%
Rolling 5-year compound return	26 out of 39	67%
Rolling 10-year compound return	31 out of 34	91%

High Price-to-Cashflow Ratios Are Dangerous

As with the other value factors, we see that stocks with high price-to-cashflow ratios are usually bad investments. Figure 7-2 and Tables 7-7 through 7-10 summarize the data. The 50 stocks with the highest price-to-cashflow ratios from All Stocks had 8 years in which they underperformed All Stocks by more than 15 percent, but only 4 years in which they beat it by 15 percent or more. Some of the periods are horrific. An investment of $10,000 in the All Stocks universe on December 31, 1972, was worth $13,167 at the end of 1977. The same $10,000 invested in the 50 highest price-to-cashflow stocks from the All Stocks universe was worth just $5249, a loss of almost 50 percent.

The same is true over the long term: $10,000 invested on December 31, 1951, in the 50 stocks with the highest price-to-cashflow ratios from All Stocks grew to just $206,805 by the end of 1994. That return is dwarfed by a simple investment in the All Stocks universe. The Sharpe ratio is a dismal 20.

Large Stocks Hit Too

Large stocks with high price-to-cashflow ratios fared little better. Here, $10,000 invested on December 31, 1951, grew to $546,816 by the end of 1994, less than half what you'd earn from an investment in the Large Stocks universe. The Sharpe ratio was a paltry 30.

Looking at the data in Table 7-10, you see why scrutinizing long-term results is the only way to understand the value of a strategy. If you saw only the data for the 10 years ending December 31, 1994, you'd be dangerously misled. The 50 Large Stocks with the highest price-to-cashflow ratios handily *beat* the Large Stocks universe by 3 percent, with a compound return of 17.19 percent. But when we review the base rates for high price-to-cashflow stocks found in Tables 7-11 and 7-12, we see those 10 years were an anomaly. The 50 high price-to-cashflow stocks from the All Stocks universe had only *one 10-year period where they beat the All Stocks universe!* Table 7-13 shows the returns by decade for both strategies while Table 7-14 catalogs the woe for the high price-to-cashflow stocks. The 50 high price-to-cashflow stocks from the Large Stocks group didn't do as poorly, but the failure rate for all rolling 10-year periods was 65 percent.

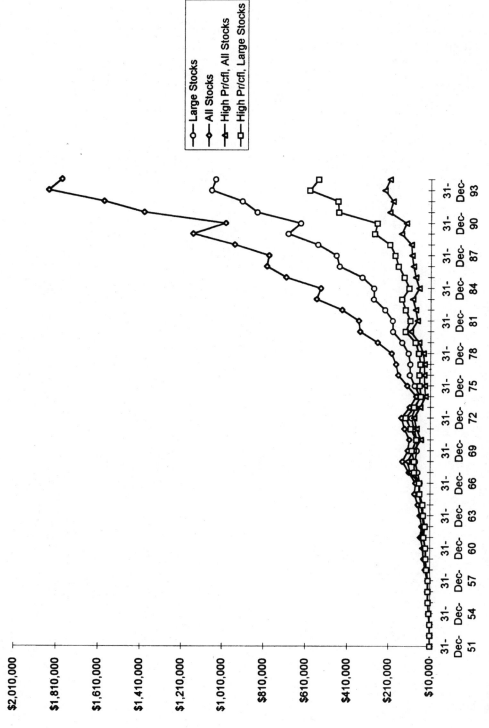

Figure 7-2. Returns on high price-to-cashflow strategies versus All Stocks and Large Stocks, 1951–1994. Year-end 1951 = $10,000.

Table 7-7. Annual performance of All Stocks versus 50 stocks with high price-to-cashflow ratios from All Stocks.

Year ending	All Stocks	Universe = All Stocks Top 50 price/cashflow	Top 50 price/cashflow Relative performance
31-Dec-52	7.90%	1.80%	−6.10%
31-Dec-53	2.90%	4.70%	1.80%
31-Dec-54	47.00%	39.80%	−7.20%
31-Dec-55	20.70%	26.30%	5.60%
31-Dec-56	17.00%	5.00%	−12.00%
31-Dec-57	−7.10%	−2.10%	5.00%
31-Dec-58	55.00%	59.70%	4.70%
31-Dec-59	23.00%	32.80%	9.80%
31-Dec-60	6.10%	11.60%	5.50%
31-Dec-61	31.20%	14.50%	−16.70%
31-Dec-62	−12.00%	−25.80%	−13.80%
31-Dec-63	18.00%	21.09%	3.09%
31-Dec-64	16.30%	5.10%	−11.20%
31-Dec-65	22.60%	28.20%	5.60%
31-Dec-66	−5.20%	−1.30%	3.90%
31-Dec-67	41.10%	67.20%	26.10%
31-Dec-68	27.40%	14.30%	−13.10%
31-Dec-69	−18.50%	−25.90%	−7.40%
31-Dec-70	−5.80%	−37.90%	−32.10%
31-Dec-71	21.30%	34.90%	13.60%
31-Dec-72	11.00%	17.10%	6.10%
31-Dec-73	−27.20%	−32.50%	−5.30%
31-Dec-74	−27.90%	−41.80%	−13.90%
31-Dec-75	55.90%	7.73%	−48.17%
31-Dec-76	35.60%	7.10%	−28.50%
31-Dec-77	6.90%	−1.10%	−8.00%
31-Dec-78	12.20%	13.00%	0.80%
31-Dec-79	34.30%	48.00%	13.70%
31-Dec-80	31.50%	60.30%	28.80%
31-Dec-81	1.70%	−30.70%	−32.40%
31-Dec-82	22.50%	12.50%	−10.00%
31-Dec-83	28.10%	16.10%	−12.00%
31-Dec-84	−3.40%	−31.40%	−28.00%
31-Dec-85	30.80%	24.00%	−6.80%
31-Dec-86	13.10%	13.90%	0.80%
31-Dec-87	−1.30%	9.10%	10.40%
31-Dec-88	21.20%	3.40%	−17.80%
31-Dec-89	21.40%	46.10%	24.70%
31-Dec-90	−13.80%	−15.70%	−1.90%
31-Dec-91	39.80%	63.30%	23.50%
31-Dec-92	13.80%	−8.10%	−21.90%
31-Dec-93	16.60%	21.10%	4.50%
31-Dec-94	−3.40%	−10.70%	−7.30%
Arithmetic average	14.61%	10.81%	−3.80%
Standard deviation	19.86%	27.19%	7.33%

Table 7-8. Annual performance of Large Stocks versus 50 stocks with high price-to-cashflow ratios drawn from Large Stocks universe.

Year ending	Large Stocks	Universe = Large Stocks Top 50 price/cashflow	Top 50 price/cashflow Relative performance
31-Dec-52	9.30%	4.60%	−4.70%
31-Dec-53	2.30%	0.90%	−1.40%
31-Dec-54	44.90%	40.40%	−4.50%
31-Dec-55	21.20%	23.50%	2.30%
31-Dec-56	9.60%	6.70%	−2.90%
31-Dec-57	−6.90%	−6.20%	0.70%
31-Dec-58	42.10%	39.60%	−2.50%
31-Dec-59	9.90%	18.40%	8.50%
31-Dec-60	4.80%	4.00%	−0.80%
31-Dec-61	27.50%	25.20%	−2.30%
31-Dec-62	−8.90%	−16.10%	−7.20%
31-Dec-63	19.50%	26.70%	7.20%
31-Dec-64	15.30%	8.10%	−7.20%
31-Dec-65	16.20%	32.80%	16.60%
31-Dec-66	−4.90%	3.10%	8.00%
31-Dec-67	21.30%	38.80%	17.50%
31-Dec-68	16.80%	0.70%	−16.10%
31-Dec-69	−9.90%	11.90%	21.80%
31-Dec-70	−0.20%	−21.10%	−20.90%
31-Dec-71	17.30%	34.40%	17.10%
31-Dec-72	14.90%	23.80%	8.90%
31-Dec-73	−18.90%	−31.20%	−12.30%
31-Dec-74	−26.70%	−36.80%	−10.10%
31-Dec-75	43.10%	9.59%	−33.51%
31-Dec-76	28.00%	3.00%	−25.00%
31-Dec-77	−2.50%	−7.70%	−5.20%
31-Dec-78	8.10%	12.80%	4.70%
31-Dec-79	27.30%	23.70%	−3.60%
31-Dec-80	30.80%	60.50%	29.70%
31-Dec-81	0.60%	−18.50%	−19.10%
31-Dec-82	19.90%	22.80%	2.90%
31-Dec-83	23.80%	13.50%	−10.30%
31-Dec-84	−0.40%	−23.70%	−23.30%
31-Dec-85	19.50%	21.60%	2.10%
31-Dec-86	32.20%	20.40%	−11.80%
31-Dec-87	3.30%	10.20%	6.90%
31-Dec-88	19.00%	14.40%	−4.60%
31-Dec-89	26.00%	35.60%	9.60%
31-Dec-90	−8.70%	−4.30%	4.40%
31-Dec-91	33.00%	68.00%	35.00%
31-Dec-92	8.70%	0.80%	−7.90%
31-Dec-93	16.30%	29.60%	13.30%
31-Dec-94	−1.90%	−7.10%	−5.20%
Arithmetic average	12.62%	12.03%	−0.59%
Standard deviation	16.18%	22.15%	5.98%

Table 7-9. Summary return results for All Stocks and 50 highest price-to-cashflow stocks from All Stocks universe: December 31, 1951–December 31, 1994.

	All Stocks	Universe = All Stocks Top 50 price/cashflow
Arithmetic average	14.61%	10.81%
Standard deviation of return	19.86%	27.19%
Sharpe risk-adjusted ratio	47.00	20.00
3-yr compounded	8.63%	−0.21%
5-yr compounded	9.09%	6.47%
10-yr compounded	12.74%	12.28%
15-yr compounded	13.55%	7.99%
20-yr compounded	16.95%	9.42%
25-yr compounded	11.51%	3.44%
30-yr compounded	11.47%	4.88%
35-yr compounded	11.39%	4.73%
40-yr compounded	12.45%	6.80%
Compound annual return	12.81%	7.30%
$10,000 becomes	$1,782,174.48	$206,805.28
Maximum return	55.90%	67.20%
Minimum return	−27.90%	−41.80%
Maximum expected return*	54.33%	65.20%
Minimum expected return**	−25.11%	−43.58%

*Maximum expected return is average return plus 2 times the standard deviation.

**Minimum expected return is average return minus 2 times the standard deviation.

Table 7-10. Summary return results for Large Stocks and 50 highest price-to-cashflow stocks from Large Stocks universe: December 31, 1951–December 31, 1994.

	Large Stocks	Universe = Large Stocks Top 50 price/cashflow
Arithmetic average	12.62%	12.03%
Standard deviation of return	16.18%	22.15%
Sharpe risk-adjusted ratio	45.00	30.00
3-yr compounded	7.44%	6.67%
5-yr compounded	8.53%	14.30%
10-yr compounded	13.93%	17.19%
15-yr compounded	14.03%	13.62%
20-yr compounded	15.42%	12.13%
25-yr compounded	11.16%	7.16%
30-yr compounded	10.48%	8.66%
35-yr compounded	10.54%	8.62%
40-yr compounded	10.97%	9.44%
Compound annual return	11.41%	9.75%
$10,000 becomes	$1,042,858.62	$546,816.15
Maximum return	44.90%	68.00%
Minimum return	−26.70%	−36.80%
Maximum expected return*	44.97%	56.33%
Minimum expected return**	−19.73%	−32.27%

*Maximum expected return is average return plus 2 times the standard deviation.

**Minimum expected return is average return minus 2 times the standard deviation.

Table 7-11. Base rates for All Stocks and 50 highest price-to-cashflow stocks from All Stocks universe: 1951–1994.

Item	50 high price-to-cashflow beat All Stocks	Percent
Single-year return	20 out of 43	47%
Rolling 5-year compound return	10 out of 39	26%
Rolling 10-year compound return	1 out of 34	3%

Table 7-12. Base rates for Large Stocks and 50 highest price-to-cashflow stocks from Large Stocks universe: 1951–1994.

Item	50 high price-to-cashflow beat Large Stocks	Percent
Single-year return	19 out of 43	44%
Rolling 5-year compound return	20 out of 39	51%
Rolling 10-year compound return	12 out of 34	35%

Table 7-13. Compound annual rates of return by decade.

Portfolio	1950s*	1960s	1970s	1980s	1990s**
Large Stocks	15.33%	8.99%	6.99%	16.89%	8.53%
50 high price-to-cashflow from Large Stocks	14.85%	12.35%	−1.85%	13.29%	14.30%
50 low price-to-cashflow from Large Stocks	17.28%	10.36%	15.40%	17.31%	12.78%
All Stocks	19.22%	11.09%	8.53%	15.85%	9.09%
50 high price-to-cashflow from All Stocks	19.30%	8.02%	−3.03%	8.77%	6.47%
50 low price-to-cashflow from All Stocks	18.71%	15.41%	13.57%	12.53%	8.93%

*Returns for 1952–1959.

**Returns for 1990–1994.

Table 7-14. Rolling compound 10-year returns for All Stocks and 50 highest price-to-cashflow stocks from All Stocks universe: December 31, 1961– December 31, 1994.

For the 10 years ending	All Stocks	Universe = All Stocks Top 50 price/cashflow	Top 50 price/cashflow Relative performance
31-Dec-61	18.97%	18.02%	−0.95%
31-Dec-62	16.57%	14.35%	−2.23%
31-Dec-63	18.18%	16.02%	−2.16%
31-Dec-64	15.44%	12.76%	−2.69%
31-Dec-65	15.63%	12.93%	−2.70%
31-Dec-66	13.22%	12.23%	−0.99%
31-Dec-67	18.05%	18.40%	0.35%
31-Dec-68	15.76%	14.51%	−1.25%
31-Dec-69	11.09%	8.02%	−3.07%
31-Dec-70	9.78%	1.87%	−7.91%
31-Dec-71	8.92%	3.55%	−5.37%
31-Dec-72	11.48%	8.38%	−3.09%
31-Dec-73	6.22%	2.23%	−3.99%
31-Dec-74	1.26%	−3.64%	−4.90%
31-Dec-75	3.72%	−5.30%	−9.02%
31-Dec-76	7.50%	−4.52%	−12.02%
31-Dec-77	4.56%	−9.40%	−13.97%
31-Dec-78	3.24%	−9.51%	−12.75%
31-Dec-79	8.53%	−3.03%	−11.55%
31-Dec-80	12.21%	6.62%	−5.59%
31-Dec-81	10.25%	−0.25%	−10.50%
31-Dec-82	11.34%	−0.65%	−11.99%
31-Dec-83	17.82%	4.89%	−12.93%
31-Dec-84	21.31%	6.63%	−14.69%
31-Dec-85	19.20%	8.14%	−11.07%
31-Dec-86	17.06%	8.80%	−8.25%
31-Dec-87	16.13%	9.88%	−6.25%
31-Dec-88	17.03%	8.91%	−8.12%
31-Dec-89	15.85%	8.77%	−7.09%
31-Dec-90	11.06%	2.00%	−9.07%
31-Dec-91	14.65%	11.12%	−3.53%
31-Dec-92	13.81%	8.90%	−4.91%
31-Dec-93	12.74%	9.36%	−3.39%
31-Dec-94	12.74%	12.28%	−0.46%
Arithmetic average	12.69%	6.27%	−6.41%

Implications

As Figures 7-3 and 7-4 show, the odds strongly favor stocks with low price-to-cashflow ratios. Unless there are additional compelling factors (e.g., the stock is selected by a successful growth model's criteria which can absorb some high price-to-cashflow risk), you should avoid stocks with the highest price-to-cashflow ratios.

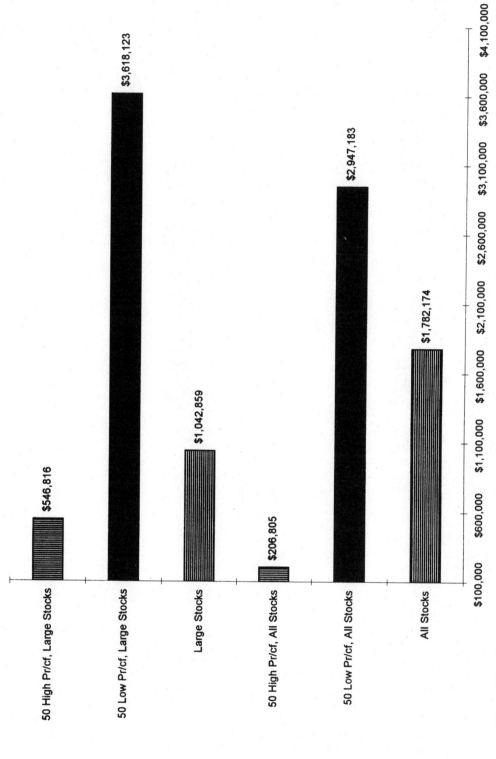

Figure 7-3. December 31, 1994, value of $10,000 invested on December 31, 1951, and annually rebalanced.

103

Figure 7-4. Sharpe risk-adjusted return ratio, 1951–1994. (Higher is better.)

8

Price-to-Sales Ratios: The King of the Value Factors

For me the greatest beauty always lay in the
greatest clarity.   —GOTTHOLD LESSING

The last individual value ratio we'll review is also the best. A stock's price-to-sales ratio (PSR) is similar to its price-to-earnings ratio, but measures the price of the company against annual sales instead of earnings. Like investors who favor low PE stocks, investors buy low PSR stocks because they believe they're getting a bargain. Ken Fisher says in his 1984 book *Super Stocks,* that a stock's PSR is "an almost perfect measure of popularity," warning that only hope and hype will increase the price of a stock with a high PSR.

As usual, we'll look at the 50 lowest PSR stocks and the 50 highest PSR stocks from both universes. All accounting data are time-lagged to avoid look-ahead bias, and the portfolios are rebalanced annually.

Starting December 31, 1951, we'll buy the 50 stocks from All Stocks with the lowest PSRs. Again, because of Compustat's ranking function, we must rank stocks by the 50 *highest* sales-to-price ratios, the inverse of the price-to-sales ratio. I'll refer to them, however, as high and low PSR stocks throughout the chapter.

The Results

An investment of $10,000 on December 31, 1951, in the 50 lowest PSR stocks from the All Stocks universe grew to $5,932,737 by December 31, 1994, a compound return of 16.01 percent. This dwarfs the $1,782,174 earned from the $10,000 invested in the All Stocks universe and beats the returns of all the value ratios we've examined. The strategy also performs well over time. With the exception of 1989 through 1991, the annual returns found in Table 8-1 show that low PSR stocks consistently beat the All Stocks universe. The low PSR stocks also do well on a risk-adjusted basis, with a Sharpe ratio of 52. Table 8-2 summarizes the returns of low PSR stocks from the All Stocks universe, and Table 8-3 compares the base rates for the strategy with All Stocks.

Large Stocks with Low Price-to-Sales Ratios Do Well

Large stocks with low PSRs also beat the Large Stocks universe, but not by as much as the smaller stocks from All Stocks. An investment of $10,000 on December 31, 1951, was worth $2,545,234 at the end of 1994, a compound return of 13.75 percent. The return was considerably better than the $1,042,859 you'd earn if you invested $10,000 in the Large Stocks universe itself. We also see consistency here and a fairly high Sharpe ratio of 49. The results are summarized in Tables 8-4 and 8-5. Table 8-6 compares the base rates for the strategy with the Large Stocks universe.

The rolling 5- and 10-year base rates for both groups of low PSR stocks are outstanding—the best of all the value ratios. For all rolling 10-year periods, both the large and smaller stock versions of the strategy beat their universes 90 percent of the time. That consistency is rare. I've reviewed rolling 10-year returns for both the large and small low PSR stocks in Tables 8-7 and 8-8. Table 8-9 gives compound returns by decades.

High PSR Stocks Are Toxic

An investment in the 50 stocks with the highest PSRs from the All Stocks universe turns in the worst performance to date: $10,000 invested on December 31, 1951, was worth just $72,552 at the end of 1994. You'd be better off with T-bills! The Sharpe ratio was 11, the bottom of the barrel.

Table 8-1. Annual performance of All Stocks versus lowest PSR stocks drawn from All Stocks universe.

Year ending	All Stocks	Universe = All Stocks Top 50 sales/price	Top 50 sales/price Relative performance
31-Dec-52	7.90%	13.40%	5.50%
31-Dec-53	2.90%	5.90%	3.00%
31-Dec-54	47.00%	59.40%	12.40%
31-Dec-55	20.70%	19.80%	−0.90%
31-Dec-56	17.00%	4.60%	−12.40%
31-Dec-57	−7.10%	−1.90%	5.20%
31-Dec-58	55.00%	73.90%	18.90%
31-Dec-59	23.00%	11.20%	−11.80%
31-Dec-60	6.10%	4.00%	−2.10%
31-Dec-61	31.20%	31.70%	0.50%
31-Dec-62	−12.00%	−12.10%	−0.10%
31-Dec-63	18.00%	14.40%	−3.60%
31-Dec-64	16.30%	27.40%	11.10%
31-Dec-65	22.60%	34.70%	12.10%
31-Dec-66	−5.20%	−17.60%	−12.40%
31-Dec-67	41.10%	48.30%	7.20%
31-Dec-68	27.40%	39.90%	12.50%
31-Dec-69	−18.50%	−28.80%	−10.30%
31-Dec-70	−5.80%	−4.50%	1.30%
31-Dec-71	21.30%	29.50%	8.20%
31-Dec-72	11.00%	−1.80%	−12.80%
31-Dec-73	−27.20%	−22.30%	4.90%
31-Dec-74	−27.90%	−12.60%	15.30%
31-Dec-75	55.90%	76.90%	21.00%
31-Dec-76	35.60%	48.40%	12.80%
31-Dec-77	6.90%	3.50%	−3.40%
31-Dec-78	12.20%	16.90%	4.70%
31-Dec-79	34.30%	51.80%	17.50%
31-Dec-80	31.50%	13.70%	−17.80%
31-Dec-81	1.70%	3.10%	1.40%
31-Dec-82	22.50%	63.30%	40.80%
31-Dec-83	28.10%	37.70%	9.60%
31-Dec-84	−3.40%	−2.60%	0.80%
31-Dec-85	30.80%	46.70%	15.90%
31-Dec-86	13.10%	9.30%	−3.80%
31-Dec-87	−1.30%	2.20%	3.50%
31-Dec-88	21.20%	42.90%	21.70%
31-Dec-89	21.40%	6.70%	−14.70%
31-Dec-90	−13.80%	−27.50%	−13.70%
31-Dec-91	39.80%	37.10%	−2.70%
31-Dec-92	13.80%	32.60%	18.80%
31-Dec-93	16.60%	24.80%	8.20%
31-Dec-94	−3.40%	8.00%	11.40%
Arithmetic average	14.61%	18.88%	4.27%
Standard deviation	19.86%	26.08%	6.22%

Table 8-2. Summary return results for All Stocks and 50 lowest PSR stocks from All Stocks universe: December 31, 1951–December 31, 1994.

	All Stocks	Universe = All Stocks Top 50 sales/price
Arithmetic average	14.61%	18.88%
Standard deviation of return	19.86%	26.08%
Sharpe risk-adjusted ratio	47.00	52.00
3-yr compounded	8.63%	21.36%
5-yr compounded	9.09%	12.18%
10-yr compounded	12.74%	16.07%
15-yr compounded	13.55%	17.61%
20-yr compounded	16.95%	22.18%
25-yr compounded	11.51%	16.48%
30-yr compounded	11.47%	15.44%
35-yr compounded	11.39%	14.93%
40-yr compounded	12.45%	15.42%
Compound annual return	12.81%	16.01%
$10,000 becomes	$1,782,174.48	$5,932,737.36
Maximum return	55.90%	76.90%
Minimum return	−27.90%	−28.80%
Maximum expected return*	54.33%	71.05%
Minimum expected return**	−25.11%	−33.29%

*Maximum expected return is average return plus 2 times the standard deviation.
**Minimum expected return is average return minus 2 times the standard deviation.

Table 8-3. Base rates for All Stocks and 50 lowest PSR stocks from All Stocks universe: 1951–1994.

Item	50 low price-to-sales beat All Stocks	Percent
Single-year return	28 out of 43	65%
Rolling 5-year compound return	26 out of 39	67%
Rolling 10-year compound return	31 out of 34	91%

Table 8-4. Annual performance of Large Stocks versus 50 lowest PSR stocks drawn from Large Stocks universe.

Year ending	Large Stocks	Universe = Large Stocks Top 50 sales/price	Top 50 sales/price Relative performance
31-Dec-52	9.30%	14.30%	5.00%
31-Dec-53	2.30%	2.00%	−0.30%
31-Dec-54	44.90%	51.90%	7.00%
31-Dec-55	21.20%	21.90%	0.70%
31-Dec-56	9.60%	10.00%	0.40%
31-Dec-57	−6.90%	−12.40%	−5.50%
31-Dec-58	42.10%	47.80%	5.70%
31-Dec-59	9.90%	9.50%	−0.40%
31-Dec-60	4.80%	−1.80%	−6.60%
31-Dec-61	27.50%	29.30%	1.80%
31-Dec-62	−8.90%	−7.40%	1.50%
31-Dec-63	19.50%	21.00%	1.50%
31-Dec-64	15.30%	22.00%	6.70%
31-Dec-65	16.20%	27.00%	10.80%
31-Dec-66	−4.90%	−10.30%	−5.40%
31-Dec-67	21.30%	33.00%	11.70%
31-Dec-68	16.80%	23.30%	6.50%
31-Dec-69	−9.90%	−23.70%	−13.80%
31-Dec-70	−0.20%	−3.00%	−2.80%
31-Dec-71	17.30%	20.60%	3.30%
31-Dec-72	14.90%	11.40%	−3.50%
31-Dec-73	−18.90%	−25.40%	−6.50%
31-Dec-74	−26.70%	−14.20%	12.50%
31-Dec-75	43.10%	64.50%	21.40%
31-Dec-76	28.00%	47.30%	19.30%
31-Dec-77	−2.50%	0.80%	3.30%
31-Dec-78	8.10%	13.60%	5.50%
31-Dec-79	27.30%	21.60%	−5.70%
31-Dec-80	30.80%	15.10%	−15.70%
31-Dec-81	0.60%	9.40%	8.80%
31-Dec-82	19.90%	34.30%	14.40%
31-Dec-83	23.80%	36.40%	12.60%
31-Dec-84	−0.40%	3.20%	3.60%
31-Dec-85	19.50%	40.90%	21.40%
31-Dec-86	32.20%	11.10%	−21.10%
31-Dec-87	3.30%	3.70%	0.40%
31-Dec-88	19.00%	39.10%	20.10%
31-Dec-89	26.00%	16.10%	−9.90%
31-Dec-90	−8.70%	−22.60%	−13.90%
31-Dec-91	33.00%	41.80%	8.80%
31-Dec-92	8.70%	22.30%	13.60%
31-Dec-93	16.30%	29.60%	13.30%
31-Dec-94	−1.90%	0.02%	1.92%
Arithmetic average	12.62%	15.70%	3.08%
Standard deviation	16.18%	20.91%	4.74%

Table 8-5. Summary return results for Large Stocks and 50
lowest PSR stocks from Large Stocks universe:
December 31, 1951–December 31, 1994.

	Large Stocks	Universe = Large Stocks Top 50 sales/price
Arithmetic average	12.62%	15.70%
Standard deviation of return	16.18%	20.91%
Sharpe risk-adjusted ratio	45.00	49.00
3-yr compounded	7.44%	16.60%
5-yr compounded	8.53%	11.71%
10-yr compounded	13.93%	16.39%
15-yr compounded	14.03%	17.23%
20-yr compounded	15.42%	19.73%
25-yr compounded	11.16%	14.66%
30-yr compounded	10.48%	13.41%
35-yr compounded	10.54%	13.15%
40-yr compounded	10.97%	13.22%
Compound annual return	11.41%	13.75%
$10,000 becomes	$1,042,858.62	$2,545,233.71
Maximum return	44.90%	64.50%
Minimum return	−26.70%	−25.40%
Maximum expected return*	44.97%	57.52%
Minimum expected return**	−19.73%	−26.12%

*Maximum expected return is average return plus 2 times the standard deviation.
**Minimum expected return is average return minus 2 times the standard deviation.

Table 8-6. Base rates for Large Stocks and 50 lowest PSR stocks from
Large Stocks universe: 1951–1994.

Item	50 low price-to-sales beat Large Stocks	Percent
Single-year return	29 out of 43	67%
Rolling 5-year compound return	27 out of 39	69%
Rolling 10-year compound return	32 out of 34	94%

Table 8-7. Rolling 10-year compound returns for low PSR stocks from the All Stocks universe.

For the 10 years ending	All Stocks	Universe = All Stocks 50 low PSR stocks	50 low PSR stocks Relative performance
31-Dec-61	18.97%	20.08%	1.10%
31-Dec-62	16.57%	17.06%	0.49%
31-Dec-63	18.18%	17.97%	−0.21%
31-Dec-64	15.44%	15.35%	−0.09%
31-Dec-65	15.63%	16.71%	1.09%
31-Dec-66	13.22%	13.96%	0.74%
31-Dec-67	18.05%	18.77%	0.72%
31-Dec-68	15.76%	16.21%	0.46%
31-Dec-69	11.09%	11.15%	0.06%
31-Dec-70	9.78%	10.20%	0.43%
31-Dec-71	8.92%	10.02%	1.10%
31-Dec-72	11.48%	11.24%	−0.23%
31-Dec-73	6.22%	7.02%	0.80%
31-Dec-74	1.26%	3.06%	1.80%
31-Dec-75	3.72%	5.91%	2.19%
31-Dec-76	7.50%	12.33%	4.82%
31-Dec-77	4.56%	8.36%	3.80%
31-Dec-78	3.24%	6.43%	3.19%
31-Dec-79	8.53%	14.80%	6.27%
31-Dec-80	12.21%	16.82%	4.61%
31-Dec-81	10.25%	14.19%	3.94%
31-Dec-82	11.34%	20.15%	8.80%
31-Dec-83	17.82%	27.22%	9.41%
31-Dec-84	21.31%	28.61%	7.30%
31-Dec-85	19.20%	26.22%	7.02%
31-Dec-86	17.06%	22.42%	5.36%
31-Dec-87	16.13%	22.27%	6.14%
31-Dec-88	17.03%	24.75%	7.72%
31-Dec-89	15.85%	20.43%	4.57%
31-Dec-90	11.06%	15.13%	4.07%
31-Dec-91	14.65%	18.46%	3.80%
31-Dec-92	13.81%	16.01%	2.20%
31-Dec-93	12.74%	14.88%	2.13%
31-Dec-94	12.74%	16.07%	3.33%

Table 8-8. Rolling 10-year compound returns for low PSR stocks from the Large Stocks universe.

For the 10 years ending	Large Stocks	Universe = Large Stocks 50 low PSR stocks	50 low PSR stocks Relative performance
31-Dec-61	15.38%	15.64%	0.26%
31-Dec-62	13.30%	13.23%	−0.07%
31-Dec-63	15.07%	15.18%	0.11%
31-Dec-64	12.47%	12.68%	0.21%
31-Dec-65	12.00%	13.14%	1.14%
31-Dec-66	10.42%	10.86%	0.44%
31-Dec-67	13.38%	15.58%	2.20%
31-Dec-68	11.18%	13.51%	2.33%
31-Dec-69	8.99%	9.48%	0.49%
31-Dec-70	8.46%	9.35%	0.88%
31-Dec-71	7.56%	8.59%	1.03%
31-Dec-72	10.09%	10.61%	0.53%
31-Dec-73	5.90%	5.39%	−0.51%
31-Dec-74	1.21%	1.75%	0.53%
31-Dec-75	3.34%	4.41%	1.07%
31-Dec-76	6.46%	9.72%	3.26%
31-Dec-77	4.16%	6.72%	2.56%
31-Dec-78	3.35%	5.85%	2.50%
31-Dec-79	6.99%	10.90%	3.91%
31-Dec-80	9.92%	12.82%	2.89%
31-Dec-81	8.25%	11.72%	3.47%
31-Dec-82	8.71%	13.83%	5.12%
31-Dec-83	13.41%	20.91%	7.50%
31-Dec-84	16.94%	23.16%	6.23%
31-Dec-85	14.85%	21.27%	6.42%
31-Dec-86	15.22%	17.90%	2.68%
31-Dec-87	15.89%	18.23%	2.35%
31-Dec-88	17.01%	20.65%	3.65%
31-Dec-89	16.89%	20.09%	3.21%
31-Dec-90	12.76%	15.42%	2.66%
31-Dec-91	15.95%	18.46%	2.50%
31-Dec-92	14.82%	17.35%	2.53%
31-Dec-93	14.10%	16.75%	2.65%
31-Dec-94	13.93%	16.39%	2.46%

Table 8-9. Compound annual rates of return by decade.

Portfolio	1950s*	1960s	1970s	1980s	1990s**
Large Stocks	15.33%	8.99%	6.99%	16.89%	8.53%
50 high price-to-sales from Large Stocks	13.21%	11.73%	3.23%	9.54%	8.30%
50 low price-to-sales from Large Stocks	16.39%	9.48%	10.90%	20.09%	11.71%
All Stocks	19.22%	11.09%	8.53%	15.85%	9.09%
50 high price-to-sales from All Stocks	14.96%	11.99%	5.82%	−2.02%	−11.80%
50 low price-to-sales from All Stocks	20.85%	11.15%	14.80%	20.43%	12.18%

*Returns for 1952–1959.
**Returns for 1990–1994.

It's painful to catalog the carnage. The All Stocks universe beat the 50 highest PSR stocks 67 percent of the time. December 31, 1980, through December 31, 1984, is particularly gruesome: $10,000 invested in the All Stocks universe grew by more than 50 percent to $15,416, but an investment in the 50 stocks with the highest PSRs fell by 70 percent, turning $10,000 into $3079.

In terms of 5-year rolling returns, the All Stocks universe beat the high PSR stocks 87 percent of the time. On a rolling 10-year basis, the All Stocks universe beat high PSR stocks 82 percent of the time.

Large Stocks Do a Little Better

The picture is only slightly brighter for Large Stocks. Here, $10,000 invested in the 50 stocks with the highest PSRs on December 31, 1951, grew to $416,189, a compound return of 9.06 percent. That's less than half what you'd earn from Large Stocks, but much better than the 50 high PSR stocks from All Stocks. The Sharpe ratio was 27, considerably below Large Stocks' 45. All base rates were negative, with the 50 highest price-to-sales ratio stocks from Large Stocks underperforming the Large Stocks universe 65 percent of the time. Tables 8-10 through 8-15 summarize the damage.

Table 8-10. Annual performance of All Stocks versus 50 stocks with high price-to-sales ratios from All Stocks.

Year ending	All Stocks	Universe = All Stocks Top 50 sales/price	Top 50 sales/price Relative performance
31-Dec-52	7.90%	5.30%	−2.60%
31-Dec-53	2.90%	1.30%	−1.60%
31-Dec-54	47.00%	33.60%	−13.40%
31-Dec-55	20.70%	14.10%	−6.60%
31-Dec-56	17.00%	10.00%	−7.00%
31-Dec-57	−7.10%	−1.00%	6.10%
31-Dec-58	55.00%	53.80%	−1.20%
31-Dec-59	23.00%	12.00%	−11.00%
31-Dec-60	6.10%	11.50%	5.40%
31-Dec-61	31.20%	23.10%	−8.10%
31-Dec-62	−12.00%	−12.70%	−0.70%
31-Dec-63	18.00%	20.90%	2.90%
31-Dec-64	16.30%	8.80%	−7.50%
31-Dec-65	22.60%	18.80%	−3.80%
31-Dec-66	−5.20%	1.90%	7.10%
31-Dec-67	41.10%	69.10%	28.00%
31-Dec-68	27.40%	26.90%	−0.50%
31-Dec-69	−18.50%	−24.20%	−5.70%
31-Dec-70	−5.80%	−25.30%	−19.50%
31-Dec-71	21.30%	29.10%	7.80%
31-Dec-72	11.00%	24.60%	13.60%
31-Dec-73	−27.20%	−13.30%	13.90%
31-Dec-74	−27.90%	−38.70%	−10.80%
31-Dec-75	55.90%	7.90%	−48.00%
31-Dec-76	35.60%	30.90%	−4.70%
31-Dec-77	6.90%	8.90%	2.00%
31-Dec-78	12.20%	6.40%	−5.80%
31-Dec-79	34.30%	68.50%	34.20%
31-Dec-80	31.50%	43.90%	12.40%
31-Dec-81	1.70%	−47.60%	−49.30%
31-Dec-82	22.50%	−11.30%	−33.80%
31-Dec-83	28.10%	1.90%	−26.20%
31-Dec-84	−3.40%	−35.00%	−31.60%
31-Dec-85	30.80%	22.20%	−8.60%
31-Dec-86	13.10%	16.00%	2.90%
31-Dec-87	−1.30%	−7.90%	−6.60%
31-Dec-88	21.20%	1.70%	−19.50%
31-Dec-89	21.40%	38.60%	17.20%
31-Dec-90	−13.80%	−18.00%	−4.20%
31-Dec-91	39.80%	47.50%	7.70%
31-Dec-92	13.80%	−25.20%	−39.00%
31-Dec-93	16.60%	−13.10%	−29.70%
31-Dec-94	−3.40%	−32.10%	−28.70%
Arithmetic average	14.61%	8.23%	−6.38%
Standard deviation	19.86%	26.95%	7.09%

Table 8-11. Summary return results for All Stocks and 50 highest price-to-sales stocks from All Stocks universe: December 31, 1951–December 31, 1994.

	All Stocks	Universe = All Stocks Top 50 sales/price
Arithmetic average	14.61%	8.23%
Standard deviation of return	19.86%	26.95%
Sharpe risk-adjusted ratio	47.00	11.00
3-yr compounded	8.63%	−23.86%
5-yr compounded	9.09%	−11.80%
10-yr compounded	12.74%	−0.18%
15-yr compounded	13.55%	−5.40%
20-yr compounded	16.95%	0.92%
25-yr compounded	11.51%	−1.06%
30-yr compounded	11.47%	1.38%
35-yr compounded	11.39%	2.51%
40-yr compounded	12.45%	4.15%
Compound annual return	12.81%	4.72%
$10,000 becomes	$1,782,174.48	$72,551.74
Maximum return	55.90%	69.10%
Minimum return	−27.90%	−47.60%
Maximum expected return*	54.33%	62.13%
Minimum expected return**	−25.11%	−45.68%

*Maximum expected return is average return plus 2 times the standard deviation.
**Minimum expected return is average return minus 2 times the standard deviation.

Table 8-12. Base rates for All Stocks and 50 highest PSR stocks from All Stocks universe: 1951–1994.

Item	50 high price-to-sales beat All Stocks	Percent
Single-year return	14 out of 43	33%
Rolling 5-year compound return	5 out of 39	13%
Rolling 10-year compound return	6 out of 34	18%

Table 8-13. Annual performance of Large Stocks versus 50 stocks with high price-to-sales ratios drawn from Large Stocks universe.

Year ending	Large Stocks	Universe = Large Stocks Top 50 sales/price	Top 50 sales/price Relative performance
31-Dec-52	9.30%	4.80%	−4.50%
31-Dec-53	2.30%	1.30%	−1.00%
31-Dec-54	44.90%	32.00%	−12.90%
31-Dec-55	21.20%	17.20%	−4.00%
31-Dec-56	9.60%	8.10%	−1.50%
31-Dec-57	−6.90%	−3.50%	3.40%
31-Dec-58	42.10%	40.60%	−1.50%
31-Dec-59	9.90%	12.00%	2.10%
31-Dec-60	4.80%	9.80%	5.00%
31-Dec-61	27.50%	23.90%	−3.60%
31-Dec-62	−8.90%	−8.30%	0.60%
31-Dec-63	19.50%	20.20%	0.70%
31-Dec-64	15.30%	14.20%	−1.10%
31-Dec-65	16.20%	17.70%	1.50%
31-Dec-66	−4.90%	1.90%	6.80%
31-Dec-67	21.30%	23.20%	1.90%
31-Dec-68	16.80%	7.90%	−8.90%
31-Dec-69	−9.90%	11.00%	20.90%
31-Dec-70	−0.20%	−17.80%	−17.60%
31-Dec-71	17.30%	25.60%	8.30%
31-Dec-72	14.90%	24.30%	9.40%
31-Dec-73	−18.90%	−20.80%	−1.90%
31-Dec-74	−26.70%	−36.80%	−10.10%
31-Dec-75	43.10%	14.50%	−28.60%
31-Dec-76	28.00%	13.50%	−14.50%
31-Dec-77	−2.50%	−2.90%	−0.40%
31-Dec-78	8.10%	15.00%	6.90%
31-Dec-79	27.30%	47.40%	20.10%
31-Dec-80	30.80%	67.52%	36.72%
31-Dec-81	0.60%	−20.60%	−21.20%
31-Dec-82	19.90%	−3.90%	−23.80%
31-Dec-83	23.80%	11.80%	−12.00%
31-Dec-84	−0.40%	−23.90%	−23.50%
31-Dec-85	19.50%	23.70%	4.20%
31-Dec-86	32.20%	19.50%	−12.70%
31-Dec-87	3.30%	10.10%	6.80%
31-Dec-88	19.00%	3.00%	−16.00%
31-Dec-89	26.00%	36.43%	10.43%
31-Dec-90	−8.70%	−6.30%	2.40%
31-Dec-91	33.00%	53.70%	20.70%
31-Dec-92	8.70%	−9.40%	−18.10%
31-Dec-93	16.30%	26.70%	10.40%
31-Dec-94	−1.90%	−9.90%	−8.00%
Arithmetic average	12.62%	11.03%	−1.58%
Standard deviation	16.18%	20.74%	4.57%

Table 8-14. Summary return results for Large Stocks and 50 highest PSR stocks from Large Stocks universe: December 31, 1951–December 31, 1994.

	Large Stocks	Universe = Large Stocks Top 50 price/sales
Arithmetic average	12.62%	11.03%
Standard deviation of return	16.18%	20.74%
Sharpe risk-adjusted ratio	45.00	27.00
3-yr compounded	7.44%	1.13%
5-yr compounded	8.53%	8.30%
10-yr compounded	13.93%	13.04%
15-yr compounded	14.03%	9.12%
20-yr compounded	15.42%	10.90%
25-yr compounded	11.16%	6.73%
30-yr compounded	10.48%	7.60%
35-yr compounded	10.54%	8.13%
40-yr compounded	10.97%	8.85%
Compound annual return	11.41%	9.06%
$10,000 becomes	$1,042,858.62	$416,189.20
Maximum return	44.90%	67.52%
Minimum return	−26.70%	−36.80%
Maximum expected return*	44.97%	52.52%
Minimum expected return**	−19.73%	−30.45%

*Maximum expected return is average return plus 2 times the standard deviation.
**Minimum expected return is average return minus 2 times the standard deviation.

Table 8-15. Base rates for Large Stocks and 50 highest PSR stocks from Large Stocks universe: 1951–1994.

Item	50 high price-to-sales beat All Stocks	Percent
Single-year return	20 out of 43	47%
Rolling 5-year compound return	17 out of 39	44%
Rolling 10-year compound return	12 out of 34	35%

Implications

Low price-to-sales ratios beat the market more than any other value ratio and do so more consistently. Low PSR stocks from both the All Stocks and Large Stocks groups beat the universes in every decade. The only time high PSR stocks beat the universes was in the 1960s, an era dominated by performance-obsessed managers who would pay any price for a stock with a good story. Indeed, 1967 was the second-best year for high PSR stocks drawn from the All Stocks universe. In his book *101 Years on Wall Street*, John Dennis Brown calls 1967 "a vintage year for speculators. About 45 percent of all issues listed at the NYSE would gain 50 percent or more." Thus, high PSR stocks perform best in frothy, speculative markets but do poorly in all other years. Amazingly, during this speculative time, *low* PSR stocks *still* did well. The results are depicted graphically in Figures 8-1 through 8-4.

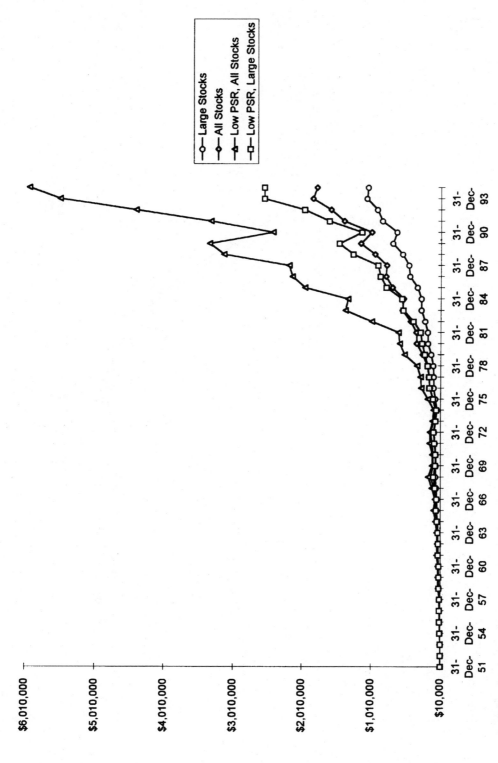

Figure 8-1. Returns on low price-to-sales strategies versus All Stocks and Large Stocks, 1951–1994. Year-end 1951 = $10,000.

Figure 8-2. Returns on high price-to-sales strategies versus All Stocks and Large Stocks, 1951–1994. Year-end 1951 = $10,000.

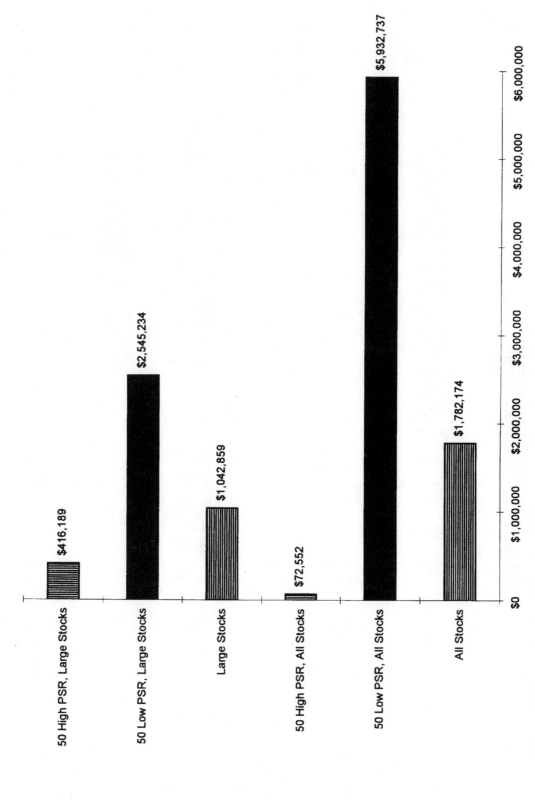

Figure 8-3. December 31, 1994, value of $10,000 invested on December 31, 1951, and annually rebalanced.

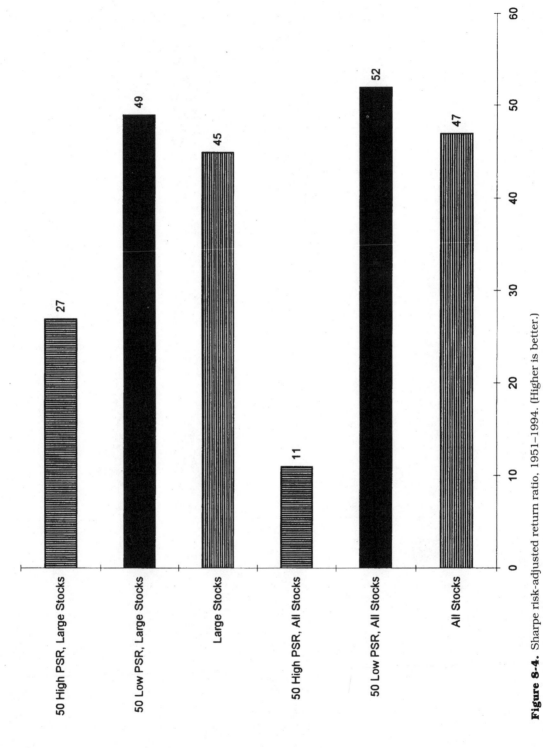

Figure 8-4. Sharpe risk-adjusted return ratio, 1951–1994. (Higher is better.)

9

Dividend Yields: Buying an Income

October. This is one of the peculiarly dangerous months to speculate in stocks. The others are July, January, September, April, November, May, March, June, December, August and February.
—MARK TWAIN

Investors who find all months peculiarly dangerous often seek redemption in stocks with high dividend yields. Since dividends often account for more than half a stock's total return, these investors think it wise to concentrate on stocks paying high dividends. What's more, it's impossible to monkey with a dividend yield, since a company must pay, defer, or cancel it.

You find a stock's dividend yield by dividing the indicated annual dividend rate by the current price of the stock. The result is then multiplied by 100 to make it a percentage. Thus, if a company pays an annual dividend of $1 and the current price of the stock is $10, the dividend yield is 10 percent.

We'll look at buying the 50 highest-yielding stocks from All Stocks and Large Stocks. We're going to *exclude* utility stocks, since they would dominate the list if included.

The Results

As Tables 9-1 through 9-7 show, the effectiveness of high dividend yields depends almost entirely on the size of the companies you buy. Reviewing Tables 9-1 and 9-3, we see that high-yielding stocks drawn from All Stocks fail to beat the universe: $10,000 invested in the 50 highest-yielding stocks from the All Stocks universe on December 31, 1951, was worth $1,112,060 at the end of 1994, $600,000 less than an investment in the All Stocks universe. The strategy also has a lower risk-adjusted return, since it took more risk. The base rate of positive returns for high-yielding stocks from the All Stocks universe shown in Table 9-5 is negative, with the strategy beating its universe just 18 percent of the time over all rolling 10-year periods.

Large Stocks Entirely Different

The returns of high-yielding large stocks are entirely different (Fig. 9-1). Here, we see the highest-yielding stocks doing twice as well as their universe with virtually the same risk: $10,000 invested in the 50 highest-yielding stocks from the Large Stocks universe on December 31, 1951, grew to $2,012,843 by the end of 1994 (Fig. 9-2). That's a compound return of 13.13 percent, some 1.72 percent better than the Large Stocks universe's return of 11.41 percent. The 50 highest-yielding stocks from the Large Stocks universe had a standard deviation of return of 17.88 percent, 1.7 percent higher than the Large Stocks universe. This, coupled with the higher absolute return, accounts for the high Sharpe ratio of 51 (Fig. 9-3). In absolute terms, the strategy is less risky than for Large Stocks overall. The largest loss was 16.5 percent in 1969, much better than the 26.7 percent drop that the Large Stocks universe suffered in 1974.

The high-yield strategy is also far more consistent when used on Large Stocks. Here the 50 highest-yielding stocks beat the universe 91 percent of the time over all rolling 10-year periods.

Implications

The difference between the returns for high-yielding stocks based on market capitalization is huge. Investors who buy higher-yielding stocks should stick to large, better-known companies, which usually have the stronger balance sheets and longer operating histories that make higher dividends possible. Indeed, in the multifactor section we'll see that

Table 9-1. Annual performance of All Stocks versus 50 stocks with highest dividend yields drawn from All Stocks universe.

Year ending	All Stocks	Universe = All Stocks Top 50 dividend yield	Top 50 dividend yield Relative performance
31-Dec-52	7.90%	14.50%	6.60%
31-Dec-53	2.90%	7.70%	4.80%
31-Dec-54	47.00%	57.80%	10.80%
31-Dec-55	20.70%	24.40%	3.70%
31-Dec-56	17.00%	10.60%	−6.40%
31-Dec-57	−7.10%	−16.60%	−9.50%
31-Dec-58	55.00%	61.00%	6.00%
31-Dec-59	23.00%	21.90%	−1.10%
31-Dec-60	6.10%	−4.40%	−10.50%
31-Dec-61	31.20%	26.50%	−4.70%
31-Dec-62	−12.00%	−8.94%	3.06%
31-Dec-63	18.00%	19.70%	1.70%
31-Dec-64	16.30%	20.70%	4.40%
31-Dec-65	22.60%	23.10%	0.50%
31-Dec-66	−5.20%	−10.60%	−5.40%
31-Dec-67	41.10%	32.40%	−8.70%
31-Dec-68	27.40%	43.10%	15.70%
31-Dec-69	−18.50%	−17.90%	0.60%
31-Dec-70	−5.80%	3.40%	9.20%
31-Dec-71	21.30%	10.10%	−11.20%
31-Dec-72	11.00%	13.10%	2.10%
31-Dec-73	−27.20%	−18.50%	8.70%
31-Dec-74	−27.90%	−40.50%	−12.60%
31-Dec-75	55.90%	51.70%	−4.20%
31-Dec-76	35.60%	42.60%	7.00%
31-Dec-77	6.90%	6.80%	−0.10%
31-Dec-78	12.20%	4.70%	−7.50%
31-Dec-79	34.30%	24.90%	−9.40%
31-Dec-80	31.50%	14.00%	−17.50%
31-Dec-81	1.70%	8.60%	6.90%
31-Dec-82	22.50%	29.50%	7.00%
31-Dec-83	28.10%	28.50%	0.40%
31-Dec-84	−3.40%	5.40%	8.80%
31-Dec-85	30.80%	19.30%	−11.50%
31-Dec-86	13.10%	7.00%	−6.10%
31-Dec-87	−1.30%	−13.80%	−12.50%
31-Dec-88	21.20%	17.00%	−4.20%
31-Dec-89	21.40%	3.40%	−18.00%
31-Dec-90	−13.80%	−15.90%	−2.10%
31-Dec-91	39.80%	47.50%	7.70%
31-Dec-92	13.80%	12.90%	−0.90%
31-Dec-93	16.60%	31.90%	15.30%
31-Dec-94	−3.40%	−7.50%	−4.10%
Arithmetic average	14.61%	13.75%	−0.87%
Standard deviation	19.86%	21.70%	1.84%

Table 9-2. Annual performance of Large Stocks versus 50 stocks with highest dividend yield drawn from Large Stocks universe.

Year ending	Large Stocks	Universe = Large Stocks Top 50 dividend yield	Top 50 dividend yield Relative performance
31-Dec-52	9.30%	12.60%	3.30%
31-Dec-53	2.30%	−5.30%	−7.60%
31-Dec-54	44.90%	56.90%	12.00%
31-Dec-55	21.20%	20.00%	−1.20%
31-Dec-56	9.60%	11.30%	1.70%
31-Dec-57	−6.90%	−11.90%	−5.00%
31-Dec-58	42.10%	44.00%	1.90%
31-Dec-59	9.90%	9.40%	−0.50%
31-Dec-60	4.80%	1.70%	−3.10%
31-Dec-61	27.50%	29.40%	1.90%
31-Dec-62	−8.90%	−3.70%	5.20%
31-Dec-63	19.50%	20.60%	1.10%
31-Dec-64	15.30%	17.70%	2.40%
31-Dec-65	16.20%	18.80%	2.60%
31-Dec-66	−4.90%	−11.10%	−6.20%
31-Dec-67	21.30%	21.30%	0.00%
31-Dec-68	16.80%	32.60%	15.80%
31-Dec-69	−9.90%	−16.50%	−6.60%
31-Dec-70	−0.20%	8.00%	8.20%
31-Dec-71	17.30%	12.70%	−4.60%
31-Dec-72	14.90%	12.10%	−2.80%
31-Dec-73	−18.90%	−10.10%	8.80%
31-Dec-74	−26.70%	−13.30%	13.40%
31-Dec-75	43.10%	51.70%	8.60%
31-Dec-76	28.00%	41.80%	13.80%
31-Dec-77	−2.50%	4.50%	7.00%
31-Dec-78	8.10%	2.80%	−5.30%
31-Dec-79	27.30%	20.20%	−7.10%
31-Dec-80	30.80%	14.90%	−15.90%
31-Dec-81	0.60%	12.70%	12.10%
31-Dec-82	19.90%	26.00%	6.10%
31-Dec-83	23.80%	33.60%	9.80%
31-Dec-84	−0.40%	2.10%	2.50%
31-Dec-85	19.50%	32.80%	13.30%
31-Dec-86	32.20%	17.80%	−14.40%
31-Dec-87	3.30%	−3.00%	−6.30%
31-Dec-88	19.00%	22.40%	3.40%
31-Dec-89	26.00%	17.80%	−8.20%
31-Dec-90	−8.70%	−10.80%	−2.10%
31-Dec-91	33.00%	44.80%	11.80%
31-Dec-92	8.70%	8.30%	−0.40%
31-Dec-93	16.30%	26.30%	10.00%
31-Dec-94	−1.90%	0.09%	1.99%
Arithmetic average	12.62%	14.51%	1.89%
Standard deviation	16.18%	17.88%	1.71%

Table 9-3. Summary return results for All Stocks and 50 highest dividend yield stocks from All Stocks universe: December 31, 1951–December 31, 1994.

	All Stocks	Universe = All Stocks Top 50 dividend yield
Arithmetic average	14.61%	13.75%
Standard deviation of return	19.86%	21.70%
Sharpe risk-adjusted ratio	47.00	39.00
3-yr compounded	8.63%	11.27%
5-yr compounded	9.09%	11.31%
10-yr compounded	12.74%	8.57%
15-yr compounded	13.55%	11.24%
20-yr compounded	16.95%	14.47%
25-yr compounded	11.51%	9.34%
30-yr compounded	11.47%	9.67%
35-yr compounded	11.39%	9.68%
40-yr compounded	12.45%	10.64%
Compound annual return	12.81%	11.58%
$10,000 becomes	$1,782,174.48	$1,112,060.04
Maximum return	55.90%	61.00%
Minimum return	−27.90%	−40.50%
Maximum expected return*	54.33%	57.15%
Minimum expected return**	−25.11%	−29.65%

*Maximum expected return is average return plus 2 times the standard deviation.

**Minimum expected return is average return minus 2 times the standard deviation.

Table 9-4. Summary return results for Large Stocks and 50 highest dividend yield stocks from Large Stocks universe: December 31, 1951–December 31, 1994.

	Large Stocks	Universe = Large Stocks Top 50 dividend yield
Arithmetic average	12.62%	14.51%
Standard deviation of return	16.18%	17.88%
Sharpe risk-adjusted ratio	45.00	51.00
3-yr compounded	7.44%	11.04%
5-yr compounded	8.53%	12.08%
10-yr compounded	13.93%	14.49%
15-yr compounded	14.03%	15.43%
20-yr compounded	15.42%	17.20%
25-yr compounded	11.16%	13.82%
30-yr compounded	10.48%	12.70%
35-yr compounded	10.54%	12.66%
40-yr compounded	10.97%	12.72%
Compound annual return	11.41%	13.13%
$10,000 becomes	$1,042,858.62	$2,012,843.01
Maximum return	44.90%	56.90%
Minimum return	−26.70%	−16.50%
Maximum expected return*	44.97%	50.28%
Minimum expected return**	−19.73%	−21.25%

*Maximum expected return is average return plus 2 times the standard deviation.
**Minimum expected return is average return minus 2 times the standard deviation.

Table 9-5. Base rates for All Stocks and 50 highest dividend yield stocks from All Stocks universe: 1951–1994.

Item	50 highest dividend yield stocks beat All Stocks	Percent
Single-year return	21 out of 43	49%
Rolling 5-year compound return	12 out of 39	31%
Rolling 10-year compound return	6 out of 34	18%

Table 9-6. Base rates for Large Stocks and 50 highest dividend yield stocks from Large Stocks universe: 1951–1994.

Item	50 highest dividend yield stocks beat Large Stocks	Percent
Single-year return	25 out of 43	67%
Rolling 5-year compound return	27 out of 39	69%
Rolling 10-year compound return	31 out of 34	91%

Table 9-7. Compound annual rates of return by decade.

Portfolio	1950s*	1960s	1970s	1980s	1990s**
Large Stocks	15.33%	8.99%	6.99%	16.89%	8.53%
50 highest dividend yield from Large Stocks	15.20%	9.82%	11.44%	17.15%	12.08%
All Stocks	19.22%	11.09%	8.53%	15.85%	9.09%
50 highest dividend yield from All Stocks	20.29%	10.54%	6.55%	11.20%	11.31%

*Returns for 1952–1959.
**Returns for 1990–1994.

when other criteria such as strong cashflows, large sales, and large numbers of shares outstanding are included, Large Stocks with high dividend yields offer the best risk-adjusted returns available.

Small stocks with high dividend yields may be in that position because their prices have fallen. Far from representing a bargain, their high dividend yields may be an indicator of more trouble to come.

Figure 9-1. Returns on high dividend yield strategy versus All Stocks and Large Stocks, 1951–1994. Year-end 1951 = $10,000.

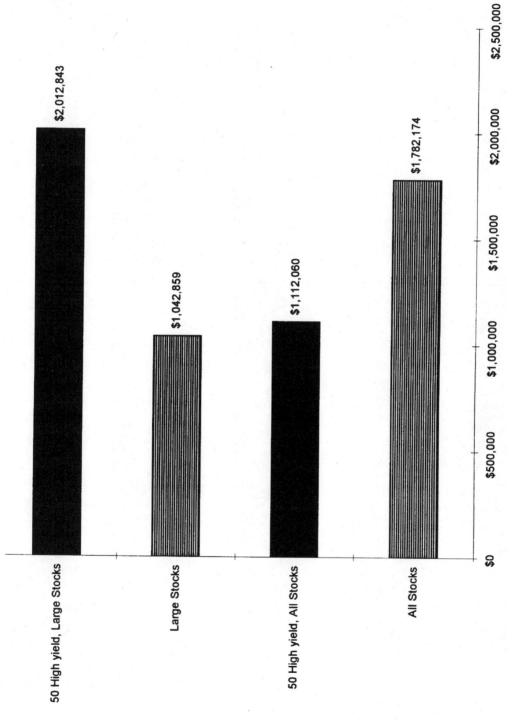

Figure 9-2. December 31, 1994, value of $10,000 invested on December 31, 1951, and annually rebalanced.

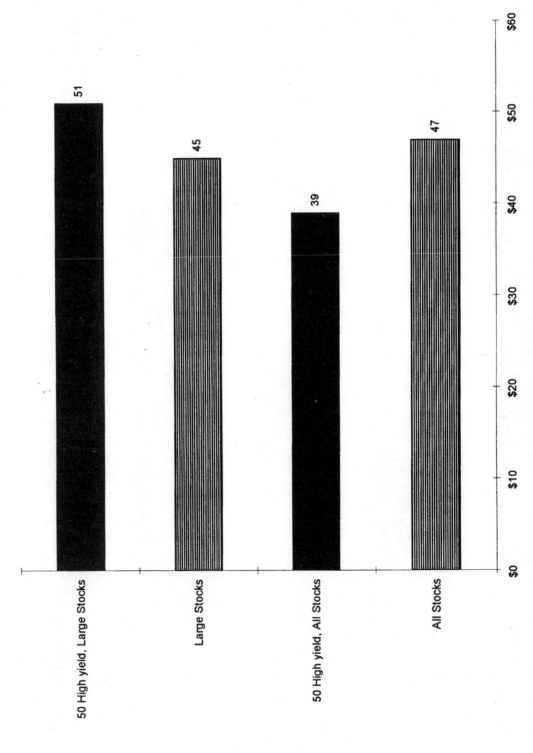

Figure 9-3. Sharpe risk-adjusted return ratio, 1951–1994. (Higher is better.)

10

The Value of Value Factors

Discovery consists in seeing what everybody has seen and thinking what nobody has thought.
—ALBERT SZENT-GYORGYI

The past 43 years show that rather than careening about like a drunken monkey, the stock market methodically rewards certain types of stocks while punishing others. Figures 10-1 through 10-4 show the results for the All Stocks universe. There's nothing random about Figure 10-1. Stocks with low price-to-book, price-to-cashflow, and price-to-sales ratios dramatically outperform the All Stocks universe. Just as important, those with *high* price-to-book, price-to-cashflow, and price-to-sales ratios do dramatically worse. The symmetry is striking.

Stocks with low price-to-earnings ratios and those with high dividend yields fail to beat All Stocks. But these factors are much more important for Large Stocks. Yet even here, the symmetry exists, with the 50 highest price-to-earnings stocks from All Stocks returning far less than the All Stocks universe and the 50 lowest price-to-earnings stocks.

Risk Doesn't Always Equal Reward

An important principle of the Capital Asset Pricing Model is that risk is compensated. It steers investors seeking higher returns to stocks with

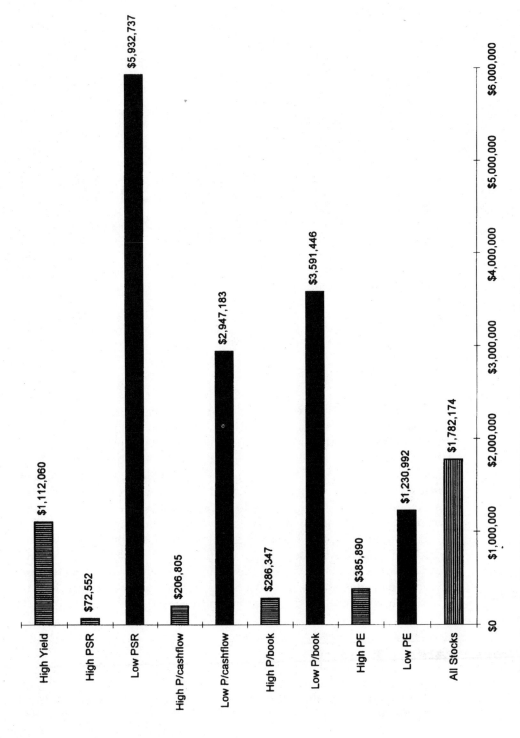

Figure 10-1. December 31, 1994, value of $10,000 invested in the various strategies using the All Stocks universe. Initial investment made December 31, 1951.

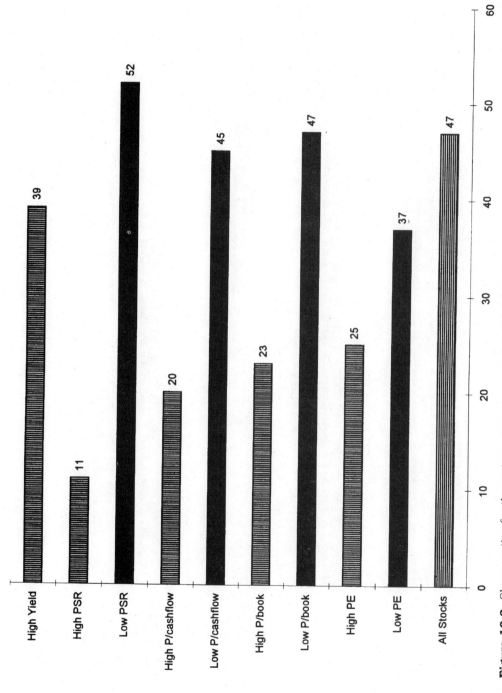

Figure 10-2. Sharpe ratios for the various strategies applied to the All Stocks universe, 1951–1994. (Higher is better.)

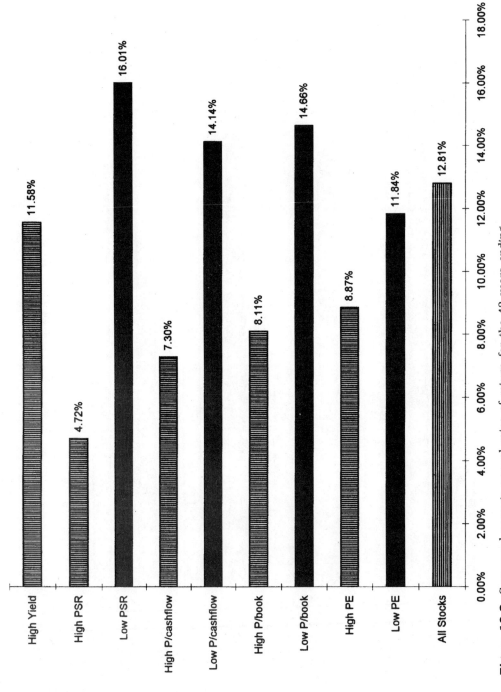

Figure 10-3. Compound average annual rates of return for the 43 years ending December 31, 1994. Results of applying strategies on the All Stocks universe.

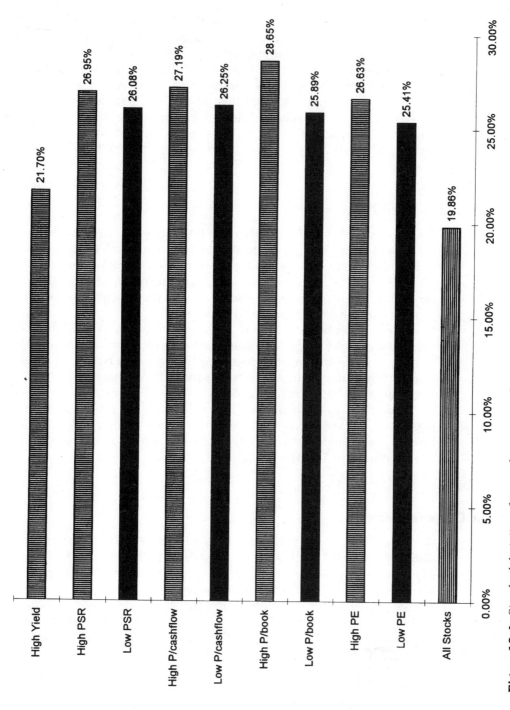

Figure 10-4. Standard deviation of return for strategies from the All Stocks universe, 1951–1994. (Higher is riskier.)

higher standard deviations. All the winning strategies thus far have higher standard deviations of return than the All Stocks universe. But the principle that higher risk equals higher rewards is not always true. As Figure 10-4 shows, the higher risk of the *high* PE, price-to-book, price-to-cashflow, and price-to-sales ratios was uncompensated. Indeed, each of the strategies significantly underperformed the All Stocks universe. Buying the 50 *lowest* price-to-sales stocks turns $10,000 into $5,932,737 with a standard deviation of return of 26.08 percent, but buying the 50 stocks with the *highest* price-to-sales ratios turns $10,000 into $72,552, *with a higher standard deviation of return of 26.95 percent.*

Is It Worth the Risk?

Risk acts like a powerful predator, culling the weak strategies from the herd. Buying the 50 stocks with the lowest price-to-sales ratios was the only strategy that beat the All Stocks universe on a risk-adjusted basis. The other value strategies came close, with the low price-to-book group matching All Stocks' Sharpe ratio of 47, and the low price-to-cashflow group close behind with a Sharpe ratio of 45.

Strategies that buy stocks with high price-to-earnings, price-to-book, price-to-cashflow, or price-to-sales ratios have abysmal risk-adjusted returns. It's as if you must endure a night at sea on a rickety ship being tossed to and fro by a powerful hurricane only to have the ship dashed upon the rocks before reaching shore.

You must *always* consider risk before investing in strategies that buy stocks significantly different from the market. High risk does not always mean high reward. Indeed, all the higher-risk strategies are eventually dashed on the rocks.

Embrace Consistency

A strategy won't help if you can't stick with it, so you must look for consistency over time. Here, all the value strategies beat the All Stocks universe more than 50 percent of the time over all rolling 10-year periods, but the records are mixed. If you bought the 50 lowest price-to-book stocks annually, you'd underperform the All Stocks universe during a *majority* of 5-year periods. Only the low price-to-sales strategy shows consistency worth betting on. *All* the high ratio strategies have horrible batting averages and should be avoided.

Large Stocks Are Different

When looking at the Large Stocks universe, we see the same results as for All Stocks. Figures 10-5 through 10-8 summarize the results. All the value strategies with low ratios beat the market and all the strategies with high ratio did considerably worse. All the high ratio strategies— save high PE—had higher standard deviations of return than and did significantly worse than their low-ratio counterparts. But the absolute amounts are more modest. With Large Stocks, the best-performing strategy is to buy the 50 stocks with the lowest price-to-cashflow ratios, with a $10,000 investment on December 31, 1951, growing to $3,618,123 by the end of 1994. We also see stocks with high dividend yields and low PE ratios beating the Large Stocks universe by wide margins. Figure 10-5 shows the returns of $10,000 invested on December 31, 1951, in the various value strategies.

The base rates for the Large Stocks value strategies are far more consistent than for the All Stocks universe. All the Large Stocks value strategies beat the universe *at least* 88 percent of the time over the 34 rolling 10-year periods. All the high-ratio strategies fail to beat the universe a majority of the time over all rolling 10-year periods, with the most successful beating the Large Stocks universe just 38 percent of the time. Tables 10-1 and 10-2 show the compound annual rates of return by decade.

Implications

Value strategies work, rewarding patient investors who stick with them through hill and valley. *All* the Large Stocks value strategies beat the Large Stocks universe on an absolute and risk-adjusted basis, and they did so at least 88 percent of the time over all rolling 10-year periods. That's an extraordinary track record.

High-ratio strategies (e.g., high PE, high price-to-book) consistently underperform their universes over the long term. They take more risk and give lower rewards. They have some spectacular runs that encourage investors to pay unwarranted prices for the stocks with the best story or most sizzle. But they consistently disappoint and should be avoided unless there are *extremely compelling* strategic reasons for buying the stock.

Now let's turn to growth variables and look for any extremely compelling strategies that might overcome the horrendous returns from high-ratio stocks.

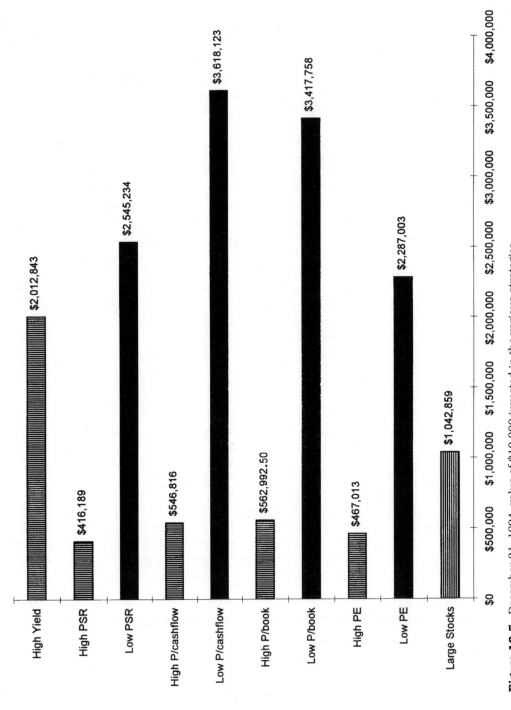

Figure 10-5. December 31, 1994, value of $10,000 invested in the various strategies using the Large Stocks universe. Initial investment made December 31, 1951.

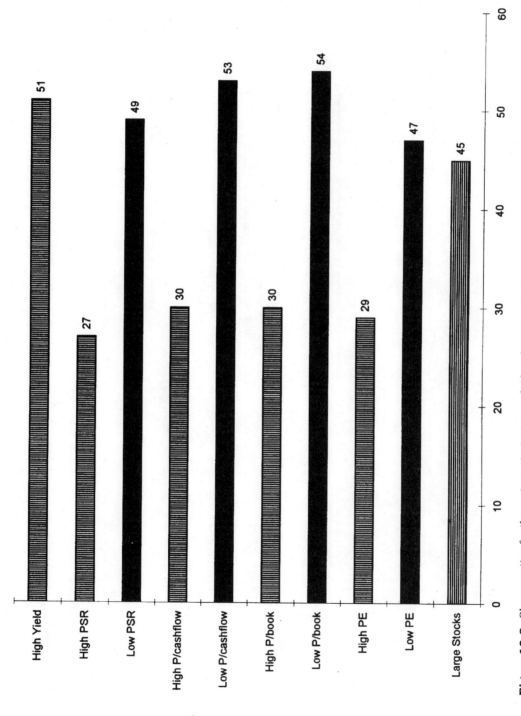

Figure 10-6. Sharpe ratios for the various strategies applied to the Large Stocks universe, 1951–1994. (Higher is better.)

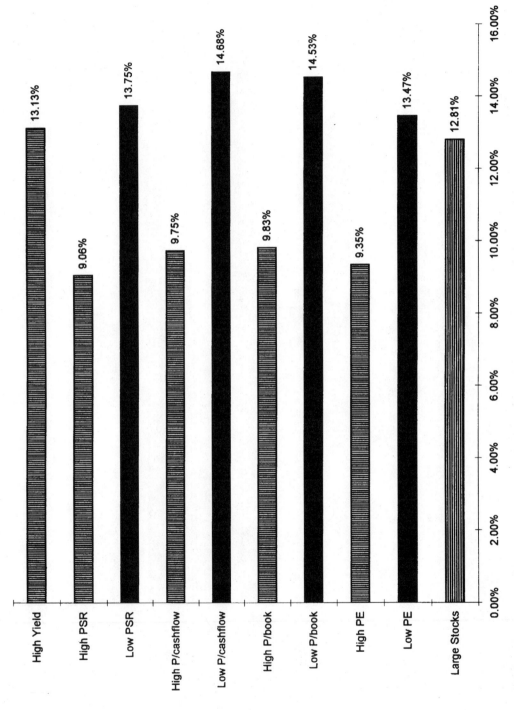

Figure 10-7. Compound average annual rates of return for the 43 years ending December 31, 1994. Results of applying strategies on the Large Stocks universe.

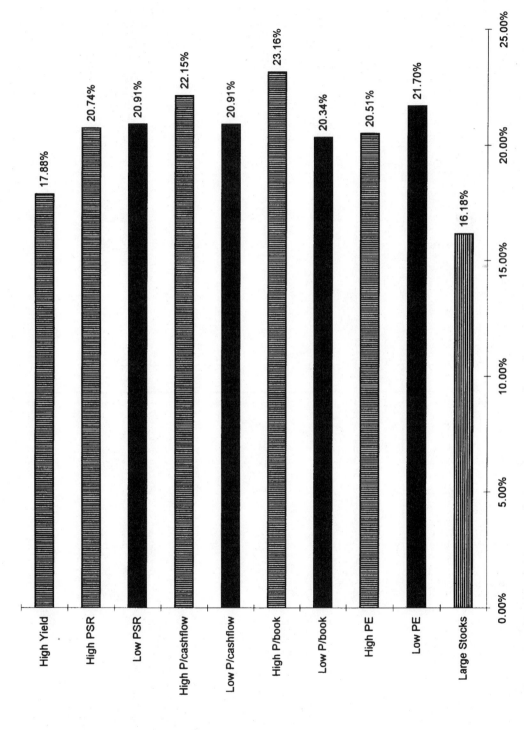

Figure 10-8. Standard deviation of return for strategies from the Large Stocks universe, 1951–1994. (Higher is riskier.)

Table 10-1. Compound annual rates of return by decade, All Stocks universe.

Portfolio	1950s*	1960s	1970s	1980s	1990s**
All Stocks	19.22%	11.09%	8.53%	15.85%	9.09%
50 low PE	21.84%	13.96%	8.89%	7.56%	7.15%
50 high PE	19.27%	10.96%	2.26%	7.99%	4.30%
50 low price-to-book ratios	18.86%	11.49%	17.06%	13.15%	12.84%
50 high price-to-book ratios	22.32%	13.13%	0.82%	1.97%	4.76%
50 low price-to-cashflow ratios	18.71%	15.41%	13.57%	12.53%	8.93%
50 high price-to-cashflow ratios	19.30%	8.02%	−3.03%	8.77%	6.47%
50 low price-to-sales ratios	20.85%	11.15%	14.80%	20.43%	12.18%
50 high price-to-sales ratios	14.96%	11.99%	5.82%	−2.02%	−11.80%
50 highest yielding stocks	20.29%	10.54%	6.55%	11.20%	11.31%

*Returns for 1952–1959.
**Returns for 1990–1994.

Table 10-2. Compound annual rates of return by decade, Large Stocks universe.

Portfolio	1950s*	1960s	1970s	1980s	1990s**
Large Stocks	15.33%	8.99%	6.99%	16.89%	8.53%
50 low PE	16.12%	11.14%	12.64%	16.19%	10.28%
50 high PE	14.77%	10.94%	0.93%	14.11%	5.98%
50 low price-to-book ratios	15.41%	9.57%	13.95%	19.99%	13.76%
50 high price-to-book ratios	16.55%	11.30%	−0.60%	14.40%	9.42%
50 low price-to-cashflow ratios	17.28%	10.36%	15.40%	17.31%	12.78%
50 high price-to-cashflow ratios	14.85%	12.35%	−1.85%	13.29%	14.30%
50 low price-to-sales ratios	16.39%	9.48%	10.90%	20.09%	11.71%
50 high price-to-sales ratios	13.21%	11.73%	3.23%	9.54%	8.30%
50 highest yielding stocks	15.20%	9.82%	11.44%	17.15%	12.08%

*Returns for 1952–1959.
**Returns for 1990–1994.

11

One-Year Earnings-Per-Share Percentage Changes: Do High Earnings Gains Mean High Performance?

It ain't so much what people know that hurts as what they know that ain't so.

—ARTEMUS WARD

Now let's look at factors commonly associated with growth investing. Generally, growth investors like *high* while value investors like *low*. Growth investors want high earnings and sales growth with prospects for more of the same. They usually don't care if a stock has a high PE ratio, reasoning that a company can grow its way out of short-term overvaluations. Growth investors often award high prices to stocks with rapidly increasing earnings.

Unfortunately, Compustat lacks long-term data on earnings forecasts. Many growth investors make substantial use of earnings forecasts when constructing their portfolios, so our inability to do a
long-term test is somewhat limiting. However, some studies have
found that forecasts are remarkably undependable. In the October 11,
1993, issue of *Forbes Magazine,* David Dreman recounts a study that
used a sample of 67,375 analysts' quarterly estimates for New York and
American Stock Exchange listed companies between 1973 and 1990. It
found that analysts' average forecast error was 40 percent and that estimates were misleading (i.e., missed their mark by more than 10 percent)
two-thirds of the time. Here, we'll look at *actual* earnings changes, not
earnings forecasts.

Examining Annual Earnings Changes

First, we'll look at buying the 50 stocks with the best and the worst
1-year earnings-per-share percentage changes from the All Stocks and
Large Stocks universes. For the rankings to work smoothly, we eliminate stocks whose annual earnings went from positive to negative.
Also, because of time-lag constraints, we must start the test on
December 31, 1952. When comparing these returns with other strategies, keep in mind that 1952 isn't included.

Let's look at the returns from buying the 50 stocks from All Stocks
with the best 1-year earnings-per-share percentage gains. As usual, we
start with $10,000 and rebalance the portfolio annually. As Tables 11-1
and 11-2 show, buying stocks with the best 1-year earnings gains is like
closing the barn door after the horse has left: $10,000 invested on
December 31, 1952, in the top 50 1-year earnings gainers from All
Stocks grew to $911,615 by the end of 1994. That's $740,076 shy of the
$1,651,691 you'd earn with a similar investment in All Stocks. The 50
highest 1-year earnings gainers also took considerably more risk—their
standard deviation was 27.52 percent compared with All Stocks' 20.07
percent. The strategy *has* had some magnificent runs, however.
Between December 31, 1962, and December 31, 1967, the strategy
almost doubled the performance of the All Stocks universe, turning
$10,000 into $38,546. It had another terrific streak between 1976 and
1980, but it lacks long-term consistency. Right after these great runs, it
went on to do significantly worse than All Stocks. The base rates in
Table 11-3 show that the strategy underperforms the All Stocks universe in each period.

Table 11-1. Annual performance of All Stocks versus 50 stocks with highest 1-year earnings gains drawn from All Stocks universe.

Year ending	All Stocks	Universe = All Stocks Top 50 1-year earnings gains	Top 50 1-year earnings gains Relative performance
31-Dec-53	2.90%	−3.80%	−6.70%
31-Dec-54	47.00%	65.70%	18.70%
31-Dec-55	20.70%	20.00%	−0.70%
31-Dec-56	17.00%	17.50%	0.50%
31-Dec-57	−7.10%	−20.80%	−13.70%
31-Dec-58	55.00%	69.60%	14.60%
31-Dec-59	23.00%	28.20%	5.20%
31-Dec-60	6.10%	3.10%	−3.00%
31-Dec-61	31.20%	21.30%	−9.90%
31-Dec-62	−12.00%	−17.80%	−5.80%
31-Dec-63	18.00%	31.19%	13.19%
31-Dec-64	16.30%	23.40%	7.10%
31-Dec-65	22.60%	35.20%	12.60%
31-Dec-66	−5.20%	−2.70%	2.50%
31-Dec-67	41.10%	81.00%	39.90%
31-Dec-68	27.40%	18.80%	−8.60%
31-Dec-69	−18.50%	−30.90%	−12.40%
31-Dec-70	−5.80%	−28.00%	−22.20%
31-Dec-71	21.30%	30.00%	8.70%
31-Dec-72	11.00%	13.20%	2.20%
31-Dec-73	−27.20%	−32.00%	−4.80%
31-Dec-74	−27.90%	−28.90%	−1.00%
31-Dec-75	55.90%	53.40%	−2.50%
31-Dec-76	35.60%	39.70%	4.10%
31-Dec-77	6.90%	17.70%	10.80%
31-Dec-78	12.20%	15.30%	3.10%
31-Dec-79	34.30%	50.70%	16.40%
31-Dec-80	31.50%	53.80%	22.30%
31-Dec-81	1.70%	−23.20%	−24.90%
31-Dec-82	22.50%	3.40%	−19.10%
31-Dec-83	28.10%	22.00%	−6.10%
31-Dec-84	−3.40%	−7.40%	−4.00%
31-Dec-85	30.80%	13.80%	−17.00%
31-Dec-86	13.10%	7.70%	−5.40%
31-Dec-87	−1.30%	−1.10%	0.20%
31-Dec-88	21.20%	17.50%	−3.70%
31-Dec-89	21.40%	16.90%	−4.50%
31-Dec-90	−13.80%	−17.40%	−3.60%
31-Dec-91	39.80%	37.20%	−2.60%
31-Dec-92	13.80%	12.50%	−1.30%
31-Dec-93	16.60%	19.30%	2.70%
31-Dec-94	−3.40%	−7.70%	−4.30%
Arithmetic average	14.77%	14.70%	−0.07%
Standard deviation	20.07%	27.52%	7.45%

Table 11-2. Summary return results for All Stocks and 50 stocks with highest 1-year earnings gains from All Stocks universe: December 31, 1952–December 31, 1994.

	All Stocks	Universe = All Stocks Top 50 highest 1-year earnings gains
Arithmetic average	14.77%	14.70%
Standard deviation of return	20.07%	27.52%
Sharpe risk-adjusted ratio	46.00	34.00
3-yr compounded	8.63%	7.40%
5-yr compounded	9.09%	7.02%
10-yr compounded	12.74%	8.86%
15-yr compounded	13.55%	8.12%
20-yr compounded	16.95%	14.16%
25-yr compounded	11.51%	8.24%
30-yr compounded	11.47%	9.23%
35-yr compounded	11.39%	9.45%
40-yr compounded	12.45%	10.65%
Compound annual return	12.93%	11.34%
$10,000 becomes	$1,651,690.90	$911,615.01
Maximum return	55.90%	81.00%
Minimum return	−27.90%	−32.00%
Maximum expected return*	54.91%	69.74%
Minimum expected return**	−25.37%	40.34%

*Maximum expected return is average return plus 2 times the standard deviation.
**Minimum expected return is average return minus 2 times the standard deviation.

Table 11-3. Base rates for All Stocks and 50 stocks with highest 1-year earnings gains from All Stocks universe: 1951–1994.

Item	50 high 1-year earnings gains beat All Stocks	Percent
Single-year return	18 out of 42	43%
Rolling 5-year compound return	11 out of 38	29%
Rolling 10-year compound return	10 out of 33	30%

Large Stocks Do Worse

As Tables 11-4 and 11-5 show, the 50 stocks with the highest 1-year earnings gains from the Large Stocks universe did worse. Here, $10,000 invested on December 31, 1952, grew to $392,549 by the end of 1994, a compound return of 9.13 percent. That's less than half the $954,125 you'd earn investing $10,000 in the Large Stocks universe, which had a return of 11.46 percent a year. The Sharpe ratio is a sorry 28 compared with Large Stocks' 44. As shown in Table 11-6, all base rates are negative, with the 50 highest 1-year earnings gainers beating Large Stocks just 12 percent of the time over all rolling 10-year periods.

The record shows that buying stocks with the highest 1-year earnings gains rarely beats the market. This probably occurs because high expectations are hard to meet. Seduced by stellar earnings gains, investors bid the stocks to unsustainable levels. When earnings growth fails to continue, investors become disenchanted and sell their shares in disgust.

Buying Stocks with the Worst Earnings Changes

Perhaps you'd be better off buying the 50 stocks with the *worst* annual earnings changes. At least expectations for these stocks are modest. Remember that we require stocks to have positive earnings, so while these stocks aren't losing money, they will have experienced substantial declines in earnings.

An investment of $10,000 on December 31, 1952, in the 50 stocks from All Stocks with the worst 1-year earnings changes grew to $1,132,754 by the end of 1994. That's better than the return from buying the *best* 50 earnings gainers, but it still falls short of the $1,651,691 you'd make investing the $10,000 in All Stocks. Risk was lower at 24.13 percent, but again, still higher than the All Stocks universe's 20.07 percent. Tables 11-7 and 11-8 summarize the results.

Large Stocks Do Better

An investment of $10,000 in the 50 Large Stocks with the worst 1-year earnings changes actually beat the Large Stocks universe, growing to $1,124,209 on December 31, 1994, a compound return of 11.90 percent. An investment of $10,000 on December 31, 1952, in the Large Stocks universe grew to $954,125, a return of 11.46 percent a year. The Sharpe ratio

Table 11-4. Annual performance of Large Stocks versus 50 stocks with highest 1-year earnings gains drawn from Large Stocks universe.

Year ending	Large Stocks	Universe = Large Stocks Top 50 1-year earnings gains	Top 50 1-year earnings gains Relative performance
31-Dec-53	2.30%	−4.40%	−6.70%
31-Dec-54	44.90%	48.10%	3.20%
31-Dec-55	21.20%	28.40%	7.20%
31-Dec-56	9.60%	8.50%	−1.10%
31-Dec-57	−6.90%	−13.90%	−7.00%
31-Dec-58	42.10%	41.40%	−0.70%
31-Dec-59	9.90%	11.10%	1.20%
31-Dec-60	4.80%	15.10%	10.30%
31-Dec-61	27.50%	16.50%	−11.00%
31-Dec-62	−8.90%	−14.60%	−5.70%
31-Dec-63	19.50%	22.70%	3.20%
31-Dec-64	15.30%	15.30%	0.00%
31-Dec-65	16.20%	26.70%	10.50%
31-Dec-66	−4.90%	−5.00%	−0.10%
31-Dec-67	21.30%	29.60%	8.30%
31-Dec-68	16.80%	9.00%	−7.80%
31-Dec-69	−9.90%	−5.60%	4.30%
31-Dec-70	−0.20%	−12.10%	−11.90%
31-Dec-71	17.30%	20.50%	3.20%
31-Dec-72	14.90%	11.00%	−3.90%
31-Dec-73	−18.90%	−31.60%	−12.70%
31-Dec-74	−26.70%	−31.80%	−5.10%
31-Dec-75	43.10%	37.80%	−5.30%
31-Dec-76	28.00%	32.30%	4.30%
31-Dec-77	−2.50%	−7.50%	−5.00%
31-Dec-78	8.10%	18.20%	10.10%
31-Dec-79	27.30%	37.10%	9.80%
31-Dec-80	30.80%	42.00%	11.20%
31-Dec-81	0.60%	−18.20%	−18.80%
31-Dec-82	19.90%	1.70%	−18.20%
31-Dec-83	23.80%	21.60%	−2.20%
31-Dec-84	−0.40%	−11.80%	−11.40%
31-Dec-85	19.50%	27.00%	7.50%
31-Dec-86	32.20%	12.20%	−20.00%
31-Dec-87	3.30%	−5.40%	−8.70%
31-Dec-88	19.00%	17.60%	−1.40%
31-Dec-89	26.00%	21.50%	−4.50%
31-Dec-90	−8.70%	−9.20%	−0.50%
31-Dec-91	33.00%	32.10%	−0.90%
31-Dec-92	8.70%	9.30%	0.60%
31-Dec-93	16.30%	19.80%	3.50%
31-Dec-94	−1.90%	−1.50%	0.40%
Arithmetic average	12.70%	10.99%	−1.71%
Standard deviation	16.36%	19.68%	3.33%

Table 11-5. Summary return results for Large Stocks and 50 stocks with highest 1-year earnings gains from Large Stocks universe: December 31, 1952–December 31, 1994.

	Large Stocks	Universe = Large Stocks Top 50 highest 1-year earnings gains
Arithmetic average	12.70%	10.99%
Standard deviation of return	16.36%	19.68%
Sharpe risk-adjusted ratio	44.00	28.00
3-yr compounded	7.44%	8.85%
5-yr compounded	8.53%	9.12%
10-yr compounded	13.93%	11.54%
15-yr compounded	14.03%	9.26%
20-yr compounded	15.42%	12.38%
25-yr compounded	11.16%	7.18%
30-yr compounded	10.48%	7.63%
35-yr compounded	10.54%	7.98%
40-yr compounded	10.97%	8.66%
Compound annual return	11.46%	9.13%
$10,000 becomes	$954,124.99	$392,549.19
Maximum return	44.90%	48.10%
Minimum return	−26.70%	−31.80%
Maximum expected return*	45.41%	50.36%
Minimum expected return**	−20.02%	−28.38%

*Maximum expected return is average return plus 2 times the standard deviation.
**Minimum expected return is average return minus 2 times the standard deviation.

Table 11-6. Base rates for Large Stocks and 50 stocks with highest 1-year earnings gains from Large Stocks universe: 1952–1994.

Item	50 highest 1-year earnings gains beat Large Stocks	Percent
Single-year return	18 out of 42	43%
Rolling 5-year compound return	8 out of 38	21%
Rolling 10-year compound return	4 out of 33	12%

Table 11-7. Annual performance of All Stocks versus 50 stocks with worst 1-year earnings changes from All Stocks.

Year ending	All Stocks	Universe = All Stocks Worst 50 1-year earnings changes	Worst 50 1-year earnings gains Relative performance
31-Dec-53	2.90%	−2.80%	−5.70%
31-Dec-54	47.00%	47.90%	0.90%
31-Dec-55	20.70%	26.40%	5.70%
31-Dec-56	17.00%	14.50%	−2.50%
31-Dec-57	−7.10%	−12.40%	−5.30%
31-Dec-58	55.00%	60.10%	5.10%
31-Dec-59	23.00%	16.20%	−6.80%
31-Dec-60	6.10%	−16.00%	−22.10%
31-Dec-61	31.20%	25.00%	−6.20%
31-Dec-62	−12.00%	−9.90%	2.10%
31-Dec-63	18.00%	23.90%	5.90%
31-Dec-64	16.30%	22.60%	6.30%
31-Dec-65	22.60%	45.00%	22.40%
31-Dec-66	−5.20%	−9.10%	−3.90%
31-Dec-67	41.10%	39.10%	−2.00%
31-Dec-68	27.40%	37.30%	9.90%
31-Dec-69	−18.50%	−32.10%	−13.60%
31-Dec-70	−5.80%	−16.00%	−10.20%
31-Dec-71	21.30%	26.20%	4.90%
31-Dec-72	11.00%	0.60%	−10.40%
31-Dec-73	−27.20%	−15.70%	11.50%
31-Dec-74	−27.90%	−26.50%	1.40%
31-Dec-75	55.90%	58.90%	3.00%
31-Dec-76	35.60%	47.10%	11.50%
31-Dec-77	6.90%	4.10%	−2.80%
31-Dec-78	12.20%	9.90%	−2.30%
31-Dec-79	34.30%	52.80%	18.50%
31-Dec-80	31.50%	45.40%	13.90%
31-Dec-81	1.70%	−10.50%	−12.20%
31-Dec-82	22.50%	19.40%	−3.10%
31-Dec-83	28.10%	30.90%	2.80%
31-Dec-84	−3.40%	−9.40%	−6.00%
31-Dec-85	30.80%	18.60%	−12.20%
31-Dec-86	13.10%	11.70%	−1.40%
31-Dec-87	−1.30%	0.90%	2.20%
31-Dec-88	21.20%	23.30%	2.10%
31-Dec-89	21.40%	15.10%	−6.30%
31-Dec-90	−13.80%	−29.70%	−15.90%
31-Dec-91	39.80%	26.60%	−13.20%
31-Dec-92	13.80%	22.60%	8.80%
31-Dec-93	16.60%	23.20%	6.60%
31-Dec-94	−3.40%	7.20%	10.60%
Arithmetic average	14.77%	14.58%	−0.19%
Standard deviation	20.07%	24.13%	4.06%

Table 11-8. Summary return results for All Stocks and 50 stocks with worst 1-year earnings changes from All Stocks universe: December 31, 1952–December 31, 1994.

	All Stocks	Universe = All Stocks Worst 50 1-year earnings gains
Arithmetic average	14.77%	14.58%
Standard deviation of return	20.07%	24.13%
Sharpe risk-adjusted ratio	46.00	38.00
3-yr compounded	8.63%	17.43%
5-yr compounded	9.09%	7.58%
10-yr compounded	12.74%	10.58%
15-yr compounded	13.55%	11.38%
20-yr compounded	16.95%	16.33%
25-yr compounded	11.51%	11.01%
30-yr compounded	11.47%	11.06%
35-yr compounded	11.39%	10.54%
40-yr compounded	12.45%	11.54%
Compound annual return	12.93%	11.92%
$10,000 becomes	$1,651,690.90	$1,132,754.19
Maximum return	55.90%	60.10%
Minimum return	−27.90%	−32.10%
Maximum expected return*	54.91%	62.83%
Minimum expected return**	−25.37%	−33.67%

*Maximum expected return is average return plus 2 times the standard deviation.

**Minimum expected return is average return minus 2 times the standard deviation.

for each was virtually identical—44 for Large Stocks and 43 for the 50 stocks with the worst 1-year earnings change. Tables 11-9 and 11-10 summarize the results.

Base rates for All Stocks and Large Stocks and compound rates of return by decade are given in Tables 11-11, 11-12, and 11-13. Figures 11-1 through 11-4 depict the results graphically for both groups.

Table 11-9. Annual performance of Large Stocks versus 50 stocks with worst 1-year earnings changes from Large Stocks.

Year ending	Large Stocks	Universe = Large Stocks Worst 50 1-year earnings changes	Worst 50 1-year earnings gains Relative performance
31-Dec-53	2.30%	2.60%	0.30%
31-Dec-54	44.90%	53.20%	8.30%
31-Dec-55	21.20%	20.20%	−1.00%
31-Dec-56	9.60%	13.10%	3.50%
31-Dec-57	−6.90%	−7.40%	−0.50%
31-Dec-58	42.10%	44.90%	2.80%
31-Dec-59	9.90%	14.00%	4.10%
31-Dec-60	4.80%	−11.10%	−15.90%
31-Dec-61	27.50%	27.70%	0.20%
31-Dec-62	−8.90%	−12.40%	−3.50%
31-Dec-63	19.50%	24.20%	4.70%
31-Dec-64	15.30%	15.90%	0.60%
31-Dec-65	16.20%	21.80%	5.60%
31-Dec-66	−4.90%	−7.00%	−2.10%
31-Dec-67	21.30%	20.00%	−1.30%
31-Dec-68	16.80%	17.40%	0.60%
31-Dec-69	−9.90%	−18.10%	−8.20%
31-Dec-70	−0.20%	−0.30%	−0.10%
31-Dec-71	17.30%	16.60%	−0.70%
31-Dec-72	14.90%	4.50%	−10.40%
31-Dec-73	−18.90%	−0.10%	18.80%
31-Dec-74	−26.70%	−23.30%	3.40%
31-Dec-75	43.10%	57.40%	14.30%
31-Dec-76	28.00%	34.60%	6.60%
31-Dec-77	−2.50%	−7.10%	−4.60%
31-Dec-78	8.10%	6.20%	−1.90%
31-Dec-79	27.30%	30.60%	3.30%
31-Dec-80	30.80%	47.20%	16.40%
31-Dec-81	0.60%	7.60%	7.00%
31-Dec-82	19.90%	24.30%	4.40%
31-Dec-83	23.80%	26.50%	2.70%
31-Dec-84	−0.40%	−9.60%	−9.20%
31-Dec-85	19.50%	22.00%	2.50%
31-Dec-86	32.20%	21.50%	−10.70%
31-Dec-87	3.30%	11.90%	8.60%
31-Dec-88	19.00%	22.80%	3.80%
31-Dec-89	26.00%	18.00%	−8.00%
31-Dec-90	−8.70%	−17.20%	−8.50%
31-Dec-91	33.00%	16.80%	−16.20%
31-Dec-92	8.70%	9.50%	0.80%
31-Dec-93	16.30%	22.10%	5.80%
31-Dec-94	−1.90%	3.40%	5.30%
Arithmetic average	12.70%	13.45%	0.75%
Standard deviation	16.36%	18.68%	2.32%

Table 11-10. Summary return results for Large Stocks and 50 stocks with worst 1-year earnings changes from Large Stocks universe: December 31, 1952–December 31, 1994.

	Large Stocks	Universe = Large Stocks Worst 50 1-year earnings changes
Arithmetic average	12.70%	13.45%
Standard deviation of return	16.36%	18.68%
Sharpe risk-adjusted ratio	44.00	43.00
3-yr compounded	7.44%	11.40%
5-yr compounded	8.53%	5.98%
10-yr compounded	13.93%	12.38%
15-yr compounded	14.03%	14.10%
20-yr compounded	15.42%	16.09%
25-yr compounded	11.16%	12.35%
30-yr compounded	10.48%	11.18%
35-yr compounded	10.54%	10.64%
40-yr compounded	10.97%	11.27%
Compound annual return	11.46%	11.90%
$10,000 becomes	$954,124.99	$1,124,208.81
Maximum return	44.90%	57.40%
Minimum return	−26.70%	−23.30%
Maximum expected return*	45.41%	50.80%
Minimum expected return**	−20.02%	−23.90%

*Maximum expected return is average return plus 2 times the standard deviation.
**Minimum expected return is average return minus 2 times the standard deviation.

Table 11-11. Base rates for All Stocks and 50 stocks with worst 1-year earnings gains stocks from All Stocks universe: 1952–1994.

Item	50 worst 1-year earnings gains beat All Stocks	Percent
Single-year return	21 out of 42	50%
Rolling 5-year compound return	15 out of 38	40%
Rolling 10-year compound return	8 out of 33	24%

Table 11-12. Base rates for Large Stocks and 50 stocks with worst 1-year earnings changes from Large Stocks universe: 1952–1994.

Item	50 worst 1-year earnings changes beat Large Stocks	Percent
Single-year return	25 out of 42	60%
Rolling 5-year compound return	20 out of 38	53%
Rolling 10-year compound return	17 out of 33	52%

Table 11-13. Compound annual rates of return by decade.

Portfolio	1950s*	1960s	1970s	1980s	1990s**
Large Stocks	16.21%	8.99%	6.99%	16.89%	8.53%
50 highest 1-year earnings gains from Large Stocks	15.05%	7.10%	9.25%	4.55%	8.95%
50 worst 1-year earnings gains from Large Stocks	18.43%	7.69%	14.14%	11.77%	10.06%
All Stocks	20.94%	11.09%	8.53%	15.85%	9.09%
50 highest 1-year earnings gains from All Stocks	21.33%	8.55%	16.97%	2.12%	2.91%
50 worst 1-year earnings gains from All Stocks	19.06%	9.40%	16.67%	5.39%	17.23%

*Returns for 1953–1959.
**Returns for 1990–1994.

Implications

Buying stocks simply because they have great earnings gains is a losing proposition. Investors get overly excited about companies with dramatic earnings gains, projecting these earnings assumptions too far into the future. It's interesting to note that the stocks with the highest 1-year earnings gains almost always have the highest price-to-earnings ratios, another indicator that poor performance lies ahead. We'll see later that *good* earnings gains coupled with strong price momentum will lead you to high-performing stocks, but for now remember that you shouldn't buy a stock just because it has outstanding 1-year earnings gains.

You're not much better off buying stocks with the worst earnings changes. While their returns are slightly higher than those with the best earnings changes, there is no compelling theory to justify buying them. History suggests you should not make investment decisions on either one of these variables.

Figure 11-1. Returns on 50 stocks with highest 1-year earnings gains versus All Stocks and Large Stocks, 1952–1994. Year-end 1952 = $10,000.

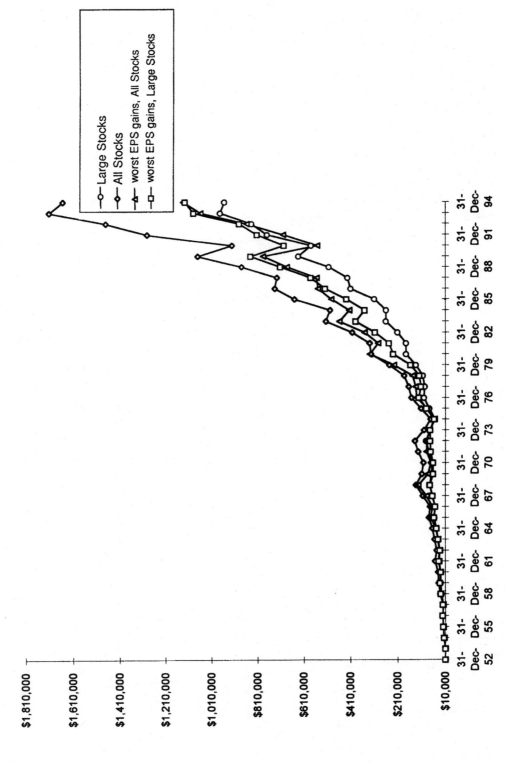

Figure 11-2. Returns on 50 stocks with worst 1-year earnings change versus All Stocks and Large Stocks, 1952–1994. Year-end 1952 = $10,000.

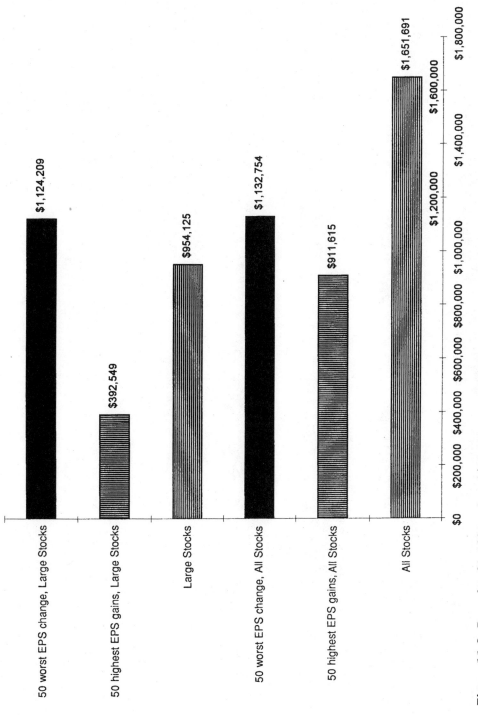

Figure 11-3. December 31, 1994, value of $10,000 invested on December 31, 1952, and annually rebalanced.

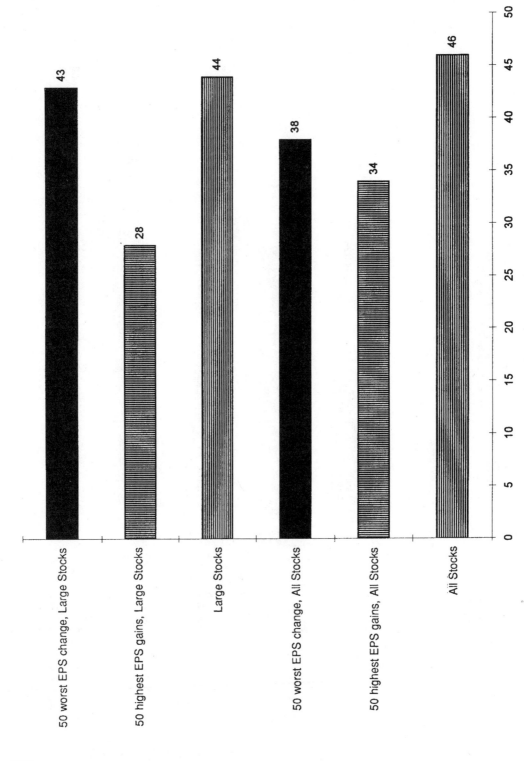

Figure 11-4. Sharpe risk-adjusted return ratio, 1952–1994. (Higher is better.)

12

Five-Year
Earnings-Per-Share
Percentage Changes

*The same thing happened today that happened
yesterday, only to different people.*
—WALTER WINCHELL

Some analysts believe that a 1-year change in earnings is meaningless
and that we should focus on 5-year growth rates. This, they argue, is
enough time to separate the one-trick pony from the true thoroughbred.

The Results

Unfortunately, 5 years of big earnings gains doesn't help us pick thoroughbreds. Starting on December 31, 1954 (we need 5 years of data to
compute the compound 5-year earnings growth rate), $10,000 invested
in the 50 stocks from All Stocks with the highest 5-year compound earnings-per-share growth rates grew to just $353,446 by the end of 1994, a
compound return of 9.32 percent. An investment of $10,000 in the All
Stocks universe on December 31, 1954, was worth $1,091,933 by
December 31, 1994, a return of 12.45 percent a year.

As with the 50 stocks with the highest 1-year earnings gains,
investors get dazzled by high 5-year earnings growth rates and bid

prices to unsustainable levels. When the future earnings are lower than expected, investors punish their former darlings and prices swoon.

The 50 stocks from All Stocks with the highest compound 5-year earnings growth rates were also risky—their standard deviation of return was 27.07 percent, well ahead of All Stocks' 19.83 percent. High risk coupled with poor return accounts for the Sharpe ratio of 26. Over the same period, the Sharpe ratio for All Stocks was 43.

All the base rates for the strategy are horrible, with the 50 stocks with the highest 5-year compound earnings growth rates beating All Stocks just 3 percent of the time over all rolling 10-year periods. Tables 12-1, 12-2, and 12-3 summarize the results.

Large Stocks Are Similar

The news is just as bad for large stocks with outstanding 5-year earnings gains—they perform about half as well as an investment in the Large Stocks universe. Starting on December 31, 1954, $10,000 invested in the 50 stocks from Large Stocks with the highest 5-year compound earnings growth rates grew to $371,937 at the end of 1994, a compound annual return of 9.46 percent. An investment of $10,000 in the Large Stocks universe grew to $643,667, an annual return of 10.97 percent. The stocks with high earnings gains were also riskier than Large Stocks, having a standard deviation of return of 21.73 percent, well ahead of Large Stocks' 15.88 percent.

The base rates are only marginally better than for All Stocks, with the strategy beating the Large Stocks universe 23 percent of the time over all rolling 10-year periods. Tables 12-4, 12-5, and 12-6 summarize the returns for Large Stocks. Table 12-7 shows returns by decades. The results for both groups are shown graphically in Figures 12-1, 12-2, and 12-3.

Implications

Like the 1-year earnings winners, we see investors consistently paying too much for stocks with outstanding 5-year gains. While we were unable to look at the 50 worst 5-year earnings changes because of the way Compustat calculates the compound returns, they are probably similar to the 1-year tests. The evidence shows it's a mistake to get overly excited by big earnings gains. Investors pay a premium for these stocks and would be better off indexing their portfolios to the Large Stocks universe.

Table 12-1. Annual performance of All Stocks versus 50 stocks with highest compound 5-year EPS growth drawn from All Stocks universe.

Year ending	All Stocks	Universe = All Stocks Top 50 5-year compound EPS growth	Top 50 5-year compound EPS growth Relative performance
31-Dec-55	20.70%	28.40%	7.70%
31-Dec-56	17.00%	19.40%	2.40%
31-Dec-57	−7.10%	−15.90%	−8.80%
31-Dec-58	55.00%	78.90%	23.90%
31-Dec-59	23.00%	37.80%	14.80%
31-Dec-60	6.10%	5.30%	−0.80%
31-Dec-61	31.20%	21.80%	−9.40%
31-Dec-62	−12.00%	−19.00%	−7.00%
31-Dec-63	18.00%	21.40%	3.40%
31-Dec-64	16.30%	3.90%	−12.40%
31-Dec-65	22.60%	22.00%	−0.60%
31-Dec-66	−5.20%	−1.90%	3.30%
31-Dec-67	41.10%	56.60%	15.50%
31-Dec-68	27.40%	20.10%	−7.30%
31-Dec-69	−18.50%	−21.40%	−2.90%
31-Dec-70	−5.80%	−34.50%	−28.70%
31-Dec-71	21.30%	35.80%	14.50%
31-Dec-72	11.00%	4.90%	−6.10%
31-Dec-73	−27.20%	−45.90%	−18.70%
31-Dec-74	−27.90%	−34.80%	−6.90%
31-Dec-75	55.90%	38.10%	−17.80%
31-Dec-76	35.60%	39.00%	3.40%
31-Dec-77	6.90%	5.90%	−1.00%
31-Dec-78	12.20%	7.30%	−4.90%
31-Dec-79	34.30%	52.50%	18.20%
31-Dec-80	31.50%	44.80%	13.30%
31-Dec-81	1.70%	−7.50%	−9.20%
31-Dec-82	22.50%	27.20%	4.70%
31-Dec-83	28.10%	20.90%	−7.20%
31-Dec-84	−3.40%	−19.40%	−16.00%
31-Dec-85	30.80%	28.40%	−2.40%
31-Dec-86	13.10%	6.60%	−6.50%
31-Dec-87	−1.30%	−16.80%	−15.50%
31-Dec-88	21.20%	21.10%	−0.10%
31-Dec-89	21.40%	30.90%	9.50%
31-Dec-90	−13.80%	−14.20%	−0.40%
31-Dec-91	39.80%	51.50%	11.70%
31-Dec-92	13.80%	5.50%	−8.30%
31-Dec-93	16.60%	13.40%	−3.20%
31-Dec-94	−3.40%	−6.00%	−2.60%
Arithmetic average	14.26%	12.80%	−1.46%
Standard deviation	19.83%	27.07%	7.24%

Table 12-2. Summary return results for All Stocks and 50 stocks with highest 5-year EPS compound growth rates from All Stocks universe: December 31, 1954–December 31, 1994.

	All Stocks	Universe = All Stocks Top 50 5-year EPS compound growth rates
Arithmetic average	14.26%	12.80%
Standard deviation of return	19.83%	27.07%
Sharpe risk-adjusted ratio	43.00	26.00
3-yr compounded	8.63%	3.99%
5-yr compounded	9.09%	7.89%
10-yr compounded	12.74%	10.19%
15-yr compounded	13.55%	10.35%
20-yr compounded	16.95%	14.33%
25-yr compounded	11.51%	6.47%
30-yr compounded	11.47%	7.39%
35-yr compounded	11.39%	7.12%
40-yr compounded	12.45%	9.32%
Compound annual return	12.45%	9.32%
$10,000 becomes	$1,091,933.19	$353,445.76
Maximum return	55.90%	78.90%
Minimum return	−27.90%	−45.90%
Maximum expected return*	53.92%	66.94%
Minimum expected return**	−25.39%	−41.33%

*Maximum expected return is average return plus 2 times the standard deviation.

**Minimum expected return is average return minus 2 times the standard deviation.

Table 12-3. Base rates for All Stocks and 50 stocks with highest 5-year EPS compound growth rates from All Stocks universe: 1954–1994.

Item	50 highest 5-year EPS growth stocks beat All Stocks	Percent
Single-year return	14 out of 40	35%
Rolling 5-year compound return	11 out of 36	31%
Rolling 10-year compound return	1 out of 31	3%

Table 12-4. Annual performance of Large Stocks versus 50 stocks with highest 5-year compound EPS growth rates drawn from Large Stocks universe.

Year ending	Large Stocks	Universe = Large Stocks Top 50 5-year compound EPS growth	Top 50 5-year compound EPS growth Relative performance
31-Dec-55	21.20%	28.10%	6.90%
31-Dec-56	9.60%	12.40%	2.80%
31-Dec-57	−6.90%	−14.70%	−7.80%
31-Dec-58	42.10%	49.00%	6.90%
31-Dec-59	9.90%	16.70%	6.80%
31-Dec-60	4.80%	5.50%	0.70%
31-Dec-61	27.50%	16.50%	−11.00%
31-Dec-62	−8.90%	−16.90%	−8.00%
31-Dec-63	19.50%	23.70%	4.20%
31-Dec-64	15.30%	10.30%	−5.00%
31-Dec-65	16.20%	30.90%	14.70%
31-Dec-66	−4.90%	3.00%	7.90%
31-Dec-67	21.30%	23.30%	2.00%
31-Dec-68	16.80%	12.50%	−4.30%
31-Dec-69	−9.90%	−15.30%	−5.40%
31-Dec-70	−0.20%	−21.60%	−21.40%
31-Dec-71	17.30%	34.80%	17.50%
31-Dec-72	14.90%	12.50%	−2.40%
31-Dec-73	−18.90%	−29.10%	−10.20%
31-Dec-74	−26.70%	−31.90%	−5.20%
31-Dec-75	43.10%	42.70%	−0.40%
31-Dec-76	28.00%	19.00%	−9.00%
31-Dec-77	−2.50%	−0.09%	2.41%
31-Dec-78	8.10%	13.20%	5.10%
31-Dec-79	27.30%	51.80%	24.50%
31-Dec-80	30.80%	51.90%	21.10%
31-Dec-81	0.60%	−9.70%	−10.30%
31-Dec-82	19.90%	26.40%	6.50%
31-Dec-83	23.80%	10.50%	−13.30%
31-Dec-84	−0.40%	−20.00%	−19.60%
31-Dec-85	19.50%	31.20%	11.70%
31-Dec-86	32.20%	16.50%	−15.70%
31-Dec-87	3.30%	−7.20%	−10.50%
31-Dec-88	19.00%	16.60%	−2.40%
31-Dec-89	26.00%	26.30%	0.30%
31-Dec-90	−8.70%	−3.60%	5.10%
31-Dec-91	33.00%	47.40%	14.40%
31-Dec-92	8.70%	6.80%	−1.90%
31-Dec-93	16.30%	1.60%	−14.70%
31-Dec-94	−1.90%	−4.50%	−2.60%
Arithmetic average	12.51%	11.66%	−0.49%
Standard deviation	15.88%	21.73%	5.85%

Table 12-5. Summary return results for Large Stocks and 50 stocks with highest 5-year EPS compound growth rates from Large Stocks universe: December 31, 1954–December 31, 1994.

	Large Stocks	Universe = Large Stockss Top 50 5-year EPS compound growth rates
Arithmetic average	12.15%	11.66%
Standard deviation of return	15.88%	21.73%
Sharpe risk-adjusted ratio	41.00	28.00
3-yr compounded	7.44%	1.19%
5-yr compounded	8.53%	8.05%
10-yr compounded	13.93%	11.89%
15-yr compounded	14.03%	10.89%
20-yr compounded	15.42%	14.00%
25-yr compounded	11.16%	8.61%
30-yr compounded	10.48%	8.78%
35-yr compounded	10.54%	8.51%
40-yr compounded	10.97%	9.46%
Compound annual return	10.97%	9.46%
$10,000 becomes	$643,667.01	$371,936.98
Maximum return	43.10%	51.90%
Minimum return	−26.70%	−31.90%
Maximum expected return*	43.90%	55.11%
Minimum expected return**	−19.60%	−31.79%

*Maximum expected return is average return plus 2 times the standard deviation.

**Minimum expected return is average return minus 2 times the standard deviation.

Table 12-6. Base rates for Large Stocks and 50 stocks with highest 5-year EPS compound growth rates from Large Stocks universe: 1954–1994.

Item	50 highest 5-year EPS growth stocks beat Large Stocks	Percent
Single-year return	19 out of 40	48%
Rolling 5-year compound return	14 out of 36	39%
Rolling 10-year compound return	7 out of 31	23%

Table 12-7. Compound annual rates of return by decade.

Portfolio	1950s*	1960s	1970s	1980s	1990s**
Large Stocks	14.07%	8.99%	6.99%	16.89%	8.53%
50 highest 5-year EPS growth rates from Large Stocks	16.39%	8.24%	5.28%	12.34%	8.05%
All Stocks	20.12%	11.09%	8.53%	15.85%	9.09%
50 highest 5-year EPS growth rates from All Stocks	26.02%	8.77%	0.91%	11.60%	7.89%

*Returns for 1955–1959.
**Returns for 1990–1994.

Persistent 5-year earnings gains are another matter. When looking at multifactor models we'll see that a record of persistent earnings gains is far more important than a record of *large* earnings gains and can be a very useful factor in a growth-oriented portfolio.

For now, remember that high 5-year compound earnings gains won't help you buy a winning stock.

Figure 12-1. Returns on highest 5-year compound earnings growth stocks versus All Stocks and Large Stocks, 1954–1994. Year-end 1954 = $10,000.

Figure 12-2. December 31, 1994, value of $10,000 invested on December 31, 1954, and annually rebalanced.

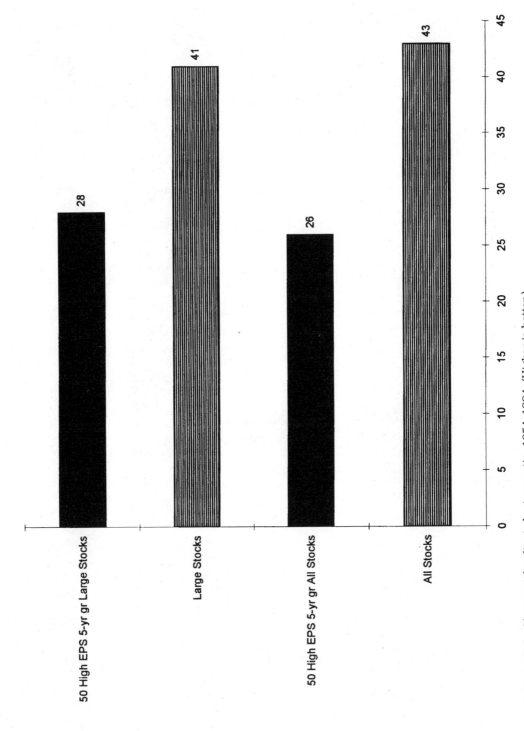

Figure 12-3. Sharpe risk-adjusted return ratio, 1954–1994. (Higher is better.)

13

Profit Margins: Do Investors Profit from Corporate Profits?

*I am a strong believer that as one moves toward
the future, the strongest and clearest way to do it
is if you have a good sense of your past. You
cannot have a very tall tree without deep roots.*
—CESAR PELLI

Net profit margins are an excellent gauge of a company's operating efficiency and ability to compete successfully with other firms in its field. Thus many believe that firms with high profit margins are better investments, since they are the leaders in their industries. You find net profit margins by dividing income before extraordinary items (a company's income after all expenses but before provisions for dividends) by net sales. This is then multiplied by 100 to get a percentage.

The Results

We'll test this strategy by buying the 50 stocks from All Stocks and Large Stocks with the highest profit margins. Here, we're able to start the test on December 31, 1951, so we're again looking at the full 43 years of data. As usual, we'll time-lag all the accounting data to avoid look-ahead bias and rebalance the portfolio annually.

An investment of $10,000 on December 31, 1951, in the 50 stocks from the All Stocks universe with the highest profit margins grew to $740,552 by the end of 1994, a compound return of 10.53 percent. That's $1 million less than you'd earn investing the money in the All Stocks universe. There, $10,000 grew to $1,782,174, a return of 12.81 percent a year.

Risk for the 50 stocks with the highest profit margins was virtually the same as that for the All Stocks universe, with a standard deviation of return of 20.86 percent, only one percent higher than All Stocks' 19.86 percent. All the base rates for the 50 stocks with the highest profit margins were negative, with the strategy beating All Stocks just 12 percent of the time over all rolling 10-year periods. Tables 13-1, 13-2, and 13-3 summarize the returns for the All Stocks version of the strategy.

Large Stocks Do Slightly Better

The 50 stocks with the highest profit margins from the Large Stocks universe did slightly better. Here, $10,000 invested on December 31, 1951, grew to $748,843 by the end of 1994. That's considerably less than the $1,042,859 you'd earn investing the money in the Large Stocks universe, but better than the return from the high profit margin stocks in All Stocks. Here, the 50 stocks with the highest profit margins were actually *less* risky than the Large Stocks universe—with a standard deviation of 16.07 percent compared with 16.16 percent for Large Stocks. This low standard deviation accounts for the strategy's fairly respectable Sharpe ratio of 40. All base rates are negative, with the 50 stocks with the highest profit margins beating the Large Stocks universe just 29 percent of the time over all rolling 10-year periods. Tables 13-4, 13-5, and 13-6 summarize the returns for the high profit margin stocks from Large Stocks. Table 13-7 shows the compound annual returns by decade for both groups. The results are depicted graphically in Figures 13-1, 13-2, and 13-3.

Implications

History shows using high profit margins as the only determinate in buying a stock will lead to disappointing results.

Table 13-1. Annual performance of All Stocks versus 50 stocks with highest profit margins drawn from All Stocks universe.

Year ending	All Stocks	Universe = All Stocks Top 50 profit margin	Top 50 profit margin Relative performance
31-Dec-52	7.90%	11.30%	3.40%
31-Dec-53	2.90%	1.40%	−1.50%
31-Dec-54	47.00%	37.80%	−9.20%
31-Dec-55	20.70%	13.90%	−6.80%
31-Dec-56	17.00%	8.40%	−8.60%
31-Dec-57	−7.10%	−0.01%	7.09%
31-Dec-58	55.00%	46.10%	−8.90%
31-Dec-59	23.00%	9.20%	−13.80%
31-Dec-60	6.10%	22.40%	16.30%
31-Dec-61	31.20%	30.60%	−0.60%
31-Dec-62	−12.00%	−3.50%	8.50%
31-Dec-63	18.00%	17.70%	−0.30%
31-Dec-64	16.30%	17.00%	0.70%
31-Dec-65	22.60%	9.90%	−12.70%
31-Dec-66	−5.20%	1.70%	6.90%
31-Dec-67	41.10%	33.40%	−7.70%
31-Dec-68	27.40%	26.30%	−1.10%
31-Dec-69	−18.50%	−15.00%	3.50%
31-Dec-70	−5.80%	−3.80%	2.00%
31-Dec-71	21.30%	5.60%	−15.70%
31-Dec-72	11.00%	15.60%	4.60%
31-Dec-73	−27.20%	−20.90%	6.30%
31-Dec-74	−27.90%	−45.70%	−17.80%
31-Dec-75	55.90%	28.10%	−27.80%
31-Dec-76	35.60%	37.50%	1.90%
31-Dec-77	6.90%	16.00%	9.10%
31-Dec-78	12.20%	14.60%	2.40%
31-Dec-79	34.30%	85.10%	50.80%
31-Dec-80	31.50%	29.40%	−2.10%
31-Dec-81	1.70%	−11.70%	−13.40%
31-Dec-82	22.50%	4.70%	−17.80%
31-Dec-83	28.10%	17.70%	−10.40%
31-Dec-84	−3.40%	−6.70%	−3.30%
31-Dec-85	30.80%	10.80%	−20.00%
31-Dec-86	13.10%	11.60%	−1.50%
31-Dec-87	−1.30%	−1.70%	−0.40%
31-Dec-88	21.20%	9.40%	−11.80%
31-Dec-89	21.40%	25.40%	4.00%
31-Dec-90	−13.80%	−13.20%	0.60%
31-Dec-91	39.80%	32.40%	−7.40%
31-Dec-92	13.80%	4.90%	−8.90%
31-Dec-93	16.60%	29.50%	12.90%
31-Dec-94	−3.40%	−4.90%	−1.50%
Arithmetic average	14.61%	12.52%	−2.09%
Standard deviation	19.86%	20.86%	1.00%

Table 13-2. Summary return results for All Stocks and 50 highest profit margin stocks from All Stocks universe: December 31, 1951–December 31, 1994.

	All Stocks	Universe = All Stocks Top 50 profit margins
Arithmetic average	14.61%	12.52%
Standard deviation of return	19.86%	20.86%
Sharpe risk-adjusted ratio	47.00	34.00
3-yr compounded	8.63%	8.91%
5-yr compounded	9.09%	8.22%
10-yr compounded	12.74%	9.49%
15-yr compounded	13.55%	8.18%
20-yr compounded	16.95%	14.14%
25-yr compounded	11.51%	8.16%
30-yr compounded	11.47%	8.44%
35-yr compounded	11.39%	9.53%
40-yr compounded	12.45%	10.14%
Compound annual return	12.81%	10.53%
$10,000 becomes	$1,782,174.48	$740,551.60
Maximum return	55.90%	85.10%
Minimum return	−27.90%	−45.70%
Maximum expected return*	54.33%	54.24%
Minimum expected return**	−25.11%	−29.20%

*Maximum expected return is average return plus 2 times the standard deviation.
**Minimum expected return is average return minus 2 times the standard deviation.

Table 13-3. Base rates for All Stocks and 50 highest profit margin stocks from All Stocks universe: 1951–1994.

Item	50 highest profit margin stocks beat All Stocks	Percent
Single-year return	17 out of 43	40%
Rolling 5-year compound return	12 out of 39	31%
Rolling 10-year compound return	4 out of 34	12%

Table 13-4. Annual performance of Large Stocks versus 50 stocks with highest profit margins drawn from Large Stocks universe.

Year ending	Large Stocks	Universe = Large Stocks Top 50 profit margin	Top 50 profit margin Relative performance
31-Dec-52	9.30%	7.80%	−1.50%
31-Dec-53	2.30%	1.30%	−1.00%
31-Dec-54	44.90%	39.60%	−5.30%
31-Dec-55	21.20%	16.20%	−5.00%
31-Dec-56	9.60%	5.40%	−4.20%
31-Dec-57	−6.90%	2.00%	8.90%
31-Dec-58	42.10%	42.20%	0.10%
31-Dec-59	9.90%	10.60%	0.70%
31-Dec-60	4.80%	17.20%	12.40%
31-Dec-61	27.50%	31.70%	4.20%
31-Dec-62	−8.90%	−0.06%	8.84%
31-Dec-63	19.50%	12.70%	−6.80%
31-Dec-64	15.30%	14.30%	−1.00%
31-Dec-65	16.20%	3.50%	−12.70%
31-Dec-66	−4.90%	−3.70%	1.20%
31-Dec-67	21.30%	2.40%	−18.90%
31-Dec-68	16.80%	8.80%	−8.00%
31-Dec-69	−9.90%	0.08%	9.98%
31-Dec-70	−0.20%	3.50%	3.70%
31-Dec-71	17.30%	9.70%	−7.60%
31-Dec-72	14.90%	17.60%	2.70%
31-Dec-73	−18.90%	−14.40%	4.50%
31-Dec-74	−26.70%	−31.70%	−5.00%
31-Dec-75	43.10%	27.90%	−15.20%
31-Dec-76	28.00%	23.20%	−4.80%
31-Dec-77	−2.50%	2.00%	4.50%
31-Dec-78	8.10%	9.00%	0.90%
31-Dec-79	27.30%	47.40%	20.10%
31-Dec-80	30.80%	38.20%	7.40%
31-Dec-81	0.60%	−11.80%	−12.40%
31-Dec-82	19.90%	2.80%	−17.10%
31-Dec-83	23.80%	16.70%	−7.10%
31-Dec-84	−0.40%	−1.80%	−1.40%
31-Dec-85	19.50%	24.70%	5.20%
31-Dec-86	32.20%	21.10%	−11.10%
31-Dec-87	3.30%	4.40%	1.10%
31-Dec-88	19.00%	11.20%	−7.80%
31-Dec-89	26.00%	30.80%	4.80%
31-Dec-90	−8.70%	−4.80%	3.90%
31-Dec-91	33.00%	40.70%	7.70%
31-Dec-92	8.70%	6.40%	−2.30%
31-Dec-93	16.30%	19.70%	3.40%
31-Dec-94	−1.90%	−0.20%	1.88%
Arithmetic average	12.62%	11.73%	−0.89%
Standard deviation	16.18%	16.07%	−0.11%

Table 13-5. Summary return results for Large Stocks and 50 highest profit margin stocks from Large Stocks universe: December 31, 1951–December 31, 1994.

	Large Stocks	Universe = Large Stocks Top 50 profit margins
Arithmetic average	12.62%	11.73%
Standard deviation of return	16.18%	16.07%
Sharpe risk-adjusted ratio	45.00	40.00
3-yr compounded	7.44%	8.39%
5-yr compounded	8.53%	11.27%
10-yr compounded	13.93%	14.61%
15-yr compounded	14.03%	12.19%
20-yr compounded	15.42%	14.31%
25-yr compounded	11.16%	10.19%
30-yr compounded	10.48%	8.81%
35-yr compounded	10.54%	9.63%
40-yr compounded	10.97%	10.23%
Compound annual return	11.41%	10.56%
$10,000 becomes	$1,042,858.62	$748,842.98
Maximum return	44.90%	47.40%
Minimum return	−26.70%	−31.70%
Maximum expected return*	44.97%	43.86%
Minimum expected return**	−19.73%	−20.40%

    *Maximum expected return is average return plus 2 times the standard deviation.
    **Minimum expected return is average return minus 2 times the standard deviation.

Table 13-6. Base rates for Large Stocks and 50 highest profit margin stocks from Large Stocks universe: 1951–1994.

Item	50 highest profit margin stocks beat Large Stocks	Percent
Single-year return	22 out of 43	51%
Rolling 5-year compound return	15 out of 39	38%
Rolling 10-year compound return	10 out of 34	29%

Table 13-7. Compound annual rates of return by decade.

Portfolio	1950s*	1960s	1970s	1980s	1990s**
Large Stocks	15.33%	8.99%	6.99%	16.89%	8.53%
50 highest profit margins from Large Stocks	14.70%	8.24%	7.26%	12.66%	11.27%
All Stocks	19.22%	11.09%	8.53%	15.85%	9.09%
50 highest profit margins from All Stocks	15.02%	13.02%	8.14%	8.16%	8.22%

*Returns for 1952–1959.
**Returns for 1990–1994.

Figure 13-1. Returns on high profit margin strategy versus All Stocks and Large Stocks, 1951–1994. Year-end 1951 = $10,000.

Figure 13-2. December 31, 1994, value of $10,000 invested on December 31, 1951, and annually rebalanced.

Figure 13-3. Sharpe risk-adjusted return ratios, 1951–1994. (Higher is better.)

14

Return on Equity

I'd rather see folks doubt what's true than accept
what isn't. —FRANK A. CLARK

High return on equity is a hallmark of a growth stock. You find return on equity by dividing common stock equity into income before extraordinary items (a company's income after all expenses but before provisions for dividends). You then multiply by 100 to express the term as a percentage. Here, we use common liquidating equity (called CEQL in Compustat) as a proxy for common equity.

As with high profit margins, many believe that a high return on equity (ROE) is an excellent gauge of how effectively a company invests shareholders' money. The higher the ROE, the better the company's ability to invest your money and, presumably, the better an investment the stock will be.

The Results

We look at the results for high ROE stocks drawn from both the All Stocks and Large Stocks universes. We start on December 31, 1951, with a $10,000 investment in the 50 stocks from All Stocks with the highest ROE. As usual, we'll rebalance the portfolio annually and time-lag all accounting data to avoid look-ahead bias.

As of December 31, 1994, $10,000 invested in the 50 stocks with the highest ROE was worth $1,713,965, a little less than the $1,782,174 you'd earn investing the money in All Stocks. But while earning a little less money, you'd take a lot more risk—the 50 stocks with the highest ROE had a standard deviation of return of 26.71 percent, considerably higher than All Stocks' 19.86 percent. This risk accounts for the 50 highest ROE stocks' Sharpe ratio of 39—8 points behind All Stocks' ratio of 47.

The base rates are almost dead even. The 50 highest ROE stocks beat the All Stocks universe 49 percent of the time over 1-year and 5-year rolling periods and 44 percent of the time over rolling 10-year periods. You may as well flip a coin. Tables 14-1, 14-2, and 14-3 summarize the returns for the All Stocks group.

Large Stocks Do a Bit Worse

The 50 highest ROE stocks from the Large Stocks universe did a bit worse. Here, $10,000 grew to $792,560 at the end of 1994, a compound return of 10.7 percent a year. That's not as good as the $1,042,859 you'd make investing the money in the Large Stocks universe itself. The 50 highest ROE stocks from Large Stocks were also riskier—their standard deviation of return was 19.82 percent, compared with 16.18 percent for the Large Stocks universe. The difference in risk and return accounts for the 50 highest ROE stocks having a Sharpe ratio of 36—9 points behind the Large Stocks universe's 45.

Base rates for the Large Stocks group are similar to those for All Stocks, with the 50 highest ROE stocks beating the Large Stocks universe 47 percent of the time in any 1-year period, 41 percent of the time in rolling 5-year periods, and 38 percent of the time in all rolling 10-year periods. Tables 14-4, 14-5, and 14-6 summarize the returns for the Large Stocks group. Table 14-7 shows returns for both groups by decades. The results are depicted graphically in Figures 14-1, 14-2, and 14-3.

Implications

Return on equity is an excellent example of the importance of looking at the long-term when judging a strategy's effectiveness. Imagine a young investor just out of college at the end of 1964. He lands a job on Wall Street and studies how stocks with high return on equity perform. The evidence from the previous decade is very encouraging—between December 31, 1951, and December 31, 1959, the 50 highest ROE stocks from both the All and Large Stocks universe outperformed their respec-

Table 14-1. Annual performance of All Stocks versus 50 stocks with highest return on equity drawn from All Stocks universe.

Year ending	All Stocks	Universe = All Stocks Top 50 ROE	Top 50 ROE Relative performance
31-Dec-52	7.90%	9.80%	1.90%
31-Dec-53	2.90%	−2.30%	−5.20%
31-Dec-54	47.00%	64.90%	17.90%
31-Dec-55	20.70%	23.30%	2.60%
31-Dec-56	17.00%	25.20%	8.20%
31-Dec-57	−7.10%	−9.70%	−2.60%
31-Dec-58	55.00%	64.20%	9.20%
31-Dec-59	23.00%	41.30%	18.30%
31-Dec-60	6.10%	26.60%	20.50%
31-Dec-61	31.20%	24.30%	−6.90%
31-Dec-62	−12.00%	−15.50%	−3.50%
31-Dec-63	18.00%	12.30%	−5.70%
31-Dec-64	16.30%	14.70%	−1.60%
31-Dec-65	22.60%	25.90%	3.30%
31-Dec-66	−5.20%	0.20%	5.22%
31-Dec-67	41.10%	96.30%	55.20%
31-Dec-68	27.40%	18.40%	−9.00%
31-Dec-69	−18.50%	−19.60%	−1.10%
31-Dec-70	−5.80%	−3.40%	2.40%
31-Dec-71	21.30%	31.00%	9.70%
31-Dec-72	11.00%	3.80%	−7.20%
31-Dec-73	−27.20%	−44.00%	−16.80%
31-Dec-74	−27.90%	−26.50%	1.40%
31-Dec-75	55.90%	49.80%	−6.10%
31-Dec-76	35.60%	32.70%	−2.90%
31-Dec-77	6.90%	18.70%	11.80%
31-Dec-78	12.20%	10.70%	−1.50%
31-Dec-79	34.30%	39.00%	4.70%
31-Dec-80	31.50%	40.60%	9.10%
31-Dec-81	1.70%	−13.50%	−15.20%
31-Dec-82	22.50%	34.00%	11.50%
31-Dec-83	28.10%	13.20%	−14.90%
31-Dec-84	−3.40%	−27.10%	−23.70%
31-Dec-85	30.80%	33.30%	2.50%
31-Dec-86	13.10%	18.70%	5.60%
31-Dec-87	−1.30%	−9.50%	−8.20%
31-Dec-88	21.20%	19.00%	−2.20%
31-Dec-89	21.40%	23.60%	2.20%
31-Dec-90	−13.80%	−18.10%	−4.30%
31-Dec-91	39.80%	31.30%	−8.50%
31-Dec-92	13.80%	8.50%	−5.30%
31-Dec-93	16.60%	23.60%	7.00%
31-Dec-94	−3.40%	−7.30%	−3.90%
Arithmetic average	14.61%	15.87%	1.25%
Standard deviation	19.86%	26.71%	6.85%

Table 14-2. Summary return results for All Stocks and 50 stocks with highest return on equity from All Stocks universe: December 31, 1951–December 31, 1994.

	All Stocks	Universe = All Stocks Top 50 ROE
Arithmetic average	14.61%	15.87%
Standard deviation of return	19.86%	26.71%
Sharpe risk-adjusted ratio	47.00	39.00
3-yr compounded	8.63%	7.52%
5-yr compounded	9.09%	5.98%
10-yr compounded	12.74%	10.91%
15-yr compounded	13.55%	9.28%
20-yr compounded	16.95%	14.00%
25-yr compounded	11.51%	8.35%
30-yr compounded	11.47%	10.01%
35-yr compounded	11.39%	10.20%
40-yr compounded	12.45%	12.11%
Compound annual return	12.81%	12.71%
$10,000 becomes	$1,782,174.48	$1,713,965.31
Maximum return	55.90%	96.30%
Minimum return	−27.90%	−44.00%
Maximum expected return*	54.33%	69.28%
Minimum expected return**	−25.11%	−37.55%

*Maximum expected return is average return plus 2 times the standard deviation.
**Minimum expected return is average return minus 2 times the standard deviation.

Table 14-3. Base rates for All Stocks and 50 stocks with highest return on equity from All Stocks universe: 1951–1994.

Item	50 highest ROE stocks beat All Stocks	Percent
Single-year return	21 out of 43	49%
Rolling 5-year compound return	19 out of 39	49%
Rolling 10-year compound return	15 out of 34	44%

Table 14-4. Annual performance of Large Stocks versus 50 stocks with highest return on equity drawn from Large Stocks universe.

Year ending	Large Stocks	Universe = Large Stocks Top 50 ROE	Top 50 ROE Relative performance
31-Dec-52	9.30%	10.10%	0.80%
31-Dec-53	2.30%	−0.07%	−2.37%
31-Dec-54	44.90%	56.20%	11.30%
31-Dec-55	21.20%	30.40%	9.20%
31-Dec-56	9.60%	11.50%	1.90%
31-Dec-57	−6.90%	−13.30%	−6.40%
31-Dec-58	42.10%	46.50%	4.40%
31-Dec-59	9.90%	16.10%	6.20%
31-Dec-60	4.80%	9.40%	4.60%
31-Dec-61	27.50%	26.00%	−1.50%
31-Dec-62	−8.90%	−17.00%	−8.10%
31-Dec-63	19.50%	19.00%	−0.50%
31-Dec-64	15.30%	11.70%	−3.60%
31-Dec-65	16.20%	19.90%	3.70%
31-Dec-66	−4.90%	2.80%	7.70%
31-Dec-67	21.30%	27.60%	6.30%
31-Dec-68	16.80%	11.70%	−5.10%
31-Dec-69	−9.90%	−1.00%	8.90%
31-Dec-70	−0.20%	−1.80%	−1.60%
31-Dec-71	17.30%	25.70%	8.40%
31-Dec-72	14.90%	15.20%	0.30%
31-Dec-73	−18.90%	−31.40%	−12.50%
31-Dec-74	−26.70%	−32.40%	−5.70%
31-Dec-75	43.10%	39.80%	−3.30%
31-Dec-76	28.00%	31.50%	3.50%
31-Dec-77	−2.50%	−4.00%	−1.50%
31-Dec-78	8.10%	4.20%	−3.90%
31-Dec-79	27.30%	38.20%	10.90%
31-Dec-80	30.80%	42.60%	11.80%
31-Dec-81	0.60%	−9.60%	−10.20%
31-Dec-82	19.90%	14.70%	−5.20%
31-Dec-83	23.80%	13.00%	−10.80%
31-Dec-84	−0.40%	−6.90%	−6.50%
31-Dec-85	19.50%	39.20%	19.70%
31-Dec-86	32.20%	17.20%	−15.00%
31-Dec-87	3.30%	−5.40%	−8.70%
31-Dec-88	19.00%	15.10%	−3.90%
31-Dec-89	26.00%	26.00%	0.00%
31-Dec-90	−8.70%	−11.20%	−2.50%
31-Dec-91	33.00%	39.00%	6.00%
31-Dec-92	8.70%	2.00%	−6.70%
31-Dec-93	16.30%	10.70%	−5.60%
31-Dec-94	−1.90%	0.00%	1.90%
Arithmetic average	12.62%	12.53%	−0.09%
Standard deviation	16.18%	19.82%	3.64%

Table 14-5. Summary return results for Large Stocks and 50 stocks with highest return on equity from Large Stocks universe: December 31, 1951–December 31, 1994.

	Large Stocks	Universe = Large Stocks Top 50 ROE
Arithmetic average	12.62%	12.53%
Standard deviation of return	16.18%	19.82%
Sharpe risk-adjusted ratio	45.00	36.00
3-yr compounded	7.44%	4.13%
5-yr compounded	8.53%	6.86%
10-yr compounded	13.93%	12.05%
15-yr compounded	14.03%	11.10%
20-yr compounded	15.42%	13.38%
25-yr compounded	11.16%	8.74%
30-yr compounded	10.48%	9.23%
35-yr compounded	10.54%	9.16%
40-yr compounded	10.97%	10.05%
Compound annual return	11.41%	10.70%
$10,000 becomes	$1,042,858.62	$792,559.64
Maximum return	44.90%	56.20%
Minimum return	−26.70%	−32.40%
Maximum expected return*	44.97%	52.17%
Minimum expected return**	−19.73%	−27.10%

*Maximum expected return is average return plus 2 times the standard deviation.
**Minimum expected return is average return minus 2 times the standard deviation.

Table 14-6. Base rates for Large Stocks and 50 stocks with highest return on equity from Large Stocks universe: 1951–1994.

Item	50 highest ROE stocks beat Large Stocks	Percent
Single-year return	20 out of 43	47%
Rolling 5-year compound return	16 out of 39	41%
Rolling 10-year compound return	13 out of 34	38%

Table 14-7. Compound annual rates of return by decade.

Portfolio	1950s*	1960s	1970s	1980s	1990s**
Large Stocks	15.33%	8.99%	6.99%	16.89%	8.53%
50 highest ROE from Large Stocks	17.71%	10.22%	5.30%	13.29%	6.86%
All Stocks	19.22%	11.09%	8.53%	15.85%	9.09%
50 highest ROE from All Stocks	24.36%	14.96%	6.98%	10.97%	5.98%

*Returns for 1952–1959.
**Returns for 1990–1994.

tive benchmarks, with the 50 from All Stocks returning 24.36 percent a year and the 50 from Large Stocks returning 17.71 percent a year.

Both the evidence and the story make sense. Buy companies that do a good job managing shareholder's money and let them manage yours. It's a simple and sensible thing to do. But our young investor is skeptical. He needs to see the evidence with his own eyes before he'll believe it. And so, he watches. In 1965 the 50 highest ROE stocks from All Stocks return 26 percent, better than the 23 percent from All Stocks. Though the next year is a bear market for All Stocks, with the group losing 5 percent, the 50 stocks with the highest ROE eked out a gain of .02 percent. Our young investor is encouraged.

Then comes 1967. The 50 stocks with the highest ROE from All Stocks soar, gaining 96 percent, 55 percent more than the All Stocks universe. Our young man is hooked. He has both the results of the last decade and the personal experience of the last 3 years to prove he's *really* on to something.

He'll go on believing that high ROE stocks are great investments for many years, yet they manage to do a bit *worse* than the market year in, year out. With access to studies that looked at the 1930s and 1940s, he probably would have seen what we see—stocks with high ROE are a good investment only 50 percent of the time. Our young investor may as well have been flipping coins!

Figure 14-1. Returns on high return on equity strategy versus All Stocks and Large Stocks, 1951–1994. Year-end 1951 = $10,000.

Figure 14-2. December 31, 1994, value of $10,000 invested on December 31, 1951, and annually rebalanced.

Figure 14-3. Sharpe risk-adjusted return ratios, 1951–1994. (Higher is better.)

15
Relative Price Strength: Winners Continue to Win

It may be that the race is not always to the swift,
nor the battle to the strong—but that's the way to
bet.   —DAMON RUNYON

"Don't fight the tape."

"Make the trend your friend."

"Cut your losses and let your winners run."

All these Wall Street maxims mean the same thing—bet on price momentum. Of all the beliefs on Wall Street, price momentum makes efficient market theorists howl the loudest. The defining principle of their theory is that you cannot use past prices to predict future prices. A stock may triple in a year, but according to efficient market theory, that will not affect next year. Efficient market theorists also hate price momentum, because it is independent of all accounting variables. If buying winning stocks works, then stock prices have "memories" and carry useful information about the future direction of a stock.

Conversely, another school of thought says you should buy stocks that have been *most* battered by the market. This is the argument of Wall Street's bottom fishers, who use absolute price change as their guide, buying issues after they've done poorly. Let's see who is right.

The Results

We'll look at buying the 50 stocks with the *best* and the *worst* 1-year price changes from both the All Stocks and the Large Stocks universes. This will contrast the results of buying last year's biggest winners with last year's biggest losers. Let's look at the winners first. (In this and future chapters, the terms *relative strength* and *price performers* will be used interchangeably. Stocks with the best relative strength are the biggest winners in terms of their previous year's price appreciation.) We'll start on December 31, 1951, and buy the 50 stocks with the largest price appreciation from the previous year. We arrive at this number by dividing this year's closing price by that from 12 months earlier. Thus, if XYZ closed this year at 10 and last year at 2, it would have a gain of 400 percent and a price index of 5 (10/2).

An investment of $10,000 on December 31, 1951, in the 50 stocks from All Stocks with the best 1-year price appreciation was worth $3,310,255 at the end of 1994, a compound return of 14.45 percent a year. This is the first 2-to-1 performance advantage over All Stocks we've seen from a growth stock variable ($10,000 invested in All Stocks was worth $1,782,174 at the end of 1994). The performance comes with a huge caveat—risk was extraordinarily high. The standard deviation of return for the 50 best 1-year price performers was 30.14 percent, the highest we've seen for an individual factor. The enormous risk pushed the Sharpe ratio to 43, below All Stocks' 47.

I cannot overstate how difficult it is to stick with volatile strategies such as this one. Investors are usually drawn to these strategies by outstanding relative performance, as when the 50 stocks with the best relative strength from All Stocks gained 101 percent in 1991. And while people *think* they can cope with volatility when a strategy is doing well, they have the wind knocked out of them when their volatile strategy is down 30 percent in a bull market. The emotional toll this takes is huge, and you *must* understand it before embracing a highly volatile strategy. As I make clear later in the book, you should have *some* exposure to volatile strategies, but they should never comprise the majority of your portfolio. Very few have the stomach for the roller coaster ride.

The base rates for the 50 stocks with the best 1-year relative strength are all positive, with the strategy beating the market 77 percent of the time over all rolling 10-year periods. Tables 15-1, 15-2, and 15-3 summarize the returns for the All Stocks group.

Table 15-1. Annual performance of All Stocks versus 50 stocks with best 1-year relative strength (RS) drawn from All Stocks universe (best price appreciation).

Year ending	All Stocks	Universe = All Stocks Top 50 1-year RS	Top 50 1-year RS Relative performance
31-Dec-52	7.90%	3.10%	−4.80%
31-Dec-53	2.90%	3.80%	0.90%
31-Dec-54	47.00%	62.30%	15.30%
31-Dec-55	20.70%	32.00%	11.30%
31-Dec-56	17.00%	29.20%	12.20%
31-Dec-57	−7.10%	−16.50%	−9.40%
31-Dec-58	55.00%	68.10%	13.10%
31-Dec-59	23.00%	39.90%	16.90%
31-Dec-60	6.10%	9.40%	3.30%
31-Dec-61	31.20%	35.20%	4.00%
31-Dec-62	−12.00%	−22.60%	−10.60%
31-Dec-63	18.00%	33.60%	15.60%
31-Dec-64	16.30%	5.30%	−11.00%
31-Dec-65	22.60%	44.40%	21.80%
31-Dec-66	−5.20%	−3.90%	1.30%
31-Dec-67	41.10%	64.30%	23.20%
31-Dec-68	27.40%	18.40%	−9.00%
31-Dec-69	−18.50%	−21.90%	−3.40%
31-Dec-70	−5.80%	−26.30%	−20.50%
31-Dec-71	21.30%	39.90%	18.60%
31-Dec-72	11.00%	20.10%	9.10%
31-Dec-73	−27.20%	−32.10%	−4.90%
31-Dec-74	−27.90%	−27.10%	0.80%
31-Dec-75	55.90%	36.00%	−19.90%
31-Dec-76	35.60%	25.30%	−10.30%
31-Dec-77	6.90%	22.50%	15.60%
31-Dec-78	12.20%	25.80%	13.60%
31-Dec-79	34.30%	50.90%	16.60%
31-Dec-80	31.50%	66.00%	34.50%
31-Dec-81	1.70%	−13.50%	−15.20%
31-Dec-82	22.50%	27.10%	4.60%
31-Dec-83	28.10%	22.80%	−5.30%
31-Dec-84	−3.40%	−19.50%	−16.10%
31-Dec-85	30.80%	40.00%	9.20%
31-Dec-86	13.10%	14.30%	1.20%
31-Dec-87	−1.30%	−3.90%	−2.60%
31-Dec-88	21.20%	8.10%	−13.10%
31-Dec-89	21.40%	39.00%	17.60%
31-Dec-90	−13.80%	−11.90%	1.90%
31-Dec-91	39.80%	101.30%	61.50%
31-Dec-92	13.80%	−7.90%	−21.70%
31-Dec-93	16.60%	26.20%	9.60%
31-Dec-94	−3.40%	−19.70%	−16.30%
Arithmetic average	14.61%	18.31%	3.70%
Standard deviation	19.86%	30.14%	10.28%

Table 15-2. Summary return results for All Stocks and 50 stocks with best 1-year relative strength (RS) from All Stocks universe: December 31, 1951–December 31, 1994.

	All Stocks	Universe = All Stocks Top 50 1-year RS
Arithmetic average	14.61%	18.31%
Standard deviation of return	19.86%	30.14%
Sharpe risk-adjusted ratio	47.00	43.00
3-yr compounded	8.63%	−2.27%
5-yr compounded	9.09%	10.60%
10-yr compounded	12.74%	14.36%
15-yr compounded	13.55%	13.74%
20-yr compounded	16.95%	17.99%
25-yr compounded	11.51%	11.94%
30-yr compounded	11.47%	12.62%
35-yr compounded	11.39%	12.24%
40-yr compounded	12.45%	14.03%
Compound annual return	12.81%	14.45%
$10,000 becomes	$1,782,174.48	$3,310,254.52
Maximum return	55.90%	101.30%
Minimum return	−27.90%	−32.10%
Maximum expected return*	54.33%	78.60%
Minimum expected return**	−25.11%	−41.97%

*Maximum expected return is average return plus 2 times the standard deviation.
**Minimum expected return is average return minus 2 times the standard deviation.

Table 15-3. Base rates for All Stocks and 50 stocks with best 1-year relative strength (RS) from All Stocks universe: 1951–1994.

Item	50 best 1-year RS beat All Stocks	Percent
Single-year return	26 out of 43	61%
Rolling 5-year compound return	26 out of 39	67%
Rolling 10-year compound return	26 out of 34	77%

Large Stocks Also Do Well

The 50 stocks from the Large Stocks universe also did well, more than doubling the return of an investment in the Large Stocks universe. Here $10,000 invested on December 31, 1951, in the 50 stocks from the Large Stocks universe with the best 1-year price performance in the previous year grew to $2,987,643, almost three times the $1,042,859 you'd earn investing in the Large Stocks universe. Risk was more manageable too, with the 50 best price performers showing a standard deviation of return of 22.46 percent, 6.28 percent higher than the Large Stocks' 16.18 percent. Because the absolute return was so much higher, the Sharpe ratio for the 50 best 1-year price performers from Large Stocks beat the universe, with a score of 49.

All the base rates are positive, with the 50 best relative strength stocks from Large Stocks beating the universe 88 percent of the time over all rolling 10-year periods. Tables 15-4, 15-5, and 15-6 summarize the results for Large Stocks.

Why Price Performance Works
While Other Measures Do Not

Price momentum conveys different information about the prospects of a stock and is a much better indicator than factors such as earnings growth rates. Many look at the disappointing results of buying stocks with the highest earnings gains and wonder why they differ from the best 1-year price performers. First, price momentum is the market putting its money where its mouth is. Second, the common belief that stocks with strong relative strength also have the highest PE ratios or earnings growth rates is wrong. When you look at the top 1-year performers over time, you find they usually have PE ratios 30 to 50 percent higher than the market, but *rarely* the highest in the market. The same is true for 5-year earnings-per-share growth rates and 1-year earnings-per-share growth rates. As a group, they are usually higher than the market, but not by extraordinary amounts.

Buying the Worst-Performing
Stocks

If you're looking for the perfect way to underperform the market, look no further: $10,000 invested on December 31, 1951, in the 50 stocks from All Stocks with the worst 1-year price performance was worth just

Table 15-4. Annual performance of Large Stocks versus 50 stocks with best 1-year relative strength (RS) drawn from Large Stocks universe (best price appreciation).

Year ending	Large Stocks	Universe = Large Stocks Top 50 1-year RS	Top 50 1-year RS Relative performance
31-Dec-52	9.30%	6.50%	−2.80%
31-Dec-53	2.30%	6.00%	3.70%
31-Dec-54	44.90%	44.40%	−0.50%
31-Dec-55	21.20%	31.60%	10.40%
31-Dec-56	9.60%	13.10%	3.50%
31-Dec-57	−6.90%	−11.50%	−4.60%
31-Dec-58	42.10%	42.40%	0.30%
31-Dec-59	9.90%	15.90%	6.00%
31-Dec-60	4.80%	1.00%	−3.80%
31-Dec-61	27.50%	32.20%	4.70%
31-Dec-62	−8.90%	−12.10%	−3.20%
31-Dec-63	19.50%	24.00%	4.50%
31-Dec-64	15.30%	20.90%	5.60%
31-Dec-65	16.20%	31.00%	14.80%
31-Dec-66	−4.90%	3.20%	8.10%
31-Dec-67	21.30%	40.60%	19.30%
31-Dec-68	16.80%	11.50%	−5.30%
31-Dec-69	−9.90%	−6.80%	3.10%
31-Dec-70	−0.20%	−13.90%	−13.70%
31-Dec-71	17.30%	21.50%	4.20%
31-Dec-72	14.90%	27.50%	12.60%
31-Dec-73	−18.90%	−16.40%	2.50%
31-Dec-74	−26.70%	−30.70%	−4.00%
31-Dec-75	43.10%	30.70%	−12.40%
31-Dec-76	28.00%	23.10%	−4.90%
31-Dec-77	−2.50%	0.03%	2.53%
31-Dec-78	8.10%	21.80%	13.70%
31-Dec-79	27.30%	28.60%	1.30%
31-Dec-80	30.80%	68.20%	37.40%
31-Dec-81	0.60%	−18.00%	−18.60%
31-Dec-82	19.90%	39.80%	19.90%
31-Dec-83	23.80%	18.90%	−4.90%
31-Dec-84	−0.40%	−10.10%	−9.70%
31-Dec-85	19.50%	45.20%	25.70%
31-Dec-86	32.20%	27.00%	−5.20%
31-Dec-87	3.30%	10.50%	7.20%
31-Dec-88	19.00%	7.00%	−12.00%
31-Dec-89	26.00%	36.50%	10.50%
31-Dec-90	−8.70%	−10.90%	−2.20%
31-Dec-91	33.00%	63.90%	30.90%
31-Dec-92	8.70%	0.70%	−8.00%
31-Dec-93	16.30%	44.10%	27.80%
31-Dec-94	−1.90%	−4.20%	−2.30%
Arithmetic average	12.62%	16.39%	3.77%
Standard deviation	16.18%	22.46%	6.28%

Table 15-5. Summary return results for Large Stocks and 50 stocks with best 1-year relative strength (RS) from Large Stocks universe: December 31, 1951–December 31, 1994.

	Large Stocks	Universe = Large Stocks Top 50 best 1-year RS
Arithmetic average	12.62%	16.39%
Standard deviation of return	16.18%	22.46%
Sharpe risk-adjusted ratio	45.00	49.00
3-yr compounded	7.44%	11.61%
5-yr compounded	8.53%	15.21%
10-yr compounded	13.93%	19.71%
15-yr compounded	14.03%	18.31%
20-yr compounded	15.42%	18.81%
25-yr compounded	11.16%	13.60%
30-yr compounded	10.48%	13.77%
35-yr compounded	10.54%	13.51%
40-yr compounded	10.97%	13.91%
Compound annual return	11.41%	14.17%
$10,000 becomes	$1,042,858.62	$2,987,646.13
Maximum return	44.90%	68.20%
Minimum return	−26.70%	−30.70%
Maximum expected return*	44.97%	61.30%
Minimum expected return**	−19.73%	−28.53%

*Maximum expected return is average return plus 2 times the standard deviation.

**Minimum expected return is average return minus 2 times the standard deviation.

Table 15-6. Base rates for Large Stocks and 50 stocks with best 1-year relative strength (RS) from Large Stocks universe: 1951–1994.

Item	50 best 1-year RS beat Large Stocks	Percent
Single-year return	25 out of 43	58%
Rolling 5-year compound return	32 out of 39	82%
Rolling 10-year compound return	30 out of 34	88%

$29,351 at the end of 1994, a compound return of 2.54 percent a year. Some *mattresses* pay better returns! The standard deviation of return for the 50 losers was 26.83 percent, considerably higher than All Stocks' 19.86 percent. With such abysmal returns, *any* risk will wreak havoc with the Sharpe ratio, and here it's a pathetic 3. Base rates are atrocious, with the 50 losers beating All Stocks in only 11 of the 43 years reviewed. The 5-year rolling returns are even worse. The 50 losers beat All Stocks only once in 39 5-year periods. But the booby prize goes to the 10-year returns, where the losers *never* beat the All Stocks universe. Tables 15-7, 15-8, and 15-9 detail the grim news.

Large Stocks Also Hit

Large stocks also suffered, but the results weren't fatal: $10,000 invested in the 50 stocks with the worst 1-year price performance from Large Stocks on December 31, 1951, grew to $485,417 by the end of 1994, a compound return of 9.45 percent a year. That's much worse than the $1,042,859 you'd earn from $10,000 invested in the Large Stocks universe, but not as damaging to your wealth as the biggest losers from All Stocks. The risk was 4 percent higher than for Large Stocks, with the standard deviation for the 50 losers at 20.88 percent. The Sharpe ratio was a fairly low 29.

The base rates are better here over the short term, but equally grim over the long term. The 50 biggest losers beat the Large Stocks universe 49 percent of the time over any single year, 33 percent over 5-year periods, and never over 10-year periods. Tables 15-10, 15-11, and 15-12 summarize the results for the 50 Large Stocks losers.

Table 15-13 gives compound rates of return by decade for both groups. The results are depicted graphically in Figures 15-1 through 15-4.

Implications

Runyon's quote is apt. Winners continue to win and losers continue to lose. Remember that when we say losers, we're talking *not* about stocks that lost some ground last year but about the 50 *worst* casualties from the entire universe. The advice is simple: Unless financial ruin is your goal, avoid the biggest 1-year losers. Buy stocks with the *best* 1-year relative strength, but understand that their volatility will continually test your emotional endurance.

Table 15-7. Annual performance of All Stocks versus 50 stocks with worst
1-year relative strength (RS) from All Stocks universe (worst price performance).

Year ending	All Stocks	Universe = All Stocks 50 worst 1-year RS	50 worst 1-year RS Relative performance
31-Dec-52	7.90%	8.10%	0.20%
31-Dec-53	2.90%	−11.00%	−13.90%
31-Dec-54	47.00%	50.80%	3.80%
31-Dec-55	20.70%	8.20%	−12.50%
31-Dec-56	17.00%	−1.90%	−18.90%
31-Dec-57	−7.10%	−9.00%	−1.90%
31-Dec-58	55.00%	63.60%	8.60%
31-Dec-59	23.00%	5.74%	−17.26%
31-Dec-60	6.10%	3.40%	−2.70%
31-Dec-61	31.20%	16.60%	−14.60%
31-Dec-62	−12.00%	−19.40%	−7.40%
31-Dec-63	18.00%	7.00%	−11.00%
31-Dec-64	16.30%	8.50%	−7.80%
31-Dec-65	22.60%	39.81%	17.21%
31-Dec-66	−5.20%	−14.30%	−9.10%
31-Dec-67	41.10%	46.80%	5.70%
31-Dec-68	27.40%	30.00%	2.60%
31-Dec-69	−18.50%	−40.90%	−22.40%
31-Dec-70	−5.80%	−18.40%	−12.60%
31-Dec-71	21.30%	0.01%	−21.29%
31-Dec-72	11.00%	−3.40%	−14.40%
31-Dec-73	−27.20%	−48.90%	−21.70%
31-Dec-74	−27.90%	−36.60%	−8.70%
31-Dec-75	55.90%	56.60%	0.70%
31-Dec-76	35.60%	27.00%	−8.60%
31-Dec-77	6.90%	−5.80%	−12.70%
31-Dec-78	12.20%	6.20%	−6.00%
31-Dec-79	34.30%	37.50%	3.20%
31-Dec-80	31.50%	8.50%	−23.00%
31-Dec-81	1.70%	−14.30%	−16.00%
31-Dec-82	22.50%	2.60%	−19.90%
31-Dec-83	28.10%	9.20%	−18.90%
31-Dec-84	−3.40%	−27.10%	−23.70%
31-Dec-85	30.80%	15.30%	−15.50%
31-Dec-86	13.10%	−21.20%	−34.30%
31-Dec-87	−1.30%	−4.20%	−2.90%
31-Dec-88	21.20%	33.90%	12.70%
31-Dec-89	21.40%	13.60%	−7.80%
31-Dec-90	−13.80%	−41.20%	−27.40%
31-Dec-91	39.80%	60.80%	21.00%
31-Dec-92	13.80%	12.70%	−1.10%
31-Dec-93	16.60%	2.00%	−14.60%
31-Dec-94	−3.40%	4.00%	7.40%
Arithmetic average	14.61%	6.07%	−8.55%
Standard deviation	19.86%	26.83%	6.97%

Table 15-8. Summary return results for All Stocks and 50 stocks with worst 1-year relative strength (RS) from All Stocks universe: December 31, 1951–December 31, 1994.

Item	All Stocks	Universe = All Stocks 50 worst 1-year RS
Arithmetic average	14.61%	6.07%
Standard deviation of return	19.86%	26.83%
Sharpe risk-adjusted ratio	47.00	3.00
3-yr compounded	8.63%	6.13%
5-yr compounded	9.09%	2.48%
10-yr compounded	12.74%	4.11%
15-yr compounded	13.55%	0.86%
20-yr compounded	16.95%	5.84%
25-yr compounded	11.51%	−0.92%
30-yr compounded	11.47%	0.24%
35-yr compounded	11.39%	0.55%
40-yr compounded	12.45%	1.78%
Compound annual return	12.81%	2.54%
$10,000 becomes	$1,782,174.48	$29,351.09
Maximum return	55.90%	63.60%
Minimum return	−27.90%	−48.90%
Maximum expected return*	54.33%	59.73%
Minimum expected return**	−25.11%	−47.60%

*Maximum expected return is average return plus 2 times the standard deviation.
**Minimum expected return is average return minus 2 times the standard deviation.

Table 15-9. Base rates for All Stocks and 50 stocks with worst 1-year relative strength (RS) from All Stocks universe: 1951–1994.

Item	50 worst 1-year RS beat All Stocks	Percent
Single-year return	11 out of 43	26%
Rolling 5-year compound return	1 out of 39	3%
Rolling 10-year compound return	0 out of 34	0%

Table 15-10. Annual performance of Large Stocks versus 50 stocks with worst 1-year relative strength (RS) from Large Stocks universe (worst price performance).

Year ending	Large Stocks	Universe = Large Stocks 50 worst 1-year RS	50 worst 1-year RS Relative performance
31-Dec-52	9.30%	12.00%	2.70%
31-Dec-53	2.30%	−3.90%	−6.20%
31-Dec-54	44.90%	53.00%	8.10%
31-Dec-55	21.20%	15.10%	−6.10%
31-Dec-56	9.60%	9.00%	−0.60%
31-Dec-57	−6.90%	−1.70%	5.20%
31-Dec-58	42.10%	47.00%	4.90%
31-Dec-59	9.90%	3.50%	−6.40%
31-Dec-60	4.80%	7.90%	3.10%
31-Dec-61	27.50%	18.80%	−8.70%
31-Dec-62	−8.90%	−13.80%	−4.90%
31-Dec-63	19.50%	20.20%	0.70%
31-Dec-64	15.30%	17.30%	2.00%
31-Dec-65	16.20%	19.20%	3.00%
31-Dec-66	−4.90%	−8.80%	−3.90%
31-Dec-67	21.30%	26.30%	5.00%
31-Dec-68	16.80%	19.50%	2.70%
31-Dec-69	−9.90%	−26.00%	−16.10%
31-Dec-70	−0.20%	−5.00%	−4.80%
31-Dec-71	17.30%	19.20%	1.90%
31-Dec-72	14.90%	8.90%	−6.00%
31-Dec-73	−18.90%	−18.60%	0.30%
31-Dec-74	−26.70%	−30.90%	−4.20%
31-Dec-75	43.10%	64.90%	21.80%
31-Dec-76	28.00%	25.40%	−2.60%
31-Dec-77	−2.50%	−2.30%	0.20%
31-Dec-78	8.10%	5.10%	−3.00%
31-Dec-79	27.30%	25.50%	−1.80%
31-Dec-80	30.80%	12.70%	−18.10%
31-Dec-81	0.60%	10.20%	9.60%
31-Dec-82	19.90%	2.90%	−17.00%
31-Dec-83	23.80%	16.70%	−7.10%
31-Dec-84	−0.40%	−15.60%	−15.20%
31-Dec-85	19.50%	25.70%	6.20%
31-Dec-86	32.20%	4.90%	−27.30%
31-Dec-87	3.30%	−1.70%	−5.00%
31-Dec-88	19.00%	38.40%	19.40%
31-Dec-89	26.00%	27.90%	1.90%
31-Dec-90	−8.70%	−25.50%	−16.80%
31-Dec-91	33.00%	55.00%	22.00%
31-Dec-92	8.70%	7.50%	−1.20%
31-Dec-93	16.30%	23.60%	7.30%
31-Dec-94	−1.90%	1.40%	3.30%
Arithmetic average	12.62%	11.42%	−1.20%
Standard deviation	16.18%	20.88%	4.70%

Table 15-11. Summary return results for Large Stocks and 50 stocks with worst 1-year relative strength (RS) from Large Stocks universe: December 31, 1951–December 31, 1994.

	Large Stocks	Universe = Large Stocks 50 worst 1-year RS
Arithmetic average	12.62%	11.42%
Standard deviation of return	16.18%	20.88%
Sharpe risk-adjusted ratio	45.00	29.00
3-yr compounded	7.44%	10.45%
5-yr compounded	8.53%	9.24%
10-yr compounded	13.93%	13.57%
15-yr compounded	14.03%	10.54%
20-yr compounded	15.42%	13.22%
25-yr compounded	11.16%	8.84%
30-yr compounded	10.48%	8.01%
35-yr compounded	10.54%	8.19%
40-yr compounded	10.97%	8.83%
Compound annual return	11.41%	9.45%
$10,000 becomes	$1,042,858.62	$485,416.93
Maximum return	44.90%	64.90%
Minimum return	−26.70%	−30.90%
Maximum expected return*	44.97%	53.17%
Minimum expected return**	−19.73%	−30.34%

*Maximum expected return is average return plus 2 times the standard deviation.
**Minimum expected return is average return minus 2 times the standard deviation.

Table 15-12. Base rates for Large Stocks and 50 stocks with worst 1-year relative strength (RS) from Large Stocks universe: 1951–1994.

Item	50 worst 1-year RS beat Large Stocks	Percent
Single-year return	21 out of 43	49%
Rolling 5-year compound return	13 out of 39	33%
Rolling 10-year compound return	0 out of 34	0%

Table 15-13. Compound annual rates of return by decade.

Portfolio	1950s*	1960s	1970s	1980s	1990s**
Large Stocks	15.33%	8.99%	6.99%	16.89%	8.53%
50 best 1-year RS from Large Stocks	17.13%	13.27%	6.90%	19.89%	15.21%
50 worst 1-year RS from Large Stocks	15.14%	6.58%	6.34%	11.19%	9.24%
All Stocks	19.22%	11.09%	8.53%	15.85%	9.09%
50 best 1-year RS from All Stocks	24.62%	13.00%	9.28%	15.35%	10.60%
50 worst 1-year RS from All Stocks	11.70%	4.31%	−3.52%	0.06%	2.48%

*Returns for 1952–1959.
**Returns for 1990–1994.

Figure 15-1. Returns on best relative strength strategies versus All Stocks and Large Stocks, 1951–1994. Year-end 1951 = $10,000.

Figure 15-2. Returns on worst 1-year relative strength strategies versus All Stocks and Large Stocks, 1951–1994. Year-end 1951 = $10,000.

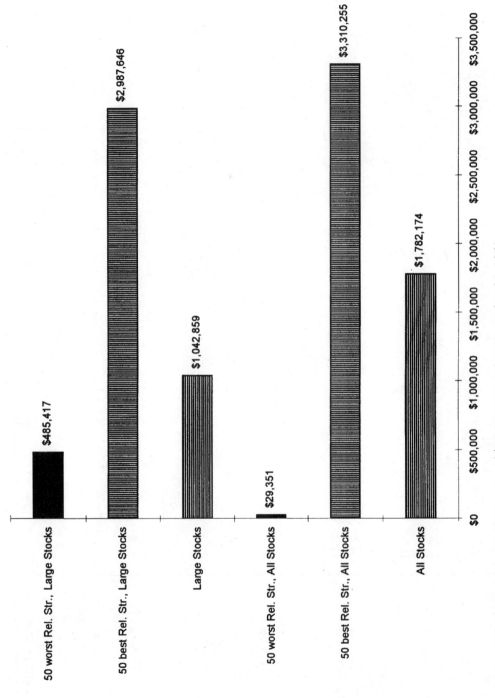

Figure 15-3. December 31, 1994, value of $10,000 invested on December 31, 1951, and annually rebalanced.

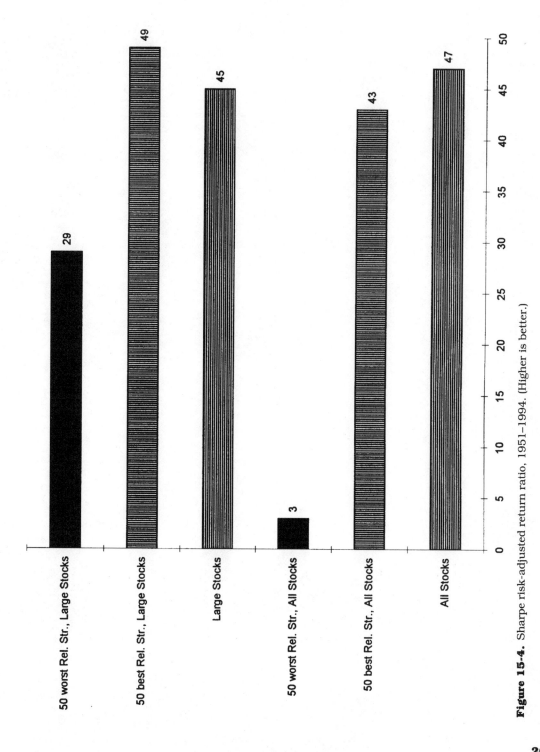

Figure 15-4. Sharpe risk-adjusted return ratio, 1951–1994. (Higher is better.)

16

Using Multifactor Models to Improve Performance

It is not who is right, but what is right, that is important.
　　　　　　　　　　　　　—THOMAS HUXLEY

Thus far, we've looked only at individual factors, such as low price-to-sales ratios and outstanding relative strength. Now we'll look at buying stocks using two or more criteria. Using several factors allows you to enhance performance *dramatically* or *substantially* reduce risk, depending on your goal. Let's look at how adding factors can improve the performance of the 50 best-performing stocks from the All Stocks universe.

Adding Value Factors

Ben Graham said anyone paying more than 20 times earnings for a stock should prepare to lose money in the long run. What happens if we remove high PE ratio stocks from the All Stocks universe and then buy the 50 biggest winners? Instead of just buying the top 50 relative strength stocks, let's also require that stocks have PE ratios below 20. Thus, we would start with the All Stocks universe and screen out stocks with PE ratios above 20, *then* buy the 50 with the best 1-year price appreciation.

If you invested $10,000 on December 31, 1951, in the 50 stocks from All Stocks with the best price appreciation from the previous year and PE ratios below 20, your investment would have grown to $8,613,730 by the end of 1994. That's $5,303,476 more than an investment in the 50 biggest winners alone! What's more, this two-factor portfolio has a standard deviation of 26.79 percent, *lower* than the 50 All Stocks winners' 30.14 percent. The Sharpe ratio for this two-factor strategy is 55, compared with 43 for the 50 best-performing stocks from All Stocks.

Risk and return aren't the only things enhanced by this model—the base rates are better as well. The 50 biggest winners from All Stocks with PE ratios below 20 beat the All Stocks universe in 28 of the 43 years of the study, or 65 percent of the time. Long term, the results get better, with this strategy outperforming All Stocks in 33 of the 39 rolling 5-year periods and 31 of the 34 rolling 10-year periods. That's a long-term success rate of 91 percent—better than relative strength alone.

What About Other Value Factors?

Adding low PE ratios is just one way to improve performance. You can enhance returns and reduce risk even more using other value factors. For instance, if you take stocks from All Stocks with price-to-book ratios below 1 and then buy the 50 stocks with the highest 1-year price appreciation, a $10,000 investment made on December 31, 1951, grows to $10,645,437 by the end of 1994, a compound return of 17.60 percent. Risk is lower, with a standard deviation of return of 24.25 percent. Base rates improve as well, with the strategy beating All Stocks in 31 of the 43 years of the study, 34 of the 39 5-year rolling periods, and 33 of the 34 10-year rolling periods. That's 97 percent of the time over all rolling 10-year periods. Table 16-1 summarizes the results for these two strategies.

Price-to-Sales Ratio Better Still

Price-to-sales ratio (PSR) also performs beautifully when joined with relative strength. If you start December 31, 1951, with the All Stocks universe and consider only stocks with PSRs below 1 and *then* buy the 50 with the best 1-year price appreciation, $10,000 grows to $14,141,980 at the end of 1994, a compound rate of return of 18.38 percent. That's

Table 16-1. Summary results for buying best 1-year price appreciation stocks with PE ratios below 20 or price-to-book ratios below 1: December 31, 1951–December 31, 1994. Universe is All Stocks.

	All Stocks	50 stocks with PE ratios below 20 and best 1-year price appreciation	50 stocks with price-to-book ratios below 1 and best 1-year price appreciation
$10,000 becomes	$1,782,174	$8,613,730	$10,645,437
Compound return	12.81%	17.02%	17.60%
Standard deviation of return (risk)	19.86%	26.79%	24.25%
Sharpe ratio	47	55	61
Percent of rolling 10-year periods beats All Stocks	NA	91%	97%

vastly better than the $1,782,174 you'd earn from an investment in All Stocks. The standard deviation of return of 26.04 percent is higher than All Stocks' 19.86 percent, but lower than the 50 best performers' 30.14 percent. The Sharpe ratio is 62 for this strategy, well ahead of All Stocks' 47. Table 16-2 compares this strategy with the All Stocks universe, while Table 16-3 compares the returns of the two relative strength strategies. Table 16-4 summarizes the returns of the low PSR relative strength strategy.

The consistency of this strategy is amazing, beating All Stocks in 33 of the 43 years of the test, or 77 percent of the time. Long term, the record can't get any better—it beat the All Stocks universe 100 percent of the time when measuring rolling 5- and 10-year periods. Table 16-5 shows the base rates. Figures 16-1 and 16-2 depict the results.

Additional Factors Add Less to Large Stocks

Using multifactor models on the Large Stocks universe does not enhance performance as much as they do with All Stocks. If you start on December 31, 1951, and require stocks from the Large Stocks universe to have PE ratios below 20 and then buy the 50 with the best 1-year price performance, $10,000 grows to $3,326,798 at the end of 1994, a 14.46 per-

Table 16-2. Annual performance of All Stocks versus 50 stocks with PSR below 1 and then the best 1-year relative strength (RS) drawn from All Stocks universe.

Year ending	All Stocks	Universe = All Stocks PSR<1 Top 50 1-year RS	Top 50 1-year RS Relative performance
31-Dec-52	7.90%	7.80%	−0.10%
31-Dec-53	2.90%	6.40%	3.50%
31-Dec-54	47.00%	56.90%	9.90%
31-Dec-55	20.70%	28.80%	8.10%
31-Dec-56	17.00%	30.50%	13.50%
31-Dec-57	−7.10%	−20.10%	−13.00%
31-Dec-58	55.00%	67.50%	12.50%
31-Dec-59	23.00%	32.00%	9.00%
31-Dec-60	6.10%	2.70%	−3.40%
31-Dec-61	31.20%	49.50%	18.30%
31-Dec-62	−12.00%	−13.30%	−1.30%
31-Dec-63	18.00%	31.80%	13.80%
31-Dec-64	16.30%	26.40%	10.10%
31-Dec-65	22.60%	55.10%	32.50%
31-Dec-66	−5.20%	−0.60%	4.60%
31-Dec-67	41.10%	59.90%	18.80%
31-Dec-68	27.40%	46.30%	18.90%
31-Dec-69	−18.50%	−33.60%	−15.10%
31-Dec-70	−5.80%	−5.20%	0.60%
31-Dec-71	21.30%	31.90%	10.60%
31-Dec-72	11.00%	14.60%	3.60%
31-Dec-73	−27.20%	−20.90%	6.30%
31-Dec-74	−27.90%	−23.90%	4.00%
31-Dec-75	55.90%	58.60%	2.70%
31-Dec-76	35.60%	39.00%	3.40%
31-Dec-77	6.90%	24.50%	17.60%
31-Dec-78	12.20%	38.40%	26.20%
31-Dec-79	34.30%	26.30%	−8.00%
31-Dec-80	31.50%	48.50%	17.00%
31-Dec-81	1.70%	−7.70%	−9.40%
31-Dec-82	22.50%	39.50%	17.00%
31-Dec-83	28.10%	35.40%	7.30%
31-Dec-84	−3.40%	−8.20%	−4.80%
31-Dec-85	30.80%	45.20%	14.40%
31-Dec-86	13.10%	19.30%	6.20%
31-Dec-87	−1.30%	−12.90%	−11.60%
31-Dec-88	21.20%	28.00%	6.80%
31-Dec-89	21.40%	30.90%	9.50%
31-Dec-90	−13.80%	−12.10%	1.70%
31-Dec-91	39.80%	43.70%	3.90%
31-Dec-92	13.80%	30.70%	16.90%
31-Dec-93	16.60%	30.40%	13.80%
31-Dec-94	−3.40%	−6.90%	−3.50%
Arithmetic average	14.61%	21.42%	6.81%
Standard deviation	19.86%	26.04%	6.18%

Table 16-3. Annual performance of 50 stocks with best 1-year relative strength (RS) versus low PSR 50 stocks with best 1-year price appreciation drawn from All Stocks universe.

Year ending	Universe = All Stocks Top 50 1-year RS	Universe = All Stocks PSR<1 Top 50 1-year RS	Low PSR top 50 1-year RS Relative performance
31-Dec-52	3.10%	7.80%	4.70%
31-Dec-53	3.80%	6.40%	2.60%
31-Dec-54	62.30%	56.90%	−5.40%
31-Dec-55	32.00%	28.80%	−3.20%
31-Dec-56	29.20%	30.50%	1.30%
31-Dec-57	−16.50%	−20.10%	−3.60%
31-Dec-58	68.10%	67.50%	−0.60%
31-Dec-59	39.90%	32.00%	−7.90%
31-Dec-60	9.40%	2.70%	−6.70%
31-Dec-61	35.20%	49.50%	14.30%
31-Dec-62	−22.60%	−13.30%	9.30%
31-Dec-63	33.60%	31.80%	−1.80%
31-Dec-64	5.30%	26.40%	21.10%
31-Dec-65	44.40%	55.10%	10.70%
31-Dec-66	−3.90%	−0.60%	3.30%
31-Dec-67	64.30%	59.90%	−4.40%
31-Dec-68	18.40%	46.30%	27.90%
31-Dec-69	−21.90%	−33.60%	−11.70%
31-Dec-70	−26.30%	−5.20%	21.10%
31-Dec-71	39.90%	31.90%	−8.00%
31-Dec-72	20.10%	14.60%	−5.50%
31-Dec-73	−32.10%	−20.90%	11.20%
31-Dec-74	−27.10%	−23.90%	3.20%
31-Dec-75	36.00%	58.60%	22.60%
31-Dec-76	25.30%	39.00%	13.70%
31-Dec-77	22.50%	24.50%	2.00%
31-Dec-78	25.80%	38.40%	12.60%
31-Dec-79	50.90%	26.30%	−24.60%
31-Dec-80	66.00%	48.50%	−17.50%
31-Dec-81	−13.50%	−7.70%	5.80%
31-Dec-82	27.10%	39.50%	12.40%
31-Dec-83	22.80%	35.40%	12.60%
31-Dec-84	−19.50%	−8.20%	11.30%
31-Dec-85	40.00%	45.20%	5.20%
31-Dec-86	14.30%	19.30%	5.00%
31-Dec-87	−3.90%	−12.90%	−9.00%
31-Dec-88	8.10%	28.00%	19.90%
31-Dec-89	39.00%	30.90%	−8.10%
31-Dec-90	−11.90%	−12.10%	−0.20%
31-Dec-91	101.30%	43.70%	−57.60%
31-Dec-92	−7.90%	30.70%	38.60%
31-Dec-93	26.20%	30.40%	4.20%
31-Dec-94	−19.70%	−6.90%	12.80%
Arithmetic average	18.31%	21.42%	3.11%
Standard deviation	30.14%	26.04%	−4.10%

Table 16-4. Summary return results for All Stocks and stocks with PSRs below 1 and then 50 biggest gains by 1-year price appreciation, drawn from All Stocks universe: December 31, 1951–December 31, 1994.

	All Stocks	Universe = All Stocks PSR<1 Top 50 1-year price appreciation
Arithmetic average	14.61%	21.42%
Standard deviation of return	19.86%	26.04%
Sharpe risk-adjusted ratio	47.00	62.00
3-yr compounded	8.63%	16.64%
5-yr compounded	9.09%	14.92%
10-yr compounded	12.74%	17.62%
15-yr compounded	13.55%	18.04%
20-yr compounded	16.95%	22.49%
25-yr compounded	11.51%	16.92%
30-yr compounded	11.47%	17.28%
35-yr compounded	11.39%	17.28%
40-yr compounded	12.45%	18.14%
Compound annual return	12.81%	18.38%
$10,000 becomes	$1,782,174.48	$14,141,979.61
Maximum return	55.90%	67.50%
Minimum return	−27.90%	−33.60%
Maximum expected return*	54.33%	73.51%
Minimum expected return**	−25.11%	−30.66%

*Maximum expected return is average return plus 2 times the standard deviation.
**Minimum expected return is average return minus 2 times the standard deviation.

Table 16-5. Base rates for All Stocks and 50 stocks with PSRs below 1 and best 1-year relative strength (RS) from All Stocks universe: 1951–1994.

Item	Stocks with PSR<1 and best 1-year RS beat All Stocks	Percent
Single-year return	33 out of 43	77%
Rolling 5-year compound return	39 out of 39	100%
Rolling 10-year compound return	39 out of 39	100%

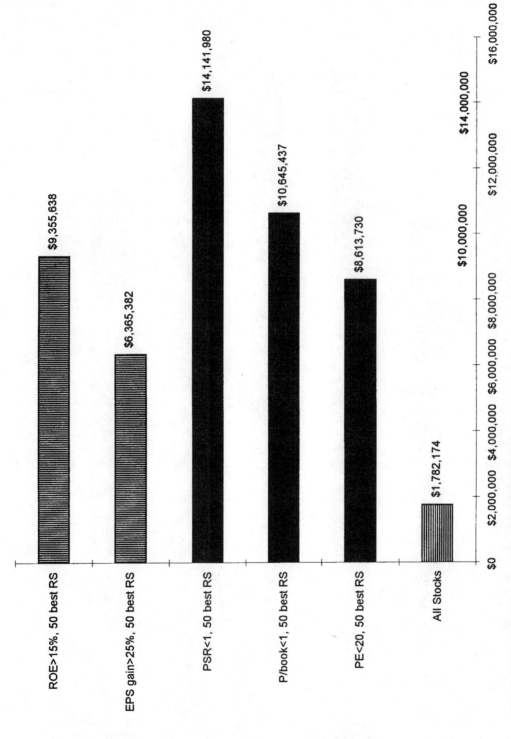

Figure 16-1. December 31, 1994, value of $10,000 invested on December 31, 1951, and annually rebalanced for different multifactor relative strength models using All Stocks as the universe.

Figure 16-2. Sharpe risk-adjusted return ratios for different multifactor relative strength models using All Stocks as the universe, 1951–1994. (Higher is better.)

cent compound annual return. Risk is relatively low—the standard deviation of 19.19 percent led to a high Sharpe ratio of 56.

Base rates for the strategy are high, beating the Large Stocks universe in 27 of the 43 years of the study, or 63 percent of the time. Longer term is even better, with the strategy beating the universe in 33 of the 39 rolling 5-year periods and 33 of the 34 rolling 10-year periods, or 97 percent of the time.

We were unable to run a test on Large Stocks using price-to-book ratios because Large Stocks rarely trade at price-to-book ratios below 1.

Price-to-Sales Ratios Still the Champs

In the Large Stocks universe, the marriage of low price-to-sales ratios to relative strength does better than buying stocks with PE ratios below 20. But here the difference is less striking than with the All Stocks universe: $10,000 invested in the 50 stocks from Large Stocks that had the best 1-year price appreciation and price-to-sales ratios below 1 grew to $3,566,132 by the end of 1994, a compound return of 14.64 percent. The standard deviation of 19.19 percent was the same for the stocks with PE ratios below 20, possibly because many of the same stocks end up in the two portfolios. The Sharpe ratio was 57, considerably better than Large Stocks' 45 and 1 point ahead of the best price performers with PE ratios below 20.

Base rates here are not as good as the relative strength stocks with PE ratios below 20. This strategy beat the Large Stocks universe in 28 of 43 years on a year-to-year basis, 30 of the 39 rolling 5-year periods, and 30 of the 34 rolling 10-year periods. Tables 16-6, 16-7, and 16-8 summarize the returns, which are also charted in Figures 16-3 and 16-4.

What About Growth Factors?

Growth factors work with relative strength too, but the returns are less consistent. For example, if you concentrated on stocks from the Large Stocks universe with PE ratios below 20 *and* positive earnings gains for the year, and then bought the 50 with the best 1-year price performance, you would actually earn $1,000,000 *less* than if you bought the low PE, high relative strength stocks alone. The addition of positive earnings gains *hurt* performance in this instance. We'll see in Chapter 19 that 5-year earnings persistence helps, but for now, understand that more factors do not necessarily mean better performance.

Table 16-6. Annual performance of Large Stocks versus 50 stocks with PSRs below 1 and the best 1-year relative strength (RS) drawn from Large Stocks universe.

Year ending	Large Stocks	Universe = Large Stocks PSR<1 Top 50 1-year RS	Top 50 1-year RS Relative performance
31-Dec-52	9.30%	13.10%	3.80%
31-Dec-53	2.30%	5.20%	2.90%
31-Dec-54	44.90%	46.60%	1.70%
31-Dec-55	21.20%	23.40%	2.20%
31-Dec-56	9.60%	8.40%	−1.20%
31-Dec-57	−6.90%	−12.10%	−5.20%
31-Dec-58	42.10%	45.40%	3.30%
31-Dec-59	9.90%	8.40%	−1.50%
31-Dec-60	4.80%	0.00%	−4.80%
31-Dec-61	27.50%	25.30%	−2.20%
31-Dec-62	−8.90%	−9.20%	−0.30%
31-Dec-63	19.50%	22.40%	2.90%
31-Dec-64	15.30%	18.60%	3.30%
31-Dec-65	16.20%	28.50%	12.30%
31-Dec-66	−4.90%	−3.60%	1.30%
31-Dec-67	21.30%	30.60%	9.30%
31-Dec-68	16.80%	13.30%	−3.50%
31-Dec-69	−9.90%	−10.40%	−0.50%
31-Dec-70	−0.20%	1.40%	1.60%
31-Dec-71	17.30%	21.70%	4.40%
31-Dec-72	14.90%	11.00%	−3.90%
31-Dec-73	−18.90%	−7.30%	11.60%
31-Dec-74	−26.70%	−21.10%	5.60%
31-Dec-75	43.10%	53.10%	10.00%
31-Dec-76	28.00%	29.20%	1.20%
31-Dec-77	−2.50%	1.50%	4.00%
31-Dec-78	8.10%	16.90%	8.80%
31-Dec-79	27.30%	28.60%	1.30%
31-Dec-80	30.80%	48.30%	17.50%
31-Dec-81	0.60%	−12.50%	−13.10%
31-Dec-82	19.90%	54.10%	34.20%
31-Dec-83	23.80%	22.80%	−1.00%
31-Dec-84	−0.40%	−5.10%	−4.70%
31-Dec-85	19.50%	45.50%	26.00%
31-Dec-86	32.20%	21.00%	−11.20%
31-Dec-87	3.30%	8.80%	5.50%
31-Dec-88	19.00%	22.10%	3.10%
31-Dec-89	26.00%	34.60%	8.60%
31-Dec-90	−8.70%	−6.90%	1.80%
31-Dec-91	33.00%	26.40%	−6.60%
31-Dec-92	8.70%	28.60%	19.90%
31-Dec-93	16.30%	24.90%	8.60%
31-Dec-94	−1.90%	−3.00%	−1.10%
Arithmetic average	12.62%	16.24%	3.63%
Standard deviation	16.18%	19.19%	3.02%

Table 16-7. Summary return results for Large Stocks and 50 stocks with PSRs below 1 and the best 1-year relative strength (RS) from Large Stocks universe: December 31, 1951–December 31, 1994.

	Large Stocks	Universe = Large Stocks PSR<1 Top 50 best 1-year RS
Arithmetic average	12.62%	16.24%
Standard deviation of return	16.18%	19.19%
Sharpe risk-adjusted ratio	45.00	57.00
3-yr compounded	7.44%	15.93%
5-yr compounded	8.53%	12.89%
10-yr compounded	13.93%	19.16%
15-yr compounded	14.03%	18.92%
20-yr compounded	15.42%	20.34%
25-yr compounded	11.16%	15.98%
30-yr compounded	10.48%	15.03%
35-yr compounded	10.54%	14.38%
40-yr compounded	10.97%	14.23%
Compound annual return	11.41%	14.64%
$10,000 becomes	$1,042,858.62	$3,566,131.73
Maximum return	44.90%	54.10%
Minimum return	−26.70%	−21.10%
Maximum expected return*	44.97%	54.63%
Minimum expected return**	−19.73%	−22.14%

*Maximum expected return is average return plus 2 times the standard deviation.
**Minimum expected return is average return minus 2 times the standard deviation.

Table 16-8. Base rates for Large Stocks and 50 stocks with PSRs below 1 and then the best 1-year relative strength (RS) from Large Stocks universe: 1951–1994.

Item	50 stocks with PSR<1 and best 1-year RS beat Large Stocks	Percent
Single-year return	28 out of 43	65%
Rolling 5-year compound return	30 out of 39	77%
Rolling 10-year compound return	30 out of 34	88%

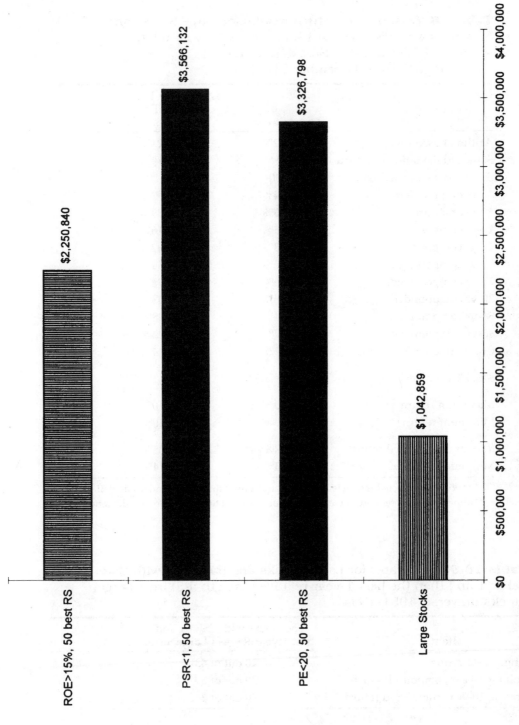

Figure 16-3. December 31, 1994, value of $10,000 invested on December 31, 1951, and annually rebalanced for different multifactor relative strength models using Large Stocks as the universe.

Figure 16-4. Sharpe risk-adjusted return ratios for different multifactor relative strength models using Large Stocks as the universe, 1951–1994. (Higher is better.)

Two Growth Models

While buying stocks with the best 1-year earnings gains doesn't beat All Stocks (see Chapter 11), buying stocks with strong 1-year earnings gains *and* strong relative price strength handily beats the All Stocks universe. A two-factor model that requires stocks from All Stocks to have 1-year earnings gains exceeding 25 percent and then buys the 50 with the best 1-year price performance turns $10,000 invested on December 31, 1952, into $6,365,382 by the end of 1994. That's a compound return of 16.62 percent a year, far ahead of All Stocks' 12.93 percent a year. Risk is high, however—the standard deviation for the strategy is 29.71 percent, much higher than All Stocks' 20.07 percent. The strategy's higher return overcomes the risk, pushing its Sharpe ratio to 50, higher than All Stocks' 46. Altogether, it's a huge improvement on buying the best 1-year earnings gainers or the best relative strength stocks alone.

Again, we weren't able to test this model on the Large Stocks universe, because in many years fewer than 50 Large Stocks had earnings gains above 25 percent.

Return on Equity Does Better Still

Other growth variables work better. In Chapter 14 we saw that buying the 50 stocks from the All Stocks universe with the best ROE didn't beat the market, but adding a high ROE factor to a relative strength model enhances returns even more than the earnings gains model.

If you start on December 31, 1951, and require stocks from the All Stocks universe to have a return on equity above 15, then buy the 50 with the best 1-year price performance, $10,000 grows to $9,355,638 by the end of 1994, a compound return of 17.25 percent. This is nearly the same as the returns from buying the 50 best-performing stocks with PE ratios below 20.

This strategy is riskier than strategies that buy cheap stocks with strong relative strength, with a standard deviation of 27.6 percent. The Sharpe ratio of 55 is similar to that for buying the best-performing low PE stocks. All base rates are positive, with the rolling 10-year results always beating the universe. Tables 16-9, 16-10, and 16-11 present the findings. Annual performance is summarized in Table 16-12.

Table 16-9. Annual performance of All Stocks versus 50 stocks with ROE above 15 and best 1-year relative strength (RS) drawn from All Stocks universe.

Year ending	All Stocks	Universe = All Stocks ROE>15 Top 50 1-year RS	Top 50 1-year RS ROE>15 Relative performance
31-Dec-52	7.90%	8.20%	0.30%
31-Dec-53	2.90%	1.90%	−1.00%
31-Dec-54	47.00%	71.50%	24.50%
31-Dec-55	20.70%	30.00%	9.30%
31-Dec-56	17.00%	30.80%	13.80%
31-Dec-57	−7.10%	−10.70%	−3.60%
31-Dec-58	55.00%	55.10%	0.10%
31-Dec-59	23.00%	37.50%	14.50%
31-Dec-60	6.10%	22.60%	16.50%
31-Dec-61	31.20%	33.90%	2.70%
31-Dec-62	−12.00%	−17.30%	−5.30%
31-Dec-63	18.00%	19.80%	1.80%
31-Dec-64	16.30%	11.10%	−5.20%
31-Dec-65	22.60%	24.90%	2.30%
31-Dec-66	−5.20%	3.40%	8.60%
31-Dec-67	41.10%	57.40%	16.30%
31-Dec-68	27.40%	39.80%	12.40%
31-Dec-69	−18.50%	−17.50%	1.00%
31-Dec-70	−5.80%	−15.60%	−9.80%
31-Dec-71	21.30%	58.10%	36.80%
31-Dec-72	11.00%	27.00%	16.00%
31-Dec-73	−27.20%	−27.50%	−0.30%
31-Dec-74	−27.90%	−29.80%	−1.90%
31-Dec-75	55.90%	36.30%	−19.60%
31-Dec-76	35.60%	21.60%	−14.00%
31-Dec-77	6.90%	20.60%	13.70%
31-Dec-78	12.20%	26.50%	14.30%
31-Dec-79	34.30%	38.90%	4.60%
31-Dec-80	31.50%	77.70%	46.20%
31-Dec-81	1.70%	−6.00%	−7.70%
31-Dec-82	22.50%	30.90%	8.40%
31-Dec-83	28.10%	21.90%	−6.20%
31-Dec-84	−3.40%	−4.30%	−0.90%
31-Dec-85	30.80%	45.20%	14.40%
31-Dec-86	13.10%	21.20%	8.10%
31-Dec-87	−1.30%	−15.60%	−14.30%
31-Dec-88	21.20%	17.10%	−4.10%
31-Dec-89	21.40%	38.40%	17.00%
31-Dec-90	−13.80%	−11.90%	1.90%
31-Dec-91	39.80%	87.30%	47.50%
31-Dec-92	13.80%	11.50%	−2.30%
31-Dec-93	16.60%	19.90%	3.30%
31-Dec-94	−3.40%	−12.10%	−8.70%
Arithmetic average	14.61%	20.46%	5.85%
Standard deviation	19.86%	27.60%	7.74%

Table 16-10. Summary return results for All Stocks and stocks with ROEs above 15 and then 50 biggest gains by 1-year price appreciation drawn from All Stocks universe: December 31, 1951–December 31, 1994.

	All Stocks	Universe = All Stocks ROE>15 Top 50 1-year price appreciation
Arithmetic average	14.61%	20.46%
Standard deviation of return	19.86%	27.60%
Sharpe risk-adjusted ratio	47.00	55.00
3-yr compounded	8.63%	5.53%
5-yr compounded	9.09%	14.16%
10-yr compounded	12.74%	16.66%
15-yr compounded	13.55%	17.96%
20-yr compounded	16.95%	20.52%
25-yr compounded	11.51%	15.42%
30-yr compounded	11.47%	15.94%
35-yr compounded	11.39%	15.45%
40-yr compounded	12.45%	16.78%
Compound annual return	12.81%	17.25%
$10,000 becomes	$1,782,174.48	$9,355,637.71
Maximum return	55.90%	87.30%
Minimum return	−27.90%	−29.80%
Maximum expected return*	54.33%	75.67%
Minimum expected return**	−25.11%	−34.75%

*Maximum expected return is average return plus 2 times the standard deviation.
**Minimum expected return is average return minus 2 times the standard deviation.

Table 16-11. Base rates for All Stocks and 50 stocks with ROE>15 and best 1-year relative strength (RS) from All Stocks universe: 1951–1994.

Item	50 stocks with ROE>15 and best 1-year RS beat All Stocks	Percent
Single-year return	27 out of 43	63%
Rolling 5-year compound return	33 out of 39	85%
Rolling 10-year compound return	34 out of 34	100%

Table 16-12. Annual performance of 50 stocks with best 1-year relative strength (RS) versus low PSR 50 stocks with best 1-year price appreciation drawn from All Stocks universe.

Year ending	Universe = All Stocks ROE>15 Top 50 1-year RS	Universe = All Stocks PSR<1 Top 50 1-year RS	Low PSR top 50 1-year RS Relative performance
31-Dec-52	8.20%	7.80%	−0.40%
31-Dec-53	1.90%	6.40%	4.50%
31-Dec-54	71.50%	56.90%	−14.60%
31-Dec-55	30.00%	28.80%	−1.20%
31-Dec-56	30.80%	30.50%	−0.30%
31-Dec-57	−10.70%	−20.10%	−9.40%
31-Dec-58	55.10%	67.50%	12.40%
31-Dec-59	37.50%	32.00%	−5.50%
31-Dec-60	22.60%	2.70%	−19.90%
31-Dec-61	33.90%	49.50%	15.60%
31-Dec-62	−17.30%	−13.30%	4.00%
31-Dec-63	19.80%	31.80%	12.00%
31-Dec-64	11.10%	26.40%	15.30%
31-Dec-65	24.90%	55.10%	30.20%
31-Dec-66	3.40%	−0.60%	−4.00%
31-Dec-67	57.40%	59.90%	2.50%
31-Dec-68	39.80%	46.30%	6.50%
31-Dec-69	−17.50%	−33.60%	−16.10%
31-Dec-70	−15.60%	−5.20%	10.40%
31-Dec-71	58.10%	31.90%	−26.20%
31-Dec-72	27.00%	14.60%	−12.40%
31-Dec-73	−27.50%	−20.90%	6.60%
31-Dec-74	−29.80%	−23.90%	5.90%
31-Dec-75	36.30%	58.60%	22.30%
31-Dec-76	21.60%	39.00%	17.40%
31-Dec-77	20.60%	24.50%	3.90%
31-Dec-78	26.50%	38.40%	11.90%
31-Dec-79	38.90%	26.30%	−12.60%
31-Dec-80	77.70%	48.50%	−29.20%
31-Dec-81	−6.00%	−7.70%	−1.70%
31-Dec-82	30.90%	39.50%	8.60%
31-Dec-83	21.90%	35.40%	13.50%
31-Dec-84	−4.30%	−8.20%	−3.90%
31-Dec-85	45.20%	45.20%	0.00%
31-Dec-86	21.20%	19.30%	−1.90%
31-Dec-87	−15.60%	−12.90%	2.70%
31-Dec-88	17.10%	28.00%	10.90%
31-Dec-89	38.40%	30.90%	−7.50%
31-Dec-90	−11.90%	−12.10%	−0.20%
31-Dec-91	87.30%	43.70%	−43.60%
31-Dec-92	11.50%	30.70%	19.20%
31-Dec-93	19.90%	30.40%	10.50%
31-Dec-94	−12.10%	−6.90%	5.20%
Arithmetic average	20.46%	21.42%	0.96%
Standard deviation	27.60%	26.04%	−1.56%

Large Stocks Are Less Dramatic

The results are less striking for Large Stocks. Here, buying the 50 best 1-year price performers that also have a return on equity higher than 15 turns $10,000 invested on December 31, 1951, into $2,250,840, a compound return of 13.42 percent a year. That's double the Large Stocks return over the same period. The standard deviation for the strategy was 22.59 percent, and the Sharpe ratio of 45 was the same as for Large Stocks.

Implications

Using multifactor models *dramatically* enhances returns. Whether your focus is All Stocks or Large Stocks, you're better off using several factors to choose stocks. When you buy the 50 stocks from All Stocks with price-to-sales ratios below 1 and the best price performance from the previous year you take virtually the same risk as when you buy the 50 stocks from All Stocks with the lowest price-to-sales ratios, yet you earn $8 million more over 43 years!

In all likelihood, adding relative strength to a value portfolio dramatically increases performance, because it picks stocks when investors have recognized the bargains and begun buying once again. All the value factors that make them good buys are still in place, but the addition of relative strength helps pinpoint when investors believe the stocks have been oversold.

Adding relative strength also helps growth stocks, but the results aren't uniform. Adding some growth factors actually reduces the gains from relative strength and should be avoided, while others, such as 1-year earnings gains above 25 percent and ROEs above 15, are helpful.

17

Two Multifactor Value Models for All Stocks

Great works are performed not by strength, but perseverance.
                    —SAMUEL JOHNSON

Buying the lowest price-to-sales stocks from All Stocks is the best-performing single value factor. It turned $10,000 invested on December 31, 1951, into $5,932,737, with a standard deviation of 26.08 percent. Now let's see if we can enhance returns or reduce risk using several value factors to pick stocks.

Using Several Value Factors

Let's see if we can approximate the returns of low price-to-sales stocks *without* using price-to-sales ratios as a factor. We'll call this Value Model 1. It requires that 50 stocks chosen from the All Stocks universe meet the following criteria:

1. Price-to-book ratios are below 1.5 (or, as Compustat will calculate it, book-to-price ratios above .66). This price-to-book ratio is typical for an extreme value stock.

2. Dividend yield must exceed the Compustat average for any given year. This effectively limits us to the upper 20 percent of the database by dividend yield.

3. Price-to-earnings ratios are below the Compustat database average for any given year.

4. Price-to-cashflow ratios are the lowest in the All Stocks universe.

The Results

An investment of $10,000 on December 31, 1951, (rebalanced annually and time-lagged to avoid look-ahead bias) grows to $5,508,987 by the end of 1994, a compound return of 15.81 percent. This handily beats the All Stocks universe, but is shy of the $5,932,737 you'd earn buying the 50 stocks with the lowest price-to-sales ratios. Risk is reduced, however. Here, the standard deviation of return is 24.21 percent, better than the 50 lowest price-to-sales ratios stocks' 26.08 percent. The multifactor portfolios' lower risk translates into a higher Sharpe ratio of 53, compared with 52 for the 50 low price-to-sales stocks. Finally, this strategy's 5-year rolling returns beat those for the low price-to-sales stocks. Tables 17-1, 17-2, and 17-3 summarize the results.

Value Factors Overlap

Importantly, we achieved these results *without* using price-to-sales as a factor. This shows that factors overlap. Many of the stocks with the lowest price-to-sales ratios *also* have low PE ratios, low price-to-book ratios, and high dividend yields. We can slightly reduce risk while maintaining similar returns when we use several factors to choose a portfolio.

A variety of value models produce similar results. For example, let low price-to-book ratios be the final factor. Leave low PE ratios out. Require that dividends went up 5 years in a row, and so on. No matter the combination, results are similar, since all end up choosing similar stocks.

A Multifactor Model Using Price-to-Sales Ratios

Let's look at a model that uses low price-to-sales ratios as its final factor. We'll call this Value Model 2. Here, we'll require that 50 stocks from the All Stocks universe meet the following criteria:

Table 17-1. Annual performance of All Stocks versus 50 stocks from Value Model 1 drawn from All Stocks universe.

Year ending	All Stocks	Universe = All Stocks Price-to-book <1.5 Yield>mean PE<mean Top 50 cashflow-to-price	Top 50 1-year RS Relative performance
31-Dec-52	7.90%	10.90%	3.00%
31-Dec-53	2.90%	−4.50%	−7.40%
31-Dec-54	47.00%	70.70%	23.70%
31-Dec-55	20.70%	25.00%	4.30%
31-Dec-56	17.00%	5.90%	−11.10%
31-Dec-57	−7.10%	−13.70%	−6.60%
31-Dec-58	55.00%	74.20%	19.20%
31-Dec-59	23.00%	20.10%	−2.90%
31-Dec-60	6.10%	−1.10%	−7.20%
31-Dec-61	31.20%	30.60%	−0.60%
31-Dec-62	−12.00%	−0.01%	11.99%
31-Dec-63	18.00%	26.70%	8.70%
31-Dec-64	16.30%	22.90%	6.60%
31-Dec-65	22.60%	29.00%	6.40%
31-Dec-66	−5.20%	−4.60%	0.60%
31-Dec-67	41.10%	44.20%	3.10%
31-Dec-68	27.40%	36.90%	9.50%
31-Dec-69	−18.50%	−19.70%	−1.20%
31-Dec-70	−5.80%	1.60%	7.40%
31-Dec-71	21.30%	14.50%	−6.80%
31-Dec-72	11.00%	13.60%	2.60%
31-Dec-73	−27.20%	−18.50%	8.70%
31-Dec-74	−27.90%	−14.30%	13.60%
31-Dec-75	55.90%	84.00%	28.10%
31-Dec-76	35.60%	47.60%	12.00%
31-Dec-77	6.90%	8.10%	1.20%
31-Dec-78	12.20%	4.80%	−7.40%
31-Dec-79	34.30%	23.80%	−10.50%
31-Dec-80	31.50%	10.20%	−21.30%
31-Dec-81	1.70%	4.70%	3.00%
31-Dec-82	22.50%	23.00%	0.50%
31-Dec-83	28.10%	42.90%	14.80%
31-Dec-84	−3.40%	0.08%	3.48%
31-Dec-85	30.80%	32.70%	1.90%
31-Dec-86	13.10%	3.70%	−9.40%
31-Dec-87	−1.30%	15.10%	16.40%
31-Dec-88	21.20%	47.10%	25.90%
31-Dec-89	21.40%	12.90%	−8.50%
31-Dec-90	−13.80%	−21.20%	−7.40%
31-Dec-91	39.80%	47.00%	7.20%
31-Dec-92	13.80%	11.60%	−2.20%
31-Dec-93	16.60%	28.90%	12.30%
31-Dec-94	−3.40%	3.90%	7.30%
Arithmetic average	14.61%	18.17%	3.56%
Standard deviation	19.86%	24.21%	4.35%

Table 17-2. Summary return results for All Stocks and 50 stocks from Value Model 1 from All Stocks universe: December 31, 1951–December 31, 1994.

	All Stocks	Universe = All Stocks Price-to-book <1.5 Yield>mean PE<mean Top 50 cashflow-to-price
Arithmetic average	14.61%	18.17%
Standard deviation of return	19.86%	24.21%
Sharpe risk-adjusted ratio	47.00	53.00
3-yr compounded	8.63%	14.33%
5-yr compounded	9.09%	11.60%
10-yr compounded	12.74%	16.37%
15-yr compounded	13.55%	15.98%
20-yr compounded	16.95%	19.49%
25-yr compounded	11.51%	14.94%
30-yr compounded	11.47%	14.83%
35-yr compounded	11.39%	14.86%
40-yr compounded	12.45%	15.37%
Compound annual return	12.81%	15.81%
$10,000 becomes	$1,782,174.48	$5,508,986.91
Maximum return	55.90%	84.00%
Minimum return	−27.90%	−21.20%
Maximum expected return*	54.33%	66.58%
Minimum expected return**	−25.11%	−30.24%

*Maximum expected return is average return plus 2 times the standard deviation.
**Minimum expected return is average return minus 2 times the standard deviation.

Table 17-3. Base rates for All Stocks and 50 from Value Model 1 from All Stocks universe: 1951–1994.

Item	50 stocks from Value Model 1 beat All Stocks	Percent
Single-year return	28 out of 43	65%
Rolling 5-year compound return	30 out of 39	77%
Rolling 10-year compound return	30 out of 34	88%

1. Dividend yields must exceed the Compustat mean.

2. The stock's price change in the previous year must be positive. (We find this by dividing the current year's price by the preceding year's price so the result is greater than 1.) This guarantees that none of the stocks' prices decreased in the previous year.

3. The stocks have the lowest price-to-sales ratios in the All Stocks universe.

   If we start on December 31, 1951, $10,000 invested in Value Model 2 grew to $7,615,257 by the end of 1994, a compound return of 16.12 percent a year. It accomplishes this with a standard deviation of return of 23.01 percent, lower than the first Value Model 1's 24.21 percent. The lower risk accounts for the higher Sharpe ratio of 59. All base rates are better than Value Model 1, with the strategy beating the All Stocks universe 88 percent of the time over all rolling 10-year periods. Tables 17-4, 17-5, and 17-6 summarize the findings. Compound returns for both value models are shown in Table 17-7. Figure 17-1 charts the results.

Implications

Multifactor models aid risk-adjusted performance. While neither of these models produced returns like those from the low price-to-sales/high relative strength model from Chapter 16, both show that you can enhance returns and reduce the risk of value strategies by adding additional criteria.

Table 17-4. Annual performance of All Stocks versus 50 stocks from Value Model 2 drawn from All Stocks universe.

Year ending	All Stocks	Universe = All Stocks Price up in previous year Yield>mean Top 50 sales-to-price	Top 50 multifactor model Relative performance
31-Dec-52	7.90%	11.90%	4.00%
31-Dec-53	2.90%	3.60%	0.70%
31-Dec-54	47.00%	66.20%	19.20%
31-Dec-55	20.70%	27.10%	6.40%
31-Dec-56	17.00%	13.50%	−3.50%
31-Dec-57	−7.10%	−17.20%	−10.10%
31-Dec-58	55.00%	43.70%	−11.30%
31-Dec-59	23.00%	18.60%	−4.40%
31-Dec-60	6.10%	−2.40%	−8.50%
31-Dec-61	31.20%	40.90%	9.70%
31-Dec-62	−12.00%	−6.30%	5.70%
31-Dec-63	18.00%	27.40%	9.40%
31-Dec-64	16.30%	23.40%	7.10%
31-Dec-65	22.60%	33.70%	11.10%
31-Dec-66	−5.20%	−12.50%	−7.30%
31-Dec-67	41.10%	54.60%	13.50%
31-Dec-68	27.40%	38.80%	11.40%
31-Dec-69	−18.50%	−26.20%	−7.70%
31-Dec-70	−5.80%	1.00%	6.80%
31-Dec-71	21.30%	23.20%	1.90%
31-Dec-72	11.00%	11.50%	0.50%
31-Dec-73	−27.20%	−19.50%	7.70%
31-Dec-74	−27.90%	−18.50%	9.40%
31-Dec-75	55.90%	72.00%	16.10%
31-Dec-76	35.60%	46.30%	10.70%
31-Dec-77	6.90%	9.30%	2.40%
31-Dec-78	12.20%	9.20%	−3.00%
31-Dec-79	34.30%	41.20%	6.90%
31-Dec-80	31.50%	25.40%	−6.10%
31-Dec-81	1.70%	16.30%	14.60%
31-Dec-82	22.50%	50.00%	27.50%
31-Dec-83	28.10%	36.90%	8.80%
31-Dec-84	−3.40%	5.40%	8.80%
31-Dec-85	30.80%	43.70%	12.90%
31-Dec-86	13.10%	19.60%	6.50%
31-Dec-87	−1.30%	8.20%	9.50%
31-Dec-88	21.20%	26.50%	5.30%
31-Dec-89	21.40%	13.30%	−8.10%
31-Dec-90	−13.80%	−18.20%	−4.40%
31-Dec-91	39.80%	21.20%	−18.60%
31-Dec-92	13.80%	24.60%	10.80%
31-Dec-93	16.60%	27.30%	10.70%
31-Dec-94	−3.40%	1.30%	4.70%
Arithmetic average	14.61%	18.98%	4.37%
Standard deviation	19.86%	23.01%	3.15%

Table 17-5. Summary return results for All Stocks and 50 stocks from Value Model 2 from All Stocks universe: December 31, 1951–December 31, 1994.

	All Stocks	Universe = All Stocks Price up in previous year Yield>mean Top 50 sales-to-price
Arithmetic average	14.61%	18.98%
Standard deviation of return	19.86%	23.01%
Sharpe risk-adjusted ratio	47.00	59.00
3-yr compounded	8.63%	17.13%
5-yr compounded	9.09%	9.76%
10-yr compounded	12.74%	15.56%
15-yr compounded	13.55%	18.89%
20-yr compounded	16.95%	22.39%
25-yr compounded	11.51%	17.10%
30-yr compounded	11.47%	16.43%
35-yr compounded	11.39%	16.25%
40-yr compounded	12.45%	16.12%
Compound annual return	12.81%	16.69%
$10,000 becomes	$1,782,174.48	$7,615,257.11
Maximum return	55.90%	72.00%
Minimum return	−27.90%	−26.20%
Maximum expected return*	54.33%	65.00%
Minimum expected return**	−25.11%	−27.04%

*Maximum expected return is average return plus 2 times the standard deviation.
**Minimum expected return is average return minus 2 times the standard deviation.

Table 17-6. Base rates for All Stocks and 50 from Value Model 2 drawn from All Stocks universe: 1951–1994.

Item	50 stocks from Value Model 2 beat All Stocks	Percent
Single-year return	31 out of 43	72%
Rolling 5-year compound return	31 out of 39	80%
Rolling 10-year compound return	30 out of 34	88%

Table 17-7. Compound annual rates of return by decade.

Portfolio	1950s*	1960s	1970s	1980s	1990s**
All Stocks	19.22%	11.09%	8.53%	15.85%	9.09%
Value Model 1	20.07%	14.65%	13.40%	18.23%	11.60%
Value Model 2	18.63%	14.14%	14.46%	23.74%	9.76%

*Returns for 1952–1959.
**Returns for 1990–1994.

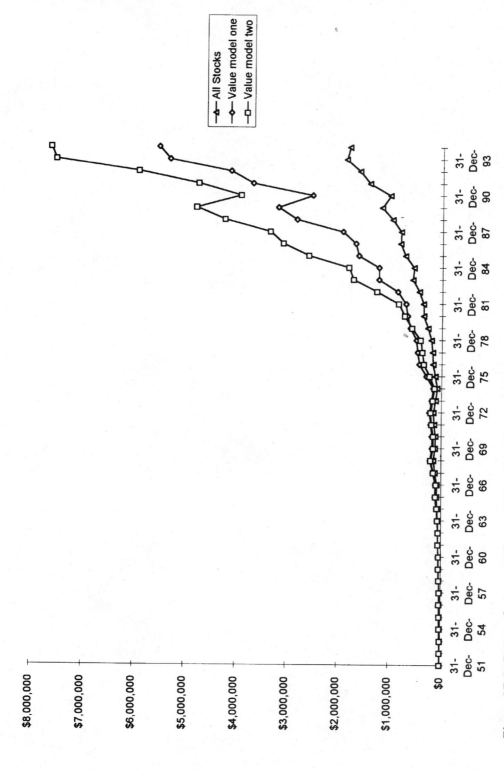

Figure 17-1. Returns for two multifactor value models versus All Stocks, 1951–1994. Year-end 1951 = $10,000.

18

Finding Value Among the Market's Leaders: A Cornerstone Value Strategy

The best way to manage anything is by making use of its own nature.
                                        —LAO TZU

Many investors are uncomfortable with any strategy that has significantly different returns from the market. They'd love to do better than the market, but cannot stomach the volatility required to do so. They can't bear a loss in their portfolio when the market is up, much less own stocks that do well in bull markets but get crushed in bear markets. These jittery investors frequently end up in index funds.

An Alternative to Indexing

There *is* an alternative to indexing. History shows that a portfolio of market-leading stocks that possess attractive value ratios—particularly those with high dividend yields—consistently beats the market at similar levels of risk. A market-leading company is a large, well-known company with sales well above the average. It usually also has strong cashflows and large numbers of shares available to the public. These market-leading firms are considerably less volatile than the market as a whole. And while we saw in Chapter 9 that high dividend yields alone do not add value to stocks from the All Stocks universe, when combined with large, market-leading firms they improve performance dramatically at risk levels that are virtually the same as the market.

Let's define market-leading stocks:

1. They come from the Large Stocks universe.

2. They have more common shares outstanding than the average stock in the Compustat database.

3. Cashflows per share exceed the Compustat mean.

4. Sales are 1.5 times the Compustat mean.

Finally, utilities are excluded so they don't dominate the list. This greatly limits the number of stocks we can consider. On December 31, 1993, only 328 of the 7919 stocks in the Compustat database met all the requirements. That's just 4 percent of the database!

High PE Ratios Hinder Even Market Leaders

All value factors are useful in sorting out which market leaders will do well. As we've seen before, high PE ratios hurt and low ones help the market leaders' performance. Tables 18-1, 18-2, and 18-3 show the results and they are dramatic: $10,000 invested on December 31, 1951, in the 50 stocks from the market-leader group with the *highest* PE ratios grew to $765,937 by the end of 1994, a compound return of just 10.62 percent. That's well behind the $1,042,859 you would earn from an investment in the Large Stocks universe. Despite a low standard deviation of 17.59 percent, the poor absolute return accounted for a Sharpe ratio of 38. The strategy beat Large Stocks in just 19 of the 43 years studied, or 44 percent of the time. Long term, the group beat the market 54 percent of the time over rolling 5-year periods and 41 percent over rolling 10-year periods.

High PE ratios pulled down even the market's leaders.

Table 18-1. Annual performance of Large Stocks versus 50 stocks with highest PE ratios drawn from the market-leaders group.

Year ending	Large Stocks	Universe = market leaders 50 highest PE ratios	Top 50 PE ratios Relative performance
31-Dec-52	9.30%	15.50%	6.20%
31-Dec-53	2.30%	0.03%	−2.27%
31-Dec-54	44.90%	50.70%	5.80%
31-Dec-55	21.20%	26.60%	5.40%
31-Dec-56	9.60%	13.00%	3.40%
31-Dec-57	−6.90%	−10.00%	−3.10%
31-Dec-58	42.10%	36.70%	−5.40%
31-Dec-59	9.90%	12.50%	2.60%
31-Dec-60	4.80%	−0.01%	−4.81%
31-Dec-61	27.50%	24.10%	−3.40%
31-Dec-62	−8.90%	−13.70%	−4.80%
31-Dec-63	19.50%	23.90%	4.40%
31-Dec-64	15.30%	13.00%	−2.30%
31-Dec-65	16.20%	24.50%	8.30%
31-Dec-66	−4.90%	−1.60%	3.30%
31-Dec-67	21.30%	35.00%	13.70%
31-Dec-68	16.80%	6.80%	−10.00%
31-Dec-69	−9.90%	0.20%	10.10%
31-Dec-70	−0.20%	−6.50%	−6.30%
31-Dec-71	17.30%	27.00%	9.70%
31-Dec-72	14.90%	24.70%	9.80%
31-Dec-73	−18.90%	−14.10%	4.80%
31-Dec-74	−26.70%	−32.90%	−6.20%
31-Dec-75	43.10%	30.10%	−13.00%
31-Dec-76	28.00%	9.20%	−18.80%
31-Dec-77	−2.50%	−12.40%	−9.90%
31-Dec-78	8.10%	12.50%	4.40%
31-Dec-79	27.30%	10.50%	−16.80%
31-Dec-80	30.80%	36.00%	5.20%
31-Dec-81	0.60%	−8.00%	−8.60%
31-Dec-82	19.90%	29.50%	9.60%
31-Dec-83	23.80%	16.90%	−6.90%
31-Dec-84	−0.40%	−4.10%	−3.70%
31-Dec-85	19.50%	32.00%	12.50%
31-Dec-86	32.20%	24.00%	−8.20%
31-Dec-87	3.30%	23.50%	20.20%
31-Dec-88	19.00%	19.40%	0.40%
31-Dec-89	26.00%	21.80%	−4.20%
31-Dec-90	−8.70%	−15.50%	−6.80%
31-Dec-91	33.00%	30.50%	−2.50%
31-Dec-92	8.70%	0.01%	−8.69%
31-Dec-93	16.30%	11.00%	−5.30%
31-Dec-94	−1.90%	−3.00%	−1.10%
Arithmetic average	12.62%	12.08%	−0.54%
Standard deviation	16.18%	17.59%	1.42%

Table 18-2. Annual performance of Large Stocks versus 50 stocks with lowest PE ratios drawn from the market-leaders group.

Year ending	Large Stocks	Universe = market leaders 50 lowest PE ratios	Low 50 PE ratios Relative performance
31-Dec-52	9.30%	15.60%	6.30%
31-Dec-53	2.30%	−0.20%	−2.50%
31-Dec-54	44.90%	51.30%	6.40%
31-Dec-55	21.20%	27.20%	6.00%
31-Dec-56	9.60%	13.30%	3.70%
31-Dec-57	−6.90%	−10.00%	−3.10%
31-Dec-58	42.10%	36.70%	−5.40%
31-Dec-59	9.90%	12.80%	2.90%
31-Dec-60	4.80%	1.10%	−3.70%
31-Dec-61	27.50%	3.60%	−23.90%
31-Dec-62	−8.90%	−4.20%	4.70%
31-Dec-63	19.50%	18.70%	−0.80%
31-Dec-64	15.30%	22.30%	7.00%
31-Dec-65	16.20%	23.30%	7.10%
31-Dec-66	−4.90%	−8.00%	−3.10%
31-Dec-67	21.30%	28.80%	7.50%
31-Dec-68	16.80%	29.60%	12.80%
31-Dec-69	−9.90%	−17.50%	−7.60%
31-Dec-70	−0.20%	7.90%	8.10%
31-Dec-71	17.30%	12.30%	−5.00%
31-Dec-72	14.90%	20.40%	5.50%
31-Dec-73	−18.90%	−10.20%	8.70%
31-Dec-74	−26.70%	−17.10%	9.60%
31-Dec-75	43.10%	88.20%	45.10%
31-Dec-76	28.00%	43.20%	15.20%
31-Dec-77	−2.50%	1.60%	4.10%
31-Dec-78	8.10%	8.20%	0.10%
31-Dec-79	27.30%	28.10%	0.80%
31-Dec-80	30.80%	18.00%	−12.80%
31-Dec-81	0.60%	2.10%	1.50%
31-Dec-82	19.90%	17.40%	−2.50%
31-Dec-83	23.80%	38.80%	15.00%
31-Dec-84	−0.40%	6.10%	6.50%
31-Dec-85	19.50%	37.20%	17.70%
31-Dec-86	32.20%	27.20%	−5.00%
31-Dec-87	3.30%	7.10%	3.80%
31-Dec-88	19.00%	26.90%	7.90%
31-Dec-89	26.00%	24.30%	−1.70%
31-Dec-90	−8.70%	−16.60%	−7.90%
31-Dec-91	33.00%	44.80%	11.80%
31-Dec-92	8.70%	5.20%	−3.50%
31-Dec-93	16.30%	25.80%	9.50%
31-Dec-94	−1.90%	3.70%	5.60%
Arithmetic average	12.62%	16.16%	3.54%
Standard deviation	16.18%	20.37%	4.20%

Table 18-3. Annual performance of 50 stocks with lowest PE ratios drawn from the market-leaders group versus the 50 highest PE stocks from the market-leaders group.

Year ending	Universe = market leaders 50 highest PE ratios	Universe = market leaders 50 lowest PE ratios	Low 50 PE ratios Relative performance
31-Dec-52	15.50%	15.60%	0.10%
31-Dec-53	0.03%	−0.20%	−0.23%
31-Dec-54	50.70%	51.30%	0.60%
31-Dec-55	26.60%	27.20%	0.60%
31-Dec-56	13.00%	13.30%	0.30%
31-Dec-57	−10.00%	−10.00%	0.00%
31-Dec-58	36.70%	36.70%	0.00%
31-Dec-59	12.50%	12.80%	0.30%
31-Dec-60	−0.01%	1.10%	1.11%
31-Dec-61	24.10%	3.60%	−20.50%
31-Dec-62	−13.70%	−4.20%	9.50%
31-Dec-63	23.90%	18.70%	−5.20%
31-Dec-64	13.00%	22.30%	9.30%
31-Dec-65	24.50%	23.30%	−1.20%
31-Dec-66	−1.60%	−8.00%	−6.40%
31-Dec-67	35.00%	28.80%	−6.20%
31-Dec-68	6.80%	29.60%	22.80%
31-Dec-69	0.20%	−17.50%	−17.70%
31-Dec-70	−6.50%	7.90%	14.40%
31-Dec-71	27.00%	12.30%	−14.70%
31-Dec-72	24.70%	20.40%	−4.30%
31-Dec-73	−14.10%	−10.20%	3.90%
31-Dec-74	−32.90%	−17.10%	15.80%
31-Dec-75	30.10%	88.20%	58.10%
31-Dec-76	9.20%	43.20%	34.00%
31-Dec-77	−12.40%	1.60%	14.00%
31-Dec-78	12.50%	8.20%	−4.30%
31-Dec-79	10.50%	28.10%	17.60%
31-Dec-80	36.00%	18.00%	−18.00%
31-Dec-81	−8.00%	2.10%	10.10%
31-Dec-82	29.50%	17.40%	−12.10%
31-Dec-83	16.90%	38.80%	21.90%
31-Dec-84	−4.10%	6.10%	10.20%
31-Dec-85	32.00%	37.20%	5.20%
31-Dec-86	24.00%	27.20%	3.20%
31-Dec-87	23.50%	7.10%	−16.40%
31-Dec-88	19.40%	26.90%	7.50%
31-Dec-89	21.80%	24.30%	2.50%
31-Dec-90	−15.50%	−16.60%	−1.10%
31-Dec-91	30.50%	44.80%	14.30%
31-Dec-92	0.01%	5.20%	5.19%
31-Dec-93	11.00%	25.80%	14.80%
31-Dec-94	−3.00%	3.70%	6.70%
Arithmetic average	12.08%	16.16%	4.09%
Standard deviation	17.59%	20.37%	2.78%

Low PE Ratios Help

Market leaders with the *lowest* PE ratios tell an entirely different story. If we start on December 31, 1951, $10,000 invested in the 50 stocks from the market-leaders group with the lowest PE ratios grows to $3,332,644 by the end of 1994, a compound return of 14.46 percent. That's $2,566,707 more than the *high* PE group from market leaders. The *only* thing separating the stocks is PE ratio. The risk is higher for the low PE group, with a standard deviation of 20.37 percent, but because of the higher total return, the Sharpe ratio is a decent 53. All base rates are considerably better, with the low PE group beating the Large Stocks universe in 28 of the 43 years studied, or 65 percent of the time. Long-term base rates are also superior, with the low PE market leaders beating Large Stocks in 30 of the 39 rolling 5-year periods and 26 of the 34 rolling 10-year periods.

High Yield Works Better Still

The best returns for market leaders come from stocks with the highest dividend yields. Buying the 50 stocks from the market leaders group with the highest dividend yields does four times as well as an investment in the Large Stocks universe, while assuming very little additional risk.

If we start on December 31, 1951, $10,000 invested in the 50 highest-yielding stocks from the market-leaders group grows to $4,141,129 by the end of 1994, a compound annual return of 15.04 percent. The remarkable thing here is risk—the standard deviation of 17.25 percent is only 1.07 percent higher than Large Stocks' 16.18 percent. Such risk-reward numbers push the Sharpe ratio for the strategy to 63, the highest we've seen thus far!

As Table 18-4 shows, the most extraordinary thing about this high-yield strategy is that the *worst* it ever did was a loss of 15 percent. That's nearly half Large Stocks' largest annual loss of 26.7 percent. This strategy outperformed Large Stocks in 8 of the 11 bear market years, and *never* had a negative 5-year return. It had only one 10-year period in which it failed to beat Large Stocks, then losing to the group only by a minuscule 0.78 percent.

Better in Bull Markets, Too

With such excellent downside protection, you would expect the strategy to perform more modestly in bull markets than Large Stocks did.

Table 18-4. Annual performance of Large Stocks versus 50 stocks with highest dividend yields drawn from the market-leaders group.

Year ending	Large Stocks	Universe = market leaders 50 highest dividend yields	Top 50 dividend yields Relative performance
31-Dec-52	9.30%	14.30%	5.00%
31-Dec-53	2.30%	1.20%	−1.10%
31-Dec-54	44.90%	52.50%	7.60%
31-Dec-55	21.20%	28.10%	6.90%
31-Dec-56	9.60%	14.80%	5.20%
31-Dec-57	−6.90%	−13.50%	−6.60%
31-Dec-58	42.10%	44.90%	2.80%
31-Dec-59	9.90%	9.60%	−0.30%
31-Dec-60	4.80%	−0.03%	−4.83%
31-Dec-61	27.50%	24.40%	−3.10%
31-Dec-62	−8.90%	−2.60%	6.30%
31-Dec-63	19.50%	18.80%	−0.70%
31-Dec-64	15.30%	20.30%	5.00%
31-Dec-65	16.20%	17.60%	1.40%
31-Dec-66	−4.90%	−10.20%	−5.30%
31-Dec-67	21.30%	23.70%	2.40%
31-Dec-68	16.80%	26.50%	9.70%
31-Dec-69	−9.90%	−15.00%	−5.10%
31-Dec-70	−0.20%	11.30%	11.50%
31-Dec-71	17.30%	15.80%	−1.50%
31-Dec-72	14.90%	14.00%	−0.90%
31-Dec-73	−18.90%	−5.90%	13.00%
31-Dec-74	−26.70%	−12.30%	14.40%
31-Dec-75	43.10%	58.20%	15.10%
31-Dec-76	28.00%	39.20%	11.20%
31-Dec-77	−2.50%	3.30%	5.80%
31-Dec-78	8.10%	3.30%	−4.80%
31-Dec-79	27.30%	25.60%	−1.70%
31-Dec-80	30.80%	20.30%	−10.50%
31-Dec-81	0.60%	12.80%	12.20%
31-Dec-82	19.90%	19.60%	−0.30%
31-Dec-83	23.80%	38.60%	14.80%
31-Dec-84	−0.40%	4.70%	5.10%
31-Dec-85	19.50%	35.00%	15.50%
31-Dec-86	32.20%	20.60%	−11.60%
31-Dec-87	3.30%	11.60%	8.30%
31-Dec-88	19.00%	26.50%	7.50%
31-Dec-89	26.00%	37.60%	11.60%
31-Dec-90	−8.70%	−7.00%	1.70%
31-Dec-91	33.00%	36.90%	3.90%
31-Dec-92	8.70%	11.60%	2.90%
31-Dec-93	16.30%	20.40%	4.10%
31-Dec-94	−1.90%	4.80%	6.70%
Arithmetic average	12.62%	16.32%	3.70%
Standard deviation	16.18%	17.25%	1.07%

But this strategy *beat* Large Stocks in 9 of the 13 years in which market gains exceeded 25 percent! Indeed, in the super bull years of 1954, 1958, and 1975—when Large Stocks gained 40 percent or more—the strategy *always* did better.

These numbers give us outstanding base rates. The high-yield strategy beat Large Stocks in 28 of the 43 years of our test, or 65 percent of the time. Long term, the news gets continually better, with the strategy beating Large Stocks 85 percent of the time over rolling 5-year periods and all but once over rolling 10-year periods. Tables 18-5 and 18-6 summarize the returns, and Tables 18-7 and 18-8 show rolling 5- and 10-year compound returns for the strategy versus the Large Stocks universe, and Table 18-9 gives compound returns by decade. Figures 18-1 through 18-4 depict the results graphically.

Implications

Large, well-known market-leading companies are much better investments when they have a value characteristic like low PE ratio or low price-to-cashflow ratio, but the best criterion is dividend yield.

The returns from buying the 50 market-leading stocks with the highest dividend yields are so outstanding that this strategy should serve as a cornerstone value strategy for all portfolios. The reasons are numerous. The strategy sticks to large, well-known companies yet does four times as well as the Large Stocks universe while taking virtually the same risk. It has the highest risk-adjusted return of all strategies examined. The *biggest* projected loss is 18.17 percent, lower than the Large Stocks' worst projected loss of 19.73 percent. The maximum projected *gain* for the strategy is 50.82 percent, compared with Large Stocks' 44.97 percent. The strategy's *actual* minimum and maximum returns are even better, with the worst year showing a loss of 15 percent and the best a gain of 58.2 percent. That compares very favorably with Large Stocks' worst loss of 26.7 percent and best gain of 44.9 percent. The strategy does better than Large Stocks in bull *and* bear markets, leading the market in most bull years and providing a cushion in bear years.

Finally, the strategy's high returns coupled with low risk and persistence of returns make it a natural replacement for investors indexing their portfolios to the S&P 500 or other Large Stocks style indexes.

Table 18-5. Summary return results for Large Stocks and 50 highest dividend yield stocks from market-leaders group: December 31, 1951–December 31, 1994.

	Large Stocks	Universe = market leaders Top 50 dividend yield
Arithmetic average	12.62%	16.32%
Standard deviation of return	16.18%	17.25%
Sharpe risk-adjusted ratio	45.00	63.00
3-yr compounded	7.44%	12.09%
5-yr compounded	8.53%	12.38%
10-yr compounded	13.93%	18.95%
15-yr compounded	14.03%	18.86%
20-yr compounded	15.42%	20.17%
25-yr compounded	11.16%	16.73%
30-yr compounded	10.48%	15.05%
35-yr compounded	10.54%	14.55%
40-yr compounded	10.97%	14.62%
Compound annual return	11.41%	15.04%
$10,000 becomes	$1,042,858.62	$4,141,128.97
Maximum return	44.90%	58.20%
Minimum return	−26.70%	−15.00%
Maximum expected return*	44.97%	50.82%
Minimum expected return**	−19.73%	−18.17%

*Maximum expected return is average return plus 2 times the standard deviation.
**Minimum expected return is average return minus 2 times the standard deviation.

Table 18-6. Base rates for Large Stocks and 50 stocks with highest dividend yields from market-leaders group, 1951–1994.

Item	50 highest dividend yield stocks beat Large Stocks	Percent
Single-year return	28 out of 43	65%
Rolling 5-year compound return	33 out of 39	85%
Rolling 10-year compound return	33 out of 34	97%

Table 18-7. Rolling 5-year compound returns for Large Stocks and 50 highest dividend yield stocks from market leaders group: December 31, 1955–December 31, 1994.

5 years ending	Large Stocks	Universe = market leaders Top 50 dividend yields	Difference
31-Dec-56	16.57%	21.00%	4.44%
31-Dec-57	12.89%	14.44%	1.56%
31-Dec-58	20.55%	22.96%	2.41%
31-Dec-59	14.07%	15.10%	1.03%
31-Dec-60	10.80%	9.53%	−1.27%
31-Dec-61	14.20%	11.31%	−2.90%
31-Dec-62	13.71%	13.98%	0.27%
31-Dec-63	9.84%	9.54%	−0.30%
31-Dec-64	10.90%	11.60%	0.70%
31-Dec-65	13.21%	15.29%	2.07%
31-Dec-66	6.76%	8.01%	1.25%
31-Dec-67	13.05%	13.30%	0.24%
31-Dec-68	12.54%	14.73%	2.19%
31-Dec-69	7.12%	7.03%	−0.09%
31-Dec-70	3.91%	5.86%	1.95%
31-Dec-71	8.37%	11.38%	3.02%
31-Dec-72	7.20%	9.58%	2.38%
31-Dec-73	−0.35	3.28%	3.63%
31-Dec-74	−4.37%	3.93%	8.30%
31-Dec-75	2.77%	11.50%	8.73%
31-Dec-76	4.58%	15.68%	11.10%
31-Dec-77	1.20%	13.42%	12.22%
31-Dec-78	7.19%	15.56%	8.37%
31-Dec-79	19.70%	24.17%	4.47%
31-Dec-80	17.57%	17.55%	−0.02%
31-Dec-81	12.04%	12.71%	0.67%
31-Dec-82	16.77%	16.06%	−0.71%
31-Dec-83	19.98%	23.09%	3.11%
31-Dec-84	14.24%	18.69%	4.45%
31-Dec-85	12.19%	21.46%	9.27%
31-Dec-86	18.49%	23.09%	4.60%
31-Dec-87	15.01%	21.40%	6.39%
31-Dec-88	14.10%	19.20%	5.10%
31-Dec-89	19.60%	25.90%	6.30%
31-Dec-90	13.33%	16.85%	3.52%
31-Dec-91	13.47%	19.85%	6.39%
31-Dec-92	14.63%	19.85%	5.22%
31-Dec-93	14.10%	18.67%	4.57%
31-Dec-94	8.53%	12.38%	3.85%
Arithmetic average	11.55%	15.10%	3.55%

Table 18-8. Rolling 10-year compound returns for Large Stocks and 50 highest dividend yield stocks from market-leaders group: December 31, 1955–December 31, 1994.

5 years ending	Large Stocks	Universe = market leaders Top 50 dividend yields	Difference
31-Dec-61	15.38%	16.05%	0.67%
31-Dec-62	13.30%	14.21%	0.91%
31-Dec-63	15.07%	16.06%	0.99%
31-Dec-64	12.47%	13.34%	0.87%
31-Dec-65	12.00%	12.37%	0.37%
31-Dec-66	10.42%	9.65%	−0.78%
31-Dec-67	13.38%	13.64%	0.26%
31-Dec-68	11.18%	12.11%	0.93%
31-Dec-69	8.99%	9.29%	0.30%
31-Dec-70	8.46%	10.47%	2.01%
31-Dec-71	7.56%	9.68%	2.12%
31-Dec-72	10.09%	11.42%	1.34%
31-Dec-73	5.90%	8.86%	2.95%
31-Dec-74	1.21%	5.47%	4.26%
31-Dec-75	3.34%	8.64%	5.30%
31-Dec-76	6.46%	13.51%	7.05%
31-Dec-77	4.16%	11.48%	7.33%
31-Dec-78	3.35%	9.25%	5.89%
31-Dec-79	6.99%	13.60%	6.61%
31-Dec-80	9.92%	14.49%	4.56%
31-Dec-81	8.25%	14.19%	5.94%
31-Dec-82	8.71%	14.73%	6.03%
31-Dec-83	13.41%	19.26%	5.86%
31-Dec-84	16.94%	21.40%	4.46%
31-Dec-85	14.85%	19.49%	4.64%
31-Dec-86	15.22%	17.78%	2.57%
31-Dec-87	15.89%	18.70%	2.81%
31-Dec-88	17.01%	21.13%	4.12%
31-Dec-89	16.89%	22.24%	5.35%
31-Dec-90	12.76%	19.13%	6.37%
31-Dec-91	15.95%	21.46%	5.51%
31-Dec-92	14.28%	20.62%	5.80%
31-Dec-93	14.10%	18.94%	4.83%
31-Dec-94	13.93%	18.95%	5.02%
Arithmetic average	11.13%	14.75%	3.63%

Table 18-9. Compound annual rates of return by decade.

Portfolio	1950s*	1960s	1970s	1980s	1990s**
Large Stocks	15.33%	8.99%	6.99%	16.89%	8.53%
50 highest dividend yield from market leaders	17.22%	9.29%	13.60%	22.24%	12.38%

*Returns for 1952–1959.

**Returns for 1990–1994.

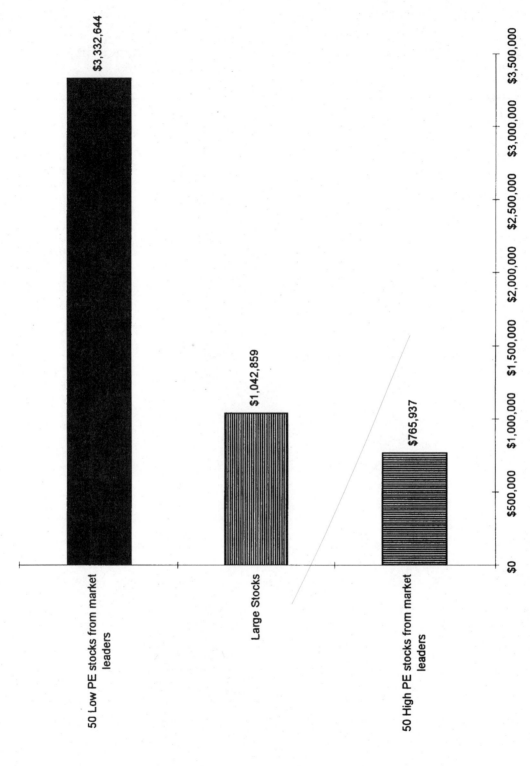

Figure 18-1. December 31, 1994, value of $10,000 invested on December 31, 1951, and annually rebalanced.

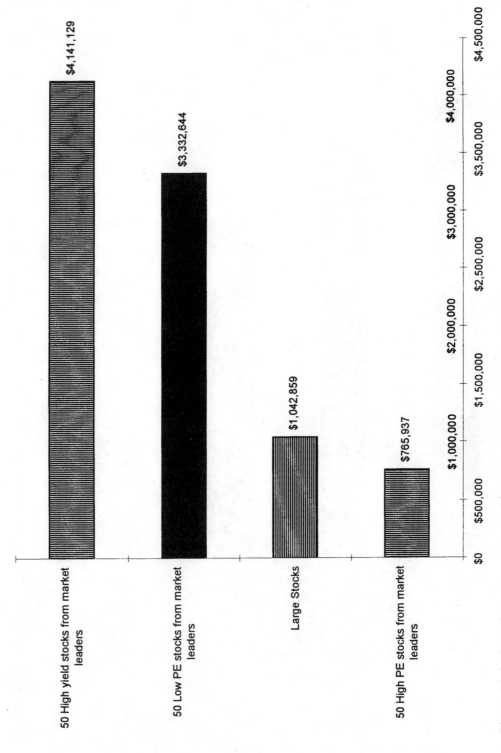

Figure 18-2. December 31, 1994, value of $10,000 invested on December 31, 1951, and annually rebalanced.

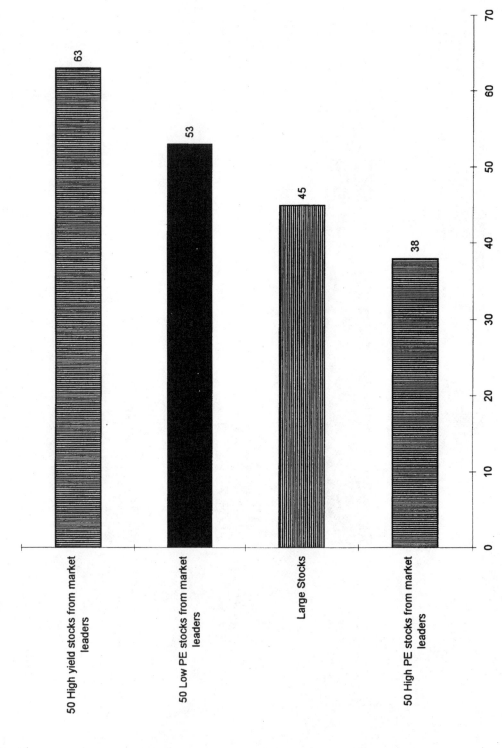

Figure 18-3. Sharpe risk-adjusted return ratios, 1951–1994. (Higher is better.)

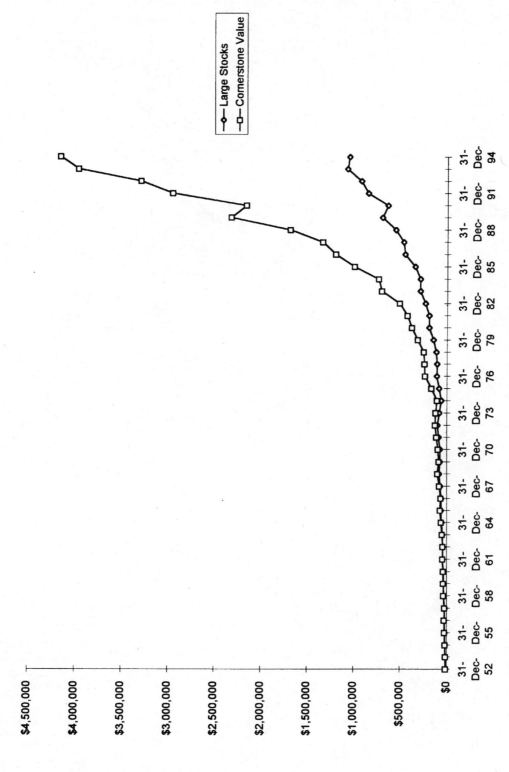

Figure 18-4. Returns on cornerstone value versus Large Stocks, 1951–1994. Year-end 1951 = $10,000.

19

Searching for a Cornerstone Growth Strategy

Facts do not cease to exist because they are ignored.
—ALDOUS HUXLEY

Now let's see if we can find a growth strategy to complement the cornerstone value strategy. With growth strategies, risk is considerably higher. The trick is putting together a portfolio that overcomes its higher standard deviation, giving you risk-adjusted returns that compensate for a wilder ride.

The best-performing strategy we've seen thus far screens the All Stocks universe for stocks with price-to-sales ratios below 1 and then buys the 50 with the best 1-year price performance. (Since we'll be using 5-year variables here, we'll adjust this strategy to the 1954–1994 period.) In this strategy, an investment of $10,000 on December 31, 1954, grew to $7,858,269 by the end of 1994, a compound return of 18.14 percent. The standard deviation was 26.22 percent and the Sharpe ratio was 59. Our objective is to find a growth strategy that offers higher returns with less risk.

Traditional Growth Factors
Fall Short

First let's use a typical group of growth factors coupled with relative strength. We'll call this Growth Model 1 and require 50 stocks to:

1. Come from the All Stocks universe
2. Have 5-year earnings-per-share growth rates exceeding the Compustat mean
3. Have profit margins exceeding the Compustat mean
4. Have earnings gains 5 years in a row
5. We'll then buy the 50 stocks with the best 1-year relative strength in the All Stocks group.

Starting on December 31, 1954, $10,000 invested in this strategy was worth $3,942,460 at the end of 1994, a compound return of 16.12 percent a year. That's well ahead of a simple investment in All Stocks, where $10,000 grew to $1,091,933 over the same period, with a return of 12.45 percent a year. Growth Model 1's risk is moderate, with a standard deviation of 22.71 percent, not much more than All Stocks' 19.83 percent. That gives it a respectable Sharpe ratio of 56, compared with All Stocks' 43. (Remember we're missing 3 years of returns here, so the figures are different from those seen earlier.)

On an absolute *and* risk-adjusted basis, this strategy falls far short of the strategy that buys low price-to-sales stocks with the best relative strength. As mentioned above, $10,000 invested on December 31, 1954, in the 50 stocks with price-to-sales ratios below 1 and the best relative strength grew to $7,858,269 by the end of 1994, almost double the returns of Growth Model 1. Risk is higher, with a standard deviation of 26.22 percent. Table 19-1 summarizes the results.

Earnings Persistence Most
Valuable

You're better off ignoring 5-year compound earnings growth rates and profit margins exceeding the Compustat mean and focusing exclusively on stocks that show *persistent* earnings growth without regard to magnitude.

We'll call this simpler strategy Growth Model 2, requiring that 50 stocks:

Table 19-1. Summary results for buying best 1-year price appreciation stocks with price-to-sales ratios below 1 and Growth Model 1: December 31, 1954– December 31, 1994. Universe is All Stocks.

	All Stocks	Growth Model 1	50 stocks with price-to-sales ratios below 1 and best 1-year price appreciation
$10,000 becomes	$1,091,933	$3,942,460	$7,858,269
Compound return	12.45%	16.12%	18.14%
Standard deviation of return (risk)	19.83%	22.71%	26.22%
Sharpe ratio	43	56	59
Percent of rolling 10-year periods beats All Stocks	NA	94%	100%
Best 1-year return	55.90%	74.40%	67.50%
Worst 1-year return	−27.90%	−30.80%	−33.60%

1. Come from the All Stocks universe
2. Have earnings gains 5 years in a row
3. Display the best 1-year price performance in the All Stocks group.

Here, $10,000 invested on December 31, 1954, grows to $5,091,746, a compound return of 16.86 percent. That's better than Growth Model 1, but the trade-off is a high standard deviation of 28.69 percent. The risk gives us a mediocre Sharpe ratio of 51, and suggests we continue our search for a cornerstone growth strategy. Table 19-2 shows the results.

Uniting the Two Models for a Cornerstone Growth Approach

Uniting earnings persistence with low price-to-sales ratios results in a strategy that performs slightly better than low price-to-sales alone while reducing risk. Here, we'll require that 50 stocks:

1. Come from the All Stocks universe
2. Have earnings gains for 5 consecutive years

3. Have price-to-sales ratios below 1.5

4. Display the best 1-year price performance in the All Stocks group.

We increase the price-to-sales minimum to 1.5 to allow more of the "growth" stocks with persistent earnings gains to make the final cut.

Starting on December 31, 1954, $10,000 invested in this cornerstone growth strategy grows to $8,074,504 by the end of 1994, a compound return of 18.22 percent. That's better than the return of the 50 best price performers with price-to-sales ratios below 1. It's slightly lower standard deviation of 25.99 percent gives it a Sharpe ratio of 60, the best for all the growth strategies we've examined. Tables 19-3 and 19-4 show the results of the cornerstone growth strategy. All base rates are high, with this cornerstone growth strategy beating All Stocks 73 percent of the time annually, 89 percent of the time for rolling 5-year periods, and 100 percent of the time over rolling 10-year periods. Table 19-5 shows base rates for the strategy, Tables 19-6 and 19-7 show rolling 5- and 10-year periods, and Table 19-8 shows compound returns. The results are depicted in Figures 19-1, 19-2, and 19-3.

Table 19-2. Summary results for buying best 1-year price appreciation stocks with price-to-sales ratios below 1 and Growth Model 2: December 31, 1954–December 31, 1994. Universe is All Stocks.

	All Stocks	Growth Model 2	50 stocks with price-to-sales ratios below 1 and best 1-year price appreciation
$10,000 becomes	$1,091,933	$5,091,746	$7,858,269
Compound return	12.45%	16.86%	18.14%
Standard deviation of return (risk)	19.83%	28.69%	26.22%
Sharpe ratio	43	51	59
Percent of rolling 10-year periods beats All Stocks	NA	100%	100%
Best 1-year return	55.90%	74.40%	67.50%
Worst 1-year return	−27.90%	−30.80%	−33.60%

Table 19-3. Annual performance of All Stocks versus cornerstone growth strategy drawn from All Stocks universe.

Year ending	All Stocks	Universe = All Stocks Top 50 cornerstone growth strategy	Top 50 cornerstone growth strategy Relative performance
31-Dec-55	20.70%	30.40%	9.70%
31-Dec-56	17.00%	18.00%	1.00%
31-Dec-57	−7.10%	−17.90%	−10.80%
31-Dec-58	55.00%	52.80%	−2.20%
31-Dec-59	23.00%	24.10%	1.10%
31-Dec-60	6.10%	12.60%	6.50%
31-Dec-61	31.20%	51.10%	19.90%
31-Dec-62	−12.00%	−17.20%	−5.20%
31-Dec-63	18.00%	20.80%	2.80%
31-Dec-64	16.30%	30.00%	13.70%
31-Dec-65	22.60%	44.10%	21.50%
31-Dec-66	−5.20%	−0.10%	5.10%
31-Dec-67	41.10%	83.30%	42.20%
31-Dec-68	27.40%	50.50%	23.10%
31-Dec-69	−18.50%	−28.10%	−9.60%
31-Dec-70	−5.80%	−2.60%	3.20%
31-Dec-71	21.30%	32.10%	10.80%
31-Dec-72	11.00%	19.70%	8.70%
31-Dec-73	−27.20%	−27.50%	−0.30%
31-Dec-74	−27.90%	−29.10%	−1.20%
31-Dec-75	55.90%	37.60%	−18.30%
31-Dec-76	35.60%	32.50%	−3.10%
31-Dec-77	6.90%	26.40%	19.50%
31-Dec-78	12.20%	38.30%	26.10%
31-Dec-79	34.30%	38.70%	4.40%
31-Dec-80	31.50%	62.70%	31.20%
31-Dec-81	1.70%	−9.00%	−10.70%
31-Dec-82	22.50%	37.10%	14.60%
31-Dec-83	28.10%	32.70%	4.60%
31-Dec-84	−3.40%	−2.00%	1.40%
31-Dec-85	30.80%	42.50%	11.70%
31-Dec-86	13.10%	17.70%	4.60%
31-Dec-87	−1.30%	−5.40%	−4.10%
31-Dec-88	21.20%	29.70%	8.50%
31-Dec-89	21.40%	23.80%	2.40%
31-Dec-90	−13.80%	−3.30%	10.50%
31-Dec-91	39.80%	51.40%	11.60%
31-Dec-92	13.80%	25.50%	11.70%
31-Dec-93	16.60%	30.30%	13.70%
31-Dec-94	−3.40%	−5.30%	−1.90%
Arithmetic average	14.26%	21.22%	6.96%
Standard deviation	19.83%	25.99%	6.16%

Table 19-4. Summary return results for All Stocks and cornerstone growth strategy from All Stocks universe: December 31, 1954–December 31, 1994.

	All Stocks	Universe = All Stocks Cornerstone growth strategy
Arithmetic average	14.26%	21.22%
Standard deviation of return	19.83%	25.99%
Sharpe risk-adjusted ratio	43.00	60.00
3-yr compounded	8.63%	15.69%
5-yr compounded	9.09%	17.79%
10-yr compounded	12.74%	19.17%
15-yr compounded	13.55%	19.92%
20-yr compounded	16.95%	23.43%
25-yr compounded	11.51%	17.24%
30-yr compounded	11.47%	18.24%
35-yr compounded	11.39%	18.09%
40-yr compounded	12.45%	18.22%
Compound annual return	12.45%	18.22%
$10,000 becomes	$1,091,933.19	$8,074,503.75
Maximum return	55.90%	83.30%
Minimum return	−27.90%	−29.10%
Maximum expected return*	53.92%	73.20%
Minimum expected return**	−25.39%	−30.75%

**Maximum expected return is average return plus 2 times the standard deviation.
**Minimum expected return is average return minus 2 times the standard deviation.

Table 19-5. Base rates for All Stocks and 50 stocks meeting cornerstone growth strategy criteria from All Stocks universe: 1954–1994.

Item	Cornerstone growth strategy stocks beat All Stocks	Percent
Single-year return	29 out of 40	73%
Rolling 5-year compound return	32 out of 36	89%
Rolling 10-year compound return	31 out of 31	100%

Table 19-6. Rolling 5-year returns for All Stocks and cornerstone growth strategy from All Stocks universe: December 31, 1954–December 31, 1994.

5 years ending	All Stocks	Universe = All Stocks Cornerstone growth strategy	Difference
31-Dec-59	20.12%	19.09%	−1.03%
31-Dec-60	17.07%	15.65%	−1.42%
31-Dec-61	19.78%	21.51%	1.73%
31-Dec-62	18.49%	21.72%	3.23%
31-Dec-63	12.20%	16.13%	3.93%
31-Dec-64	10.95%	17.21%	6.26%
31-Dec-65	14.20%	23.14%	8.94%
31-Dec-66	7.02%	13.36%	6.34%
31-Dec-67	17.61%	32.89%	15.27%
31-Dec-68	19.43%	38.86%	19.43%
31-Dec-69	11.23%	23.35%	12.12%
31-Dec-70	5.52%	14.05%	8.53%
31-Dec-71	10.85%	20.61%	9.75%
31-Dec-72	5.66%	10.76%	5.09%
31-Dec-73	−5.53%	−4.30%	1.23%
31-Dec-74	−7.81%	−4.56%	3.25%
31-Dec-75	1.96%	2.26%	0.31%
31-Dec-76	4.26%	2.33%	−1.93%
31-Dec-77	3.47%	3.45%	−0.03%
31-Dec-78	12.82%	17.71%	4.88%
31-Dec-79	27.77%	34.62%	6.85%
31-Dec-80	23.49%	39.20%	15.71%
31-Dec-81	16.59%	29.13%	12.54%
31-Dec-82	19.81%	31.24%	11.43%
31-Dec-83	23.03%	30.16%	7.13%
31-Dec-84	15.18%	21.43%	6.25%
31-Dec-85	15.06%	18.25%	3.19%
31-Dec-86	17.53%	24.49%	6.96%
31-Dec-87	12.56%	15.59%	3.03%
31-Dec-88	11.32%	15.06%	3.74%
31-Dec-89	16.53%	20.57%	4.04%
31-Dec-90	7.20%	11.57%	4.37%
31-Dec-91	11.84%	17.33%	5.49%
31-Dec-92	15.07%	24.16%	9.08%
31-Dec-93	14.19%	24.27%	10.09%
31-Dec-94	9.09%	17.79%	8.70%
Arithmetic average	12.65%	18.89%	6.24%

Table 19-7. Rolling 10-year returns for All Stocks and cornerstone growth strategy from All Stocks universe: December 31, 1954–December 31, 1994.

10 years ending	All Stocks	Universe = All Stocks Cornerstone growth strategy	Difference
31-Dec-64	15.44%	18.15%	2.70%
31-Dec-65	15.63%	19.33%	3.71%
31-Dec-66	13.22%	17.36%	4.15%
31-Dec-67	18.05%	27.18%	9.13%
31-Dec-68	15.76%	26.99%	11.23%
31-Dec-69	11.09%	20.24%	9.15%
31-Dec-70	9.78%	18.51%	8.73%
31-Dec-71	8.92%	16.93%	8.01%
31-Dec-72	11.48%	21.32%	9.84%
31-Dec-73	6.22%	15.28%	9.06%
31-Dec-74	1.26%	8.50%	7.24%
31-Dec-75	3.72%	8.00%	4.27%
31-Dec-76	7.50%	11.09%	3.59%
31-Dec-77	4.56%	7.04%	2.48%
31-Dec-78	3.24%	6.14%	2.90%
31-Dec-79	8.53%	13.34%	4.82%
31-Dec-80	12.21%	19.31%	7.10%
31-Dec-81	10.25%	14.95%	4.70%
31-Dec-82	11.34%	16.52%	5.18%
31-Dec-83	17.82%	23.78%	5.96%
31-Dec-84	21.31%	27.85%	6.54%
31-Dec-85	19.20%	28.30%	9.10%
31-Dec-86	17.06%	26.79%	9.73%
31-Dec-87	16.13%	23.17%	7.04%
31-Dec-88	17.03%	22.38%	5.35%
31-Dec-89	15.85%	21.00%	5.14%
31-Dec-90	11.06%	14.86%	3.80%
31-Dec-91	14.65%	20.86%	6.21%
31-Dec-92	13.81%	19.80%	5.99%
31-Dec-93	12.74%	19.58%	6.83%
31-Dec-94	12.74%	19.17%	6.42%
Arithmetic average	12.18%	18.51%	6.33%

Table 19-8. Compound annual rates of return by decade.

Portfolio	1950s*	1960s	1970s	1980s	1990s**
All Stocks	20.12%	11.09%	8.53%	15.85%	9.09%
Cornerstone growth stocks from All Stocks	19.09%	20.24%	13.34%	21.00%	17.79%

*Returns for 1955–1959.

**Returns for 1990–1994.

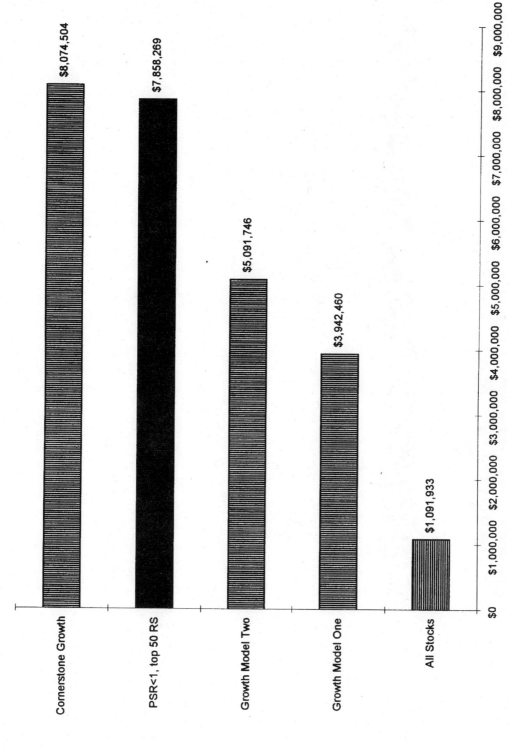

Figure 19-1. December 31, 1994, value of $10,000 invested on December 31, 1954, and annually rebalanced.

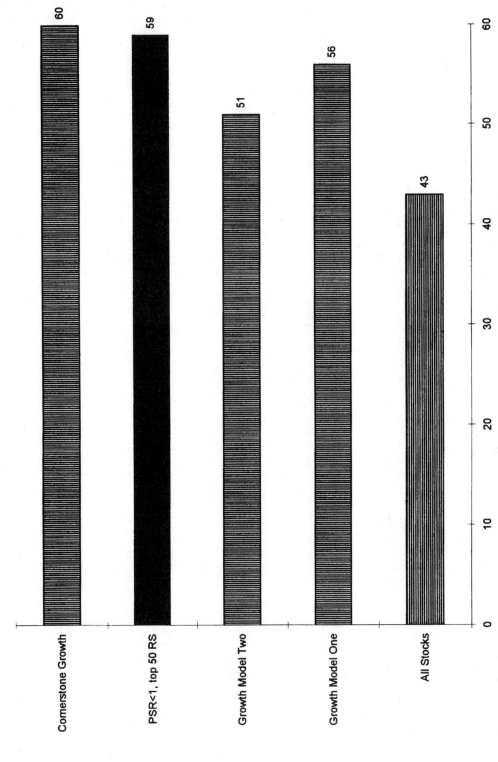

Figure 19-2. Sharpe risk-adjusted return ratios, 1954–1994. (Higher is better.)

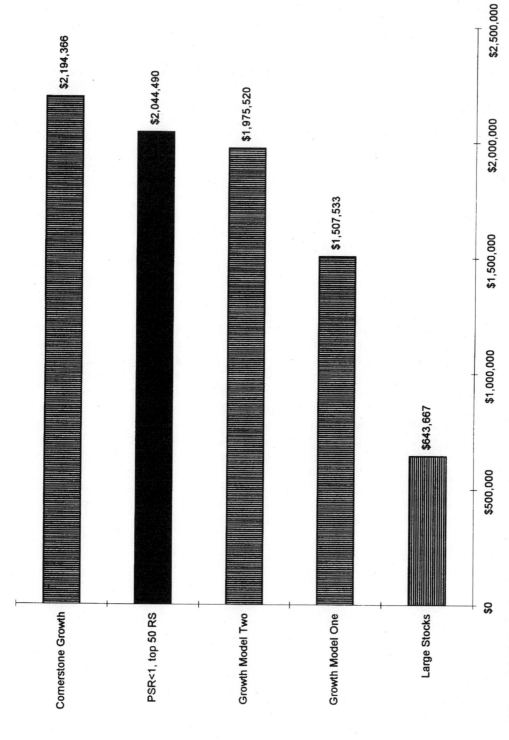

Figure 19-3. December 31, 1994, value of $10,000 invested on December 31, 1954, and annually rebalanced. Strategies are used only on Large Stocks.

Growth Strategies Are Less
Effective with Large Stocks

We won't spend much time reviewing the Large Stocks version of these strategies, since you're much better off using the All Stocks universe when pursuing growth strategies. Figure 19-4 shows the 1994 value of $10,000 invested on December 31, 1954, in the strategies using the Large Stocks universe instead of All Stocks, and Figure 19-5 shows the Sharpe ratios. The strategies all beat the Large Stocks universe handily, yet it's pointless to limit yourself to big companies when buying growth stocks. Unlike the market leaders from the cornerstone value strategy, many growth stocks are young, smaller companies that aren't included in the Large Stocks universe. While these smaller stocks are riskier, the difference between the All Stocks and Large Stocks versions of the strategy make it clear you're well compensated for the additional risk.

Implications

If you can tolerate higher risk, you can beat the market with a strategy like cornerstone growth. It's worth noting that our best growth strategy includes a low price-to-sales requirement, traditionally a value factor. The best time to buy growth stocks is when they are cheap, not when the investment herd is clamoring to buy. This strategy will never buy a Netscape or Genetech or Polaroid at 165 times earnings. That's why it works so well. It forces you to buy stocks just when the market realizes the companies have been overlooked. That's the beauty of using relative strength as your final factor. It gets you to buy just as the market is embracing the stocks, while the price-to-sales constraint ensures that they are still reasonably priced. Indeed, the evidence in this book shows that *all* the most successful strategies include at least one value factor, keeping investors from paying too much for a stock.

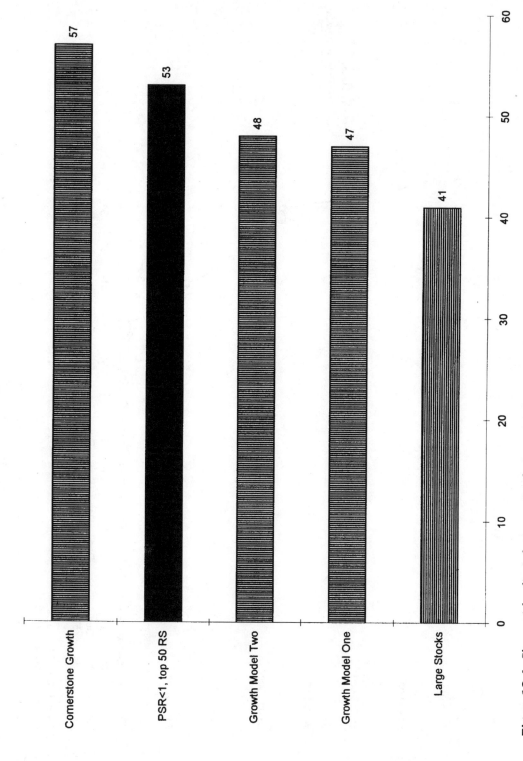

Figure 19-4. Sharpe risk-adjusted return ratios for Large Stocks version of strategies, 1954–1994. (Higher is better.)

Figure 19-5. Returns on Cornerstone Growth versus All Stocks, 1954-1994.
Year-end 1954 = $10,000.

20

Uniting Strategies for the Best Risk-Adjusted Performance

If you only keep adding little by little, it will soon become a big heap. —HESIOD

Thus far, we've looked only at results from one style or strategy. Yet the most effective way to diversify your portfolio and enhance risk-adjusted returns is to unite growth and value strategies. Joining growth with value substantially reduces the volatility of growth strategies and increases the capital appreciation potential of less volatile value strategies. It also ensures a diversified portfolio, giving you the chance to perform well regardless of what style is in favor on Wall Street.

Let's look at the returns of a portfolio that unites our cornerstone growth and value strategies. Here, we'll start on December 31, 1954, and split a $10,000 investment between cornerstone growth and cornerstone value, investing $5000 in each. We'll rebalance the portfolio annually so it always reflects a 50-50 split between the growth and value strategies. Obviously, investors who are nearer retirement will allocate less money to the growth strategy and younger investors might allocate more, but the 50-50 mix is a good example to study.

The Results

The united portfolio does almost five times as well as the All Stocks universe. Tables 20-1 and 20-2 compare the results with All Stocks. Table 20-3 shows the base rates. Starting on December 31, 1954, $10,000 invested in the combined growth and value cornerstone strategies grows to $4,887,389 by the end of 1994, a compound return of 16.74 percent. (An investment of $10,000 in All Stocks grows to $1,091,933 over the same period, a compound return of 12.45 percent.) The amazing thing is that the combined portfolio achieved this performance while taking *virtually the same risk as All Stocks!* The standard deviation for the united strategies was 19.94 percent, a scant 0.11 percent higher than All Stocks' 19.83 percent. This is extraordinary, accounting for a Sharpe ratio of 65, the highest seen to date.

Uniting the strategies gives us the best chance to beat the market in any given year. The combined strategies beat All Stocks in 33 of the 40 years of our test, or 83 percent of the time. Longer term, combining the strategies also hits a home run, with the united strategies beating All Stocks in 32 of the 36 rolling 5-year periods and 100 percent of the rolling 10-year periods.

The united strategies do so well in any given year because if one is coasting, the other is often soaring. Consider 1967, a frothy, speculative year. Had you invested only in the market-leading stocks from the cornerstone value strategy, you'd have gained 23.7 percent. That beat Large Stocks' return of 21.30 percent, but did only half as well as the All Stocks gain of 41.1 percent. By adding the cornerstone growth stocks, which soared 83.3 percent, you increase your overall return to 53.5 percent, beating both the All Stocks and Large Stocks groups. That's with *half* your portfolio safely invested in large, conservative market-leading companies paying high dividends.

Conversely, when growth stocks are getting clobbered, the conservative, high-yielding stocks from cornerstone value buffer the portfolio's performance. Cornerstone growth really suffered during the bear market of 1973–1975, but the market leaders from cornerstone value fared much better. Splitting your money between the two strategies allowed you to do better than both the Large and All Stocks universes during the 2-year debacle.

The United Strategy Also Outperforms Large Stocks

We used the All Stocks universe in our first comparison because it outperformed Large Stocks over time, so it's no surprise that the combined

Table 20-1. Annual performance for cornerstone growth and cornerstone value plus results of investing 50 percent of the portfolio into each strategy with annual rebalancing.

Year ending	All Stocks	Cornerstone value	Cornerstone growth	United
31-Dec-55	20.70%	28.10%	30.40%	29.25%
31-Dec-56	17.00%	14.80%	18.00%	16.40%
31-Dec-57	−7.10%	−13.50%	−17.90%	−15.70%
31-Dec-58	55.00%	44.90%	52.80%	48.85%
31-Dec-59	23.00%	9.60%	24.10%	16.85%
31-Dec-60	6.10%	−0.03%	12.60%	6.29%
31-Dec-61	31.20%	24.40%	51.10%	37.75%
31-Dec-62	−12.00%	−2.60%	−17.20%	−9.90%
31-Dec-63	18.00%	18.80%	20.80%	19.80%
31-Dec-64	16.30%	20.30%	30.00%	25.15%
31-Dec-65	22.60%	17.60%	44.10%	30.85%
31-Dec-66	−5.20%	−10.20%	−0.10%	−5.15%
31-Dec-67	41.10%	23.70%	83.30%	53.50%
31-Dec-68	27.40%	26.50%	50.50%	38.50%
31-Dec-69	−18.50%	−15.00%	−28.10%	−21.55%
31-Dec-70	−5.80%	11.30%	−2.60%	4.35%
31-Dec-71	21.30%	15.80%	32.10%	23.95%
31-Dec-72	11.00%	14.00%	19.70%	16.85%
31-Dec-73	−27.20%	−5.90%	−27.50%	−16.70%
31-Dec-74	−27.90%	−12.30%	−29.10%	−20.70%
31-Dec-75	55.90%	58.20%	37.60%	47.90%
31-Dec-76	35.60%	39.20%	32.50%	35.85%
31-Dec-77	6.90%	3.30%	26.40%	14.85%
31-Dec-78	12.20%	3.30%	38.30%	20.80%
31-Dec-79	34.30%	25.60%	38.70%	32.15%
31-Dec-80	31.50%	20.30%	62.70%	41.50%
31-Dec-81	1.70%	12.80%	−9.00%	1.90%
31-Dec-82	22.50%	19.60%	37.10%	28.35%
31-Dec-83	28.10%	38.60%	32.70%	35.65%
31-Dec-84	−3.40%	4.70%	−2.00%	1.35%
31-Dec-85	30.80%	35.00%	42.50%	38.75%
31-Dec-86	13.10%	20.60%	17.70%	19.15%
31-Dec-87	−1.30%	11.60%	−5.40%	3.10%
31-Dec-88	21.20%	26.50%	29.70%	28.10%
31-Dec-89	21.40%	37.60%	23.80%	30.70%
31-Dec-90	−13.80%	−7.00%	−3.30%	−5.15%
31-Dec-91	39.80%	36.90%	51.40%	44.15%
31-Dec-92	13.80%	11.60%	25.50%	18.55%
31-Dec-93	16.60%	20.40%	30.30%	25.35%
31-Dec-94	−3.40%	4.80%	−5.30%	−0.25%
Arithmetic average	14.26%	15.85%	21.22%	18.53%
Standard deviation of return	19.83%	16.76%	25.99%	19.94%

Table 20-2. Summary return results for cornerstone growth and cornerstone value plus results of investing 50 percent of the portfolio into each strategy with annual rebalancing: December 31, 1954–December 31, 1994.

	All Stocks	Cornerstone value	Cornerstone growth	United
Arithmetic average	14.26%	15.85%	21.22%	18.53%
Standard deviation of return	19.83%	16.76%	25.99%	19.94%
Sharpe risk-adjusted ratio	43.00	61.00	60.00	65.00
3-yr compounded	8.63%	12.09%	15.69%	14.02%
5-yr compounded	9.09%	12.38%	17.79%	15.17%
10-yr compounded	12.74%	18.95%	19.17%	19.18%
15-yr compounded	13.55%	18.86%	19.92%	19.63%
20-yr compounded	16.95%	20.17%	23.43%	22.10%
25-yr compounded	11.51%	16.73%	17.24%	17.31%
30-yr compounded	11.47%	15.05%	18.24%	17.03%
35-yr compounded	11.39%	14.55%	18.09%	16.68%
40-yr compounded	12.45%	14.62%	18.22%	16.74%
Compound annual return	12.45%	14.62%	18.22%	16.74%
$10,000 becomes	$1,091,933.00	$2,347,560.00	$8,074,504.00	$4,887,389.29
Maximum return	55.90%	58.20%	83.30%	53.50%
Minimum return	−27.90%	−15.00%	−29.10%	−21.55%
Maximum expected return*	53.92%	49.38%	73.20%	58.41%
Minimum expected return**	−25.39%	−17.68%	−30.75%	−21.34%

*Maximum expected return is average return plus 2 times the standard deviation.
**Minimum expected return is average return minus 2 times the standard deviation.

Table 20-3. Base rates for All Stocks and combined cornerstone growth and value strategies, 1954–1994.

Item	United cornerstone strategies beat All Stocks	Percent
Single-year return	33 out of 40	83%
Rolling 5-year compound return	32 out of 36	89%
Rolling 10-year compound return	31 out of 31	100%

strategies also handily beat Large Stocks. Tables 20-4 and 20-5 compare the united strategies with the Large Stocks universe. In all instances, the combined portfolio did vastly better than Large Stocks. Table 20-6 shows the base rates, with the united growth and value strategy beating Large Stocks in 34 of the 40 1-year periods, and 100 percent of the time over rolling 5- and 10-year periods.

Implications

Table 20-7 compares the returns of the united cornerstone strategies with the All and Large Stocks universes by decade, and Tables 20-8 and 20-9 show the rolling 5- and 10-year returns versus All Stocks. The results are charted in Figures 20-1 and 20-2. This is truly an impressive strategy. Uniting growth and value stocks is the best way to diversify your portfolio and improve your risk-adjusted return. The 50-50 split is most appropriate for younger investors with average risk tolerance. As retirement approaches, you should reduce the amount of money you allocate to the growth strategy and increase the allocation to the more conservative stocks from cornerstone value. Other than for investors *very* near retirement, *all* investors benefit from diversifying their investments by style. Even the *most* aggressive younger investors should have some money in the cornerstone value strategy, bolstering the portfolio during the inevitable periods when larger stocks outperform their smaller brethren from cornerstone growth.

Higher returns at reduced levels of risk is the most important thing style diversification achieves. Wall Streeters often joke that you should decide how to invest on the basis of whether you want to eat well or sleep well. Splitting your portfolio between growth and value strategies lets you do both, because it provides vastly higher absolute returns than the market at similar levels of risk.

Table 20-4. Annual performance of strategies versus the Large Stocks universe.

Year ending	Large Stocks	Cornerstone value	Cornerstone growth	United
31-Dec-55	21.20%	28.10%	30.40%	29.25%
31-Dec-56	9.60%	14.80%	18.00%	16.40%
31-Dec-57	−6.90%	−13.50%	−17.90%	−15.70%
31-Dec-58	42.10%	44.90%	52.80%	48.85%
31-Dec-59	9.90%	9.60%	24.10%	16.85%
31-Dec-60	4.80%	−0.03%	12.60%	6.29%
31-Dec-61	27.50%	24.40%	51.10%	37.75%
31-Dec-62	−8.90%	−2.60%	−17.20%	−9.90%
31-Dec-63	19.50%	18.80%	20.80%	19.80%
31-Dec-64	15.30%	20.30%	30.00%	25.15%
31-Dec-65	16.20%	17.60%	44.10%	30.85%
31-Dec-66	−4.90%	−10.20%	−0.10%	−5.15%
31-Dec-67	21.30%	23.70%	83.30%	53.50%
31-Dec-68	16.80%	26.50%	50.50%	38.50%
31-Dec-69	−9.90%	−15.00%	−28.10%	−21.55%
31-Dec-70	−0.20%	11.30%	−2.60%	4.35%
31-Dec-71	17.30%	15.80%	32.10%	23.95%
31-Dec-72	14.90%	14.00%	19.70%	16.85%
31-Dec-73	−18.90%	−5.90%	−27.50%	−16.70%
31-Dec-74	−26.70%	−12.30%	−29.10%	−20.70%
31-Dec-75	43.10%	58.20%	37.60%	47.90%
31-Dec-76	28.00%	39.20%	32.50%	35.85%
31-Dec-77	−2.50%	3.30%	26.40%	14.85%
31-Dec-78	8.10%	3.30%	38.30%	20.80%
31-Dec-79	27.30%	25.60%	38.70%	32.15%
31-Dec-80	30.80%	20.30%	62.70%	41.50%
31-Dec-81	0.60%	12.80%	−9.00%	1.90%
31-Dec-82	19.90%	19.60%	37.10%	28.35%
31-Dec-83	23.80%	38.60%	32.70%	35.65%
31-Dec-84	−0.40%	4.70%	−2.00%	1.35%
31-Dec-85	19.50%	35.00%	42.50%	38.75%
31-Dec-86	32.20%	20.60%	17.70%	19.15%
31-Dec-87	3.30%	11.60%	−5.40%	3.10%
31-Dec-88	19.00%	26.50%	29.70%	28.10%
31-Dec-89	26.00%	37.60%	23.80%	30.70%
31-Dec-90	−8.70%	−7.00%	−3.30%	−5.15%
31-Dec-91	33.00%	36.90%	51.40%	44.15%
31-Dec-92	8.70%	11.60%	25.50%	18.55%
31-Dec-93	16.30%	20.40%	30.30%	25.35%
31-Dec-94	−1.90%	4.80%	−5.30%	−0.25%
Arithmetic average	12.15%	15.85%	21.22%	18.53%
Standard deviation of return	15.88%	16.76%	25.99%	19.94%

Table 20-5. Summary return results for strategies versus Large Stocks universe: December 31, 1954–December 31, 1994.

	Large Stocks	Cornerstone value	Cornerstone growth	United
Arithmetic average	12.15%	15.85%	21.22%	18.53%
Standard deviation of return	15.88%	16.76%	25.99%	19.94%
Sharpe risk-adjusted ratio	41.00	61.00	60.00	65.00
3-yr compounded	7.44%	12.09%	15.69%	14.02%
5-yr compounded	8.53%	12.38%	17.79%	15.17%
10-yr compounded	13.93%	18.95%	19.17%	19.18%
15-yr compounded	14.03%	18.86%	19.92%	19.63%
20-yr compounded	15.42%	20.17%	23.43%	22.10%
25-yr compounded	11.16%	16.73%	17.24%	17.31%
30-yr compounded	10.48%	15.05%	18.24%	17.03%
35-yr compounded	10.54%	14.55%	18.09%	16.68%
40-yr compounded	10.97%	14.62%	18.22%	16.74%
Compound annual return	10.97%	14.62%	18.22%	16.74%
$10,000 becomes	$643,667.01	$2,347,560.00	$8,074,504.00	$4,887,389.29
Maximum return	43.10%	58.20%	83.30%	53.50%
Minimum return	−26.70%	−15.00%	−29.10%	−21.55%
Maximum expected return*	43.90%	49.38%	73.20%	58.41%
Minimum expected return**	−19.60%	−17.68%	−30.75%	−21.34%

*Maximum expected return is average return plus 2 times the standard deviation.
**Minimum expected return is average return minus 2 times the standard deviation.

Table 20-6. Base rates for Large Stocks and united growth and value cornerstone strategies, 1954–1994.

Item	United cornerstone strategies beat Large Stocks	Percent
Single-year return	34 out of 40	85%
Rolling 5-year compound return	36 out of 36	100%
Rolling 10-year compound return	31 out of 31	100%

Table 20-7. Compound annual rates of return by decade.

Portfolio	1950s*	1960s	1970s	1980s	1990s**
Large Stocks	14.07%	8.99%	6.99%	16.89%	8.53%
United cornerstone growth and value strategies	17.14%	15.14%	13.91%	21.93%	15.17%
All Stocks	20.12%	11.09%	8.53%	15.85%	9.09%

*Returns for 1955–1959.
**Returns for 1990–1994.

Table 20-8. Rolling 5-year returns, united cornerstone growth and value strategies versus All Stocks.

5 years ending	All Stocks	United cornerstone strategies	Difference
31-Dec-59	20.12%	17.14%	−2.98%
31-Dec-60	17.07%	12.65%	−4.42%
31-Dec-61	19.78%	16.51%	−3.27%
31-Dec-62	18.49%	18.07%	−0.42%
31-Dec-63	12.20%	13.05%	0.85%
31-Dec-64	10.95%	14.61%	3.67%
31-Dec-65	14.20%	19.48%	5.28%
31-Dec-66	7.02%	10.89%	3.87%
31-Dec-67	17.61%	23.36%	5.74%
31-Dec-68	19.43%	26.99%	7.56%
31-Dec-69	11.23%	15.66%	4.43%
31-Dec-70	5.52%	10.54%	5.02%
31-Dec-71	10.85%	16.62%	5.77%
31-Dec-72	5.66%	10.43%	4.77%
31-Dec-73	−5.53%	−0.25%	5.28%
31-Dec-74	−7.81%	−0.03%	7.78%
31-Dec-75	1.96%	7.19%	5.23%
31-Dec-76	4.26%	9.17%	4.92%
31-Dec-77	3.47%	8.80%	5.32%
31-Dec-78	12.82%	17.19%	4.37%
31-Dec-79	27.77%	29.80%	2.20%
31-Dec-80	23.49%	28.65%	5.16%
31-Dec-81	16.59%	21.46%	4.87%
31-Dec-82	19.81%	24.19%	4.38%
31-Dec-83	23.03%	27.11%	4.08%
31-Dec-84	15.18%	20.54%	5.35%
31-Dec-85	15.06%	20.06%	5.00%
31-Dec-86	17.53%	23.88%	6.35%
31-Dec-87	12.56%	18.57%	6.01%
31-Dec-88	11.32%	17.22%	5.90%
31-Dec-89	16.53%	23.33%	6.81%
31-Dec-90	7.20%	14.30%	7.10%
31-Dec-91	11.84%	18.74%	6.89%
31-Dec-92	15.07%	22.10%	7.03%
31-Dec-93	14.19%	21.57%	7.38%
31-Dec-94	9.09%	15.17%	6.09%
Arithmetic average	12.65%	17.08%	4.42%

Table 20-9. Rolling 10-year returns, united cornerstone growth and value strategies versus All Stocks.

10 years ending	All Stocks	United cornerstone strategies	Difference
31-Dec-64	15.44%	15.87%	0.43%
31-Dec-65	15.63%	16.01%	0.39%
31-Dec-66	13.22%	13.66%	0.45%
31-Dec-67	18.05%	20.68%	2.63%
31-Dec-68	15.76%	19.82%	4.06%
31-Dec-69	11.09%	15.14%	4.05%
31-Dec-70	9.78%	14.93%	5.15%
31-Dec-71	8.92%	13.72%	4.80%
31-Dec-72	11.48%	16.71%	5.24%
31-Dec-73	6.22%	12.55%	6.33%
31-Dec-74	1.26%	7.53%	6.27%
31-Dec-75	3.72%	8.85%	5.13%
31-Dec-76	7.50%	12.84%	5.33%
31-Dec-77	4.56%	9.61%	5.05%
31-Dec-78	3.24%	8.12%	4.88%
31-Dec-79	8.53%	13.91%	5.38%
31-Dec-80	12.21%	17.43%	5.22%
31-Dec-81	10.25%	15.15%	4.90%
31-Dec-82	11.34%	16.24%	4.90%
31-Dec-83	17.82%	22.05%	4.23%
31-Dec-84	21.31%	25.08%	3.77%
31-Dec-85	19.20%	24.28%	5.08%
31-Dec-86	17.06%	22.66%	5.61%
31-Dec-87	16.13%	21.35%	5.22%
31-Dec-88	17.03%	22.06%	5.03%
31-Dec-89	15.85%	21.93%	6.07%
31-Dec-90	11.06%	17.15%	6.09%
31-Dec-91	14.65%	21.28%	6.63%
31-Dec-92	13.81%	20.32%	6.51%
31-Dec-93	12.74%	19.37%	6.63%
31-Dec-94	12.74%	19.18%	6.44%
Arithmetic average	12.18%	16.95%	4.77%

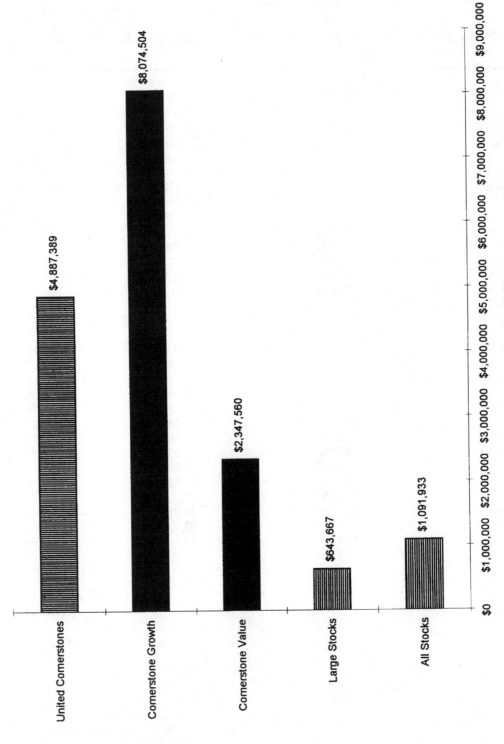

Figure 20-1. December 31, 1994, value of $10,000 invested on December 31, 1954.

Figure 20-2. Sharpe risk-adjusted return rankings, 1954–1994. (Higher is better.)

21
Ranking the Strategies

I know of no way of judging of the future but by
the past.   —PATRICK HENRY

It's time to rank all the strategies' returns on both an absolute and a
risk-adjusted basis. Several of our strategies use 5-year variables, so for
simplicity's sake we'll compare returns starting December 31, 1954.
(Because of the missing 3 years, the numbers are often different from
those in the individual chapters.) While the rankings may differ
slightly, the same lessons emerge.

The Results

Forty years of data prove that the market follows a purposeful stride,
not a random walk. The stock market consistently rewards some strategies and consistently punishes others. The strategies found near the top
or the bottom of our list possess similar attributes that are easily iden-
tified. Each of the five best-performing strategies, for example, include
a relative strength criterion. All but one of the five worst-performing
strategies buy stocks that investors have bid to unsustainable prices,
giving them astronomical price-to-earnings, price-to-book, price-to-
sales, or price-to-cashflow ratios. These factors usually reflect high
hopes on the part of investors. History shows that high hopes are

dashed, and that investors are better off buying reasonably priced stocks with good relative strength.

All the best-performing strategies are riskier than the market as a whole, but a handful do *much better* than the market while taking only slightly more risk. Most of the *worst*-performing strategies are actually riskier than the best-performing strategies. The results prove that the market doesn't always award high returns to portfolios with higher risk.

Absolute Returns

Table 21-1 ranks all the strategies by absolute return, and Figures 21-1 and 21-2 show the five best and worst performers. The cornerstone growth strategy, which buys stocks with persistent earnings gains, low price-to-sales ratios, and strong relative strength, was the best-performing of all the strategies. It turned $10,000 invested on December 31, 1954, into $8,074,504 by the end of 1994, a compound return of 18.22 percent. Again, note that the top five strategies buy stocks with the best relative price strength. Relative strength is one of the criteria in all top 10 performing strategies, proving the maxim that you should never fight the tape.

Fighting the tape leads to our worst-performing strategy, which buys the 50 stocks from All Stocks with the worst 1-year price performance: $10,000 invested in these stocks on December 31, 1954, and annually rebalanced was worth just $20,231 by the end of 1994, a pathetic return of 1.78 percent a year! Heed the market's advice and avoid last year's biggest losers.

The other four losing strategies buy stocks whose prices have been pushed to unsustainable levels by investors' huge expectations. This is reflected by the stocks' high multiples. With strategies like cornerstone growth available, there's no reason to buy stocks with the highest price-to-earnings, price-to-book, price-to-sales, or price-to-cashflow ratio. The odds for such stocks are about as bad as the story is good. Investors who buy these stocks always brag about the handful that work out and conveniently forget the majority that don't. The evidence is painfully clear—if you habitually buy stocks with good stories but the highest multiples, you'll do much worse than the market.

In the absence of stories, investors look at the base rates. But let one Netscape in the door, and many investors will jettison common sense and sound research, believing it's different this time. It isn't.

Table 21-1. Summary returns for all strategies, 1954–1994, ranked by absolute return.

Strategy	$10,000 becomes	Compound return	Standard deviation	Sharpe ratio
Cornerstone growth, All Stocks	$8,074,504	18.22%	25.99%	60
PSR<1, high rel. str., All Stocks	$7,858,269	18.14%	26.22%	59
Pbook<1, high rel. str., All Stocks	$5,862,803	17.27%	23.65%	59
EPS up 5 yrs in a row, best rel. str., All Stocks	$5,091,746	16.86%	28.69%	51
ROE>15, high rel. str., All Stocks	$4,947,751	16.78%	27.23%	52
United cornerstone strategies	$4,887,389	16.74%	19.94%	65
PE<20, high rel. str., All Stocks	$4,745,447	16.66%	26.71%	53
Yield>mean, positive rel. str., lowest PSR, All Stocks	$3,952,426	16.12%	22.49%	56
5-yr EPS ch>mean, Pmargin>mean, EPS up 5 yrs in a row, best rel. str., All Stocks	$3,942,460	16.12%	22.71%	56
1-yr EPS ch>25%, high rel. str., All Stocks	$3,866,729	16.06%	29.04%	48
Low PSR, All Stocks	$3,099,258	15.42%	26.17%	48
Pbook<1.5, yield>mean, PE<mean, lowest PCfl, All Stocks	$3,047,216	15.37%	23.38%	51
Market leaders, high yield	$2,347,590	14.62%	16.76%	61
Cornerstone value	$2,347,590	14.62%	16.76%	61
EPS up 5 yrs in a row, PSR<1.5, high rel. str., Large Stocks	$2,194,366	14.43%	17.89%	57
Low Pbook, All Stocks	$2,156,845	14.38%	25.63%	45
PE<20, high rel. str., Large Stocks	$2,068,256	14.26%	19.19%	53
PSR<1, high rel. str., Large Stocks	$2,044,490	14.23%	19.22%	53
EPS up 5 yrs in a row, high rel. str., Large Stocks	$1,975,520	14.13%	22.23%	48
Low PCfl, Large Stocks	$1,928,230	14.06%	20.11%	50
Market leaders, low PE	$1,909,245	14.03%	20.21%	50
High 1-yr rel. str., All Stocks	$1,905,842	14.03%	30.28%	41
Low Pbook, Large Stocks	$1,887,298	14.00%	19.79%	51
High 1-yr rel. str., Large Stocks	$1,832,764	13.91%	22.75%	46
Low PCfl, All Stocks	$1,628,222	13.58%	25.53%	42
5-yr EPS ch>mean, Pmargin>mean, EPS up 5 yrs in a row, best rel. str., Large Stocks	$1,507,533	13.36%	20.14%	47

(Continued)

Table 21-1. Summary returns for all strategies, 1954–1994, ranked by absolute return. (*Continued*)

Strategy	$10,000 becomes	Compound return	Standard deviation	Sharpe ratio
Low PSR, Large Stocks	$1,437,221	13.22%	20.79%	46
Low PE, Large Stocks	$1,281,467	12.90%	20.88%	44
ROE>15, high rel. str., Large Stocks	$1,275,027	12.89%	22.08%	42
High yield, Large Stocks	$1,203,091	12.72%	16.99%	49
All Stocks	*$1,091,933*	*12.45%*	*19.83%*	*43*
$25M<capitalization<$100M	$1,010,388	12.23%	24.70%	38
High ROE, All Stocks	$968,912	12.11%	26.40%	36
$100M<capitalization<$250M	$833,784	11.69%	20.14%	39
$250M<capitalization<$500M	$793,780	11.56%	17.53%	42
Low 1-yr EPS gain, All Stocks	$789,115	11.54%	23.99%	36
Low 1-yr EPS gain, Large Stocks	$715,222	11.27%	17.98%	39
Low PE, All Stocks	$693,695	11.18%	24.67%	33
Large Stocks	*$643,667*	*10.97%*	*15.88%*	*41*
High 1-yr EPS gain, All Stocks	$571,829	10.65%	26.85%	31
High yield, All Stocks	$571,479	10.64%	21.35%	33
High Pmargin, Large Stocks	$491,221	10.23%	15.96%	36
High Pmargin, All Stocks	$476,182	10.14%	21.18%	31
$500M<capitalization<$1bil.	$472,190	10.12%	16.12%	35
High ROE, Large Stocks	$461,177	10.05%	19.23%	32
Capitalization>$1bil.	$442,609	9.94%	15.52%	35
Market leaders, High PE	$439,913	9.92%	17.06%	33
High 5-yr EPS gain, Large Stocks	$371,937	9.46%	21.73%	28
High PCfl, Large Stocks	$369,021	9.44%	22.42%	27
High Pbook, Large Stocks	$367,914	9.43%	23.40%	27
High 5-yr EPS gain, All Stocks	$353,446	9.32%	27.07%	26
High PE, Large Stocks	$310,219	8.97%	20.79%	26
High PSR, Large Stocks	$296,993	8.85%	21.17%	25
Low 1-yr rel. str., Large Stocks	$294,769	8.83%	20.47%	25
High, 1-yr EPS gain, Large Stocks	$277,256	8.66%	19.14%	25
High PE, All Stocks	$254,601	8.43%	27.09%	23
High Pbook, All Stocks	$178,166	7.47%	29.04%	20
High PCfl, All Stocks	$138,791	6.80%	27.76%	17
High PSR, All Stocks	$50,910	4.15%	27.63%	8
Low 1-yr rel. str., All Stocks	$20,231	1.78%	26.76%	−1

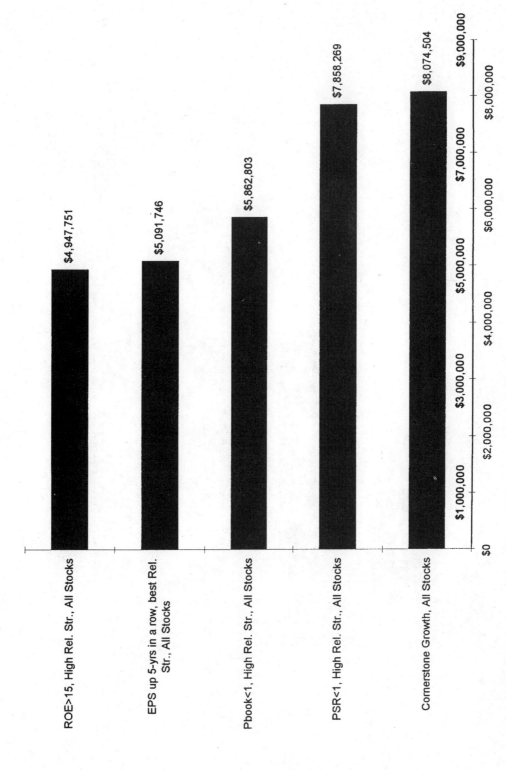

Figure 21-1. The five strategies with the highest absolute returns, 1954–1994.

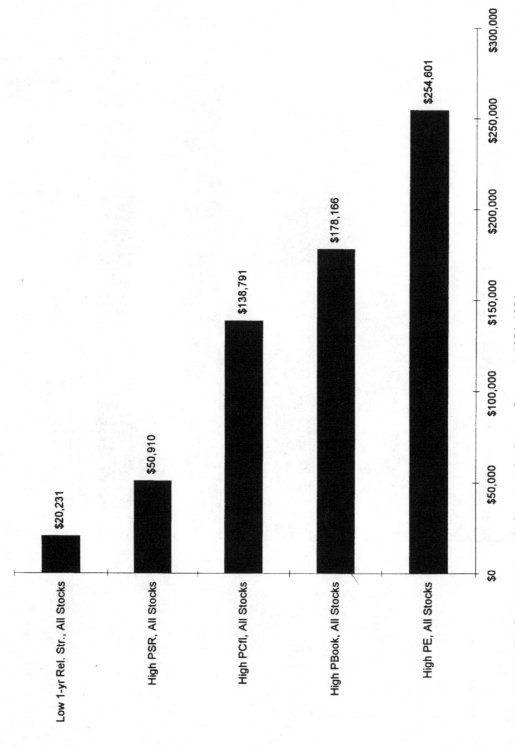

Figure 21-2. The five strategies with the worst absolute performance, 1954–1994.

Risk

Table 21-2 ranks the strategies by standard deviation, and Figures 21-3 and 21-4 show the five strategies with the highest and lowest risk. Buying the 50 best-performing stocks from All Stocks is the riskiest strategy, with a standard deviation of 30.28 percent. Such risk is unacceptable, but can be dramatically lowered by adding other factors. Three of the five strategies with the highest standard deviations offered good absolute performance, at least. The other two, stocks with high price-to-book ratios and high price-to-cashflow ratios, add insult to injury by giving investors both high risk *and* dismal returns.

All these strategies should be avoided, because the risk is too high. Indeed, you should never use a strategy with an annual standard deviation above 25 percent *unless* its performance is so fantastic that it pushes the Sharpe ratio well above All Stocks' ratio of 43. Unless the potential rewards are vastly higher than the market, the emotional toll of high-risk strategies outweighs their benefits. *No one* should invest an entire portfolio in the riskiest strategies, no matter how good their absolute return. You'll capitulate to your fears, usually near a strategy's bottom. This brings nothing but misery and will probably send you into the arms of the nearest index fund. The best use of high-risk strategies is to blend them with lower-risk ones, bringing overall risk to acceptable levels.

The five strategies with the lowest risk all come from the Large Stocks universe. The least risky buys the biggest stocks in the Compustat database, with market capitalizations above $1 billion. This strategy has a standard deviation of 15.52 percent. Of the five lowest-risk strategies, only cornerstone value—buying market leaders with high dividend yields—*also* provides high absolute returns. The cornerstone value strategy proves that investors needn't take huge risks to handily outperform the market, and the strategy should be used by anyone considering a large capitalization index fund.

Risk-Adjusted Return

Table 21-3 ranks the strategies by their Sharpe ratios, and Figures 21-5 and 21-6 show the five strategies with the best and worst risk-adjusted returns. This is the most important table of all, since it puts return into perspective. Buying the 50 stocks from All Stocks with the best relative strength is a good example. This strategy beats All Stocks on an absolute basis, but fails when risk is taken into account. Risk-adjusted

Table 21-2. Summary returns for all strategies, 1954–1994, ranked by risk.

Strategy	Standard deviation	$10,000 becomes	Compound return	Sharpe ratio
High 1-yr rel. str., All Stocks	30.28%	$1,905,842	14.03%	41
1-yr EPS ch>25%, high rel. str., All Stocks	29.04%	$3,866,729	16.06%	48
High Pbook, All Stocks	29.04%	$178,166	7.47%	20
EPS up 5 yrs in a row, best rel. str., All Stocks	28.69%	$5,091,746	16.86%	51
High PCfl, All Stocks	27.76%	$138,791	6.80%	17
High PSR, All Stocks	27.63%	$50,910	4.15%	8
ROE>15, high rel. str., All Stocks	27.23%	$4,947,751	16.78%	52
High PE, All Stocks	27.09%	$254,601	8.43%	23
High 5-yr EPS gain, All Stocks	27.07%	$353,446	9.32%	26
High 1-yr EPS gain, All Stocks	26.85%	$571,829	10.65%	31
Low 1-yr rel. str., All Stocks	26.76%	$20,231	1.78%	−1
PE<20, high rel. str., All Stocks	26.71%	$4,745,447	16.66%	53
High ROE, All Stocks	26.40%	$968,912	12.11%	36
PSR<1, high rel. str., All Stocks	26.22%	$7,858,269	18.14%	59
Low PSR, All Stocks	26.17%	$3,099,258	15.42%	48
Cornerstone growth, All Stocks	25.99%	$8,074,504	18.22%	60
Low Pbook, All Stocks	25.63%	$2,156,845	14.38%	45
Low PCfl, All Stocks	25.53%	$1,628,222	13.58%	42
$25M<capitalization<$100M	24.70%	$1,010,388	12.23%	38
Low PE, All Stocks	24.67%	$693,695	11.18%	33
Low 1-yr EPS gain, All Stocks	23.99%	$789,115	11.54%	36
Pbook<1, high rel. str., All Stocks	23.65%	$5,862,803	17.27%	59
High Pbook, Large Stocks	23.40%	$367,914	9.43%	27
Pbook<1.5, yield>mean, PE<mean, lowest PCfl, All Stocks	23.38%	$3,047,216	15.37%	51
High 1-yr rel. str., Large Stocks	22.75%	$1,832,764	13.91%	46
5-yr EPS ch>mean, Pmargin>mean, EPS up 5 yrs in a row, best rel. str., All Stocks	22.71%	$3,942,460	16.12%	56
Yield>mean, positive rel. str., lowest PSR, All Stocks	22.49%	$3,952,426	16.12%	56
High PCfl, Large Stocks	22.42%	$369,021	9.44%	27
EPS up 5 yrs in a row, high rel. str., Large Stocks	22.23%	$1,975,520	14.13%	48
ROE>15, high rel. str., Large Stocks	22.08%	$1,275,027	12.89%	42
High 5-yr EPS gain, Large Stocks	21.73%	$371,937	9.46%	28
High yield, All Stocks	21.35%	$571,479	10.64%	33
High Pmargin, All Stocks	21.18%	$476,182	10.14%	31
High PSR, Large Stocks	21.17%	$296,993	8.85%	25
Low PE, Large Stocks	20.88%	$1,281,467	12.90%	44
Low PSR, Large Stocks	20.79%	$1,437,221	13.22%	46

Table 21-2. Summary returns for all strategies, 1954–1994, ranked by risk. (*Continued*)

Strategy	Standard deviation	$10,000 becomes	Compound return	Sharpe ratio
High PE, Large Stocks	20.79%	$310,219	8.97%	26
Low 1-yr rel. str., Large Stocks	20.47%	$294,769	8.83%	25
Market leaders, low PE	20.21%	$1,909,245	14.03%	50
5-yr EPS ch>mean, Pmargin>mean, EPS up 5 yrs in a row, best rel. str., Large Stocks	20.14%	$1,507,533	13.36%	47
$100M<capitalization<$250M	20.14%	$833,784	11.69%	39
Low PCfl, Large Stocks	20.11%	$1,928,230	14.60%	50
United cornerstone strategies	19.94%	$4,887,389	16.74%	65
All Stocks	*19.83%*	*$1,091,933*	*12.45%*	*43*
Low Pbook, Large Stocks	19.79%	$1,887,298	14.00%	51
High ROE, Large Stocks	19.23%	$461,177	10.55%	32
PSR<1, high rel. str., Large Stocks	19.22%	$2,044,490	14.23%	53
PE<20, high rel. str., Large Stocks	19.19%	$2,068,256	14.26%	53
High 1-yr EPS gain, Large Stocks	19.14%	$277,256	8.66%	25
Low 1-yr EPS gain, Large Stocks	17.98%	$715,222	11.27%	39
EPS up 5 yrs in a row, PSR<1.5, high rel. str., Large Stocks	17.89%	$2,194,366	14.43%	57
$250M<capitalization<$500M	17.53%	$793,780	11.56%	42
Market leaders, high PE	17.06%	$439,913	9.92%	33
High yield, Large Stocks	16.99%	$1,203,091	12.72%	49
Market leaders, high yield	16.76%	$2,347,590	14.62%	61
Cornerstone value	16.76%	$2,347,590	14.62%	61
$500M<capitalization<$1bil.	16.12%	$472,190	10.12%	35
High Pmargin, Large Stocks	15.96%	$491,221	10.23%	36
Large Stocks	*15.88%*	*$643,667*	*10.97%*	*41*
Capitalization>$1bil.	15.52%	$442,609	9.94%	35

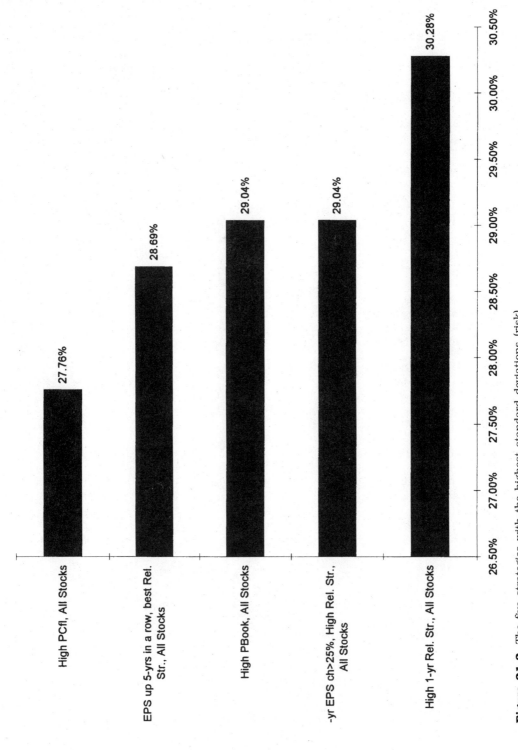

Figure 21-3. The five strategies with the highest standard deviations (risk), 1954–1994.

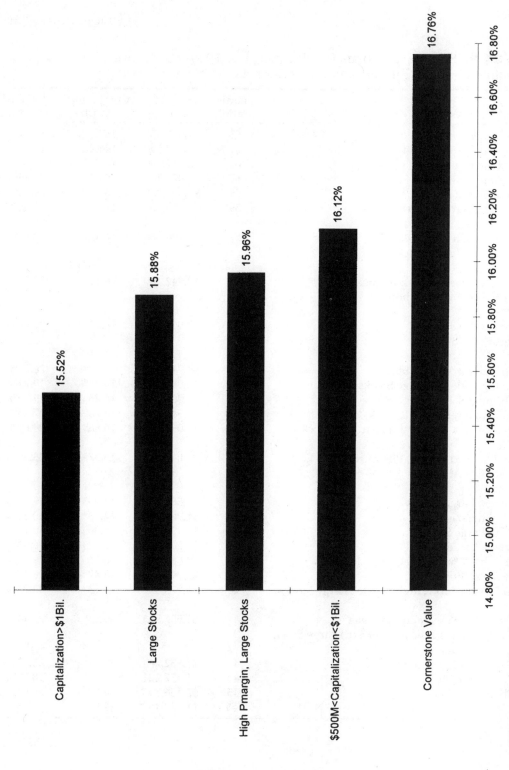

Figure 21-4. The five strategies with the lowest standard deviations (risk), 1954-1994.

Table 21-3. Summary returns for all strategies, 1954–1994, ranked by Sharpe risk-adjusted return ratio. (Higher is better.)

Strategy	Sharpe ratio	$10,000 becomes	Compound return	Standard deviation
United cornerstone strategies	65	$4,887,389	16.74%	19.94%
Market leaders, high yield	61	$2,347,590	14.62%	16.76%
Cornerstone value	61	$2,347,590	14.62%	16.76%
Cornerstone growth, All Stocks	60	$8,074,504	18.22%	25.99%
PSR<1, high rel. str., All Stocks	59	$7,858,269	18.14%	26.22%
Pbook<1, high rel. str., All Stocks	59	$5,862,803	17.27%	23.65%
EPS up 5 yrs in a row, PSR<1.5, high rel. str., Large Stocks	57	$2,194,366	14.43%	17.89%
5-yr EPS ch>mean, Pmargin>mean, EPS up 5 yrs in a row, best rel. str., All Stocks	56	$3,942,460	16.12%	22.71%
Yield>mean, positive rel. str., lowest PSR, All Stocks	56	$3,952,426	16.12%	22.49%
PE<20, high rel. str., All Stocks	53	$4,745,447	16.66%	26.71%
PSR<1, high rel. str., Large Stocks	53	$2,044,490	14.23%	19.22%
PE<20, high rel. str., Large Stocks	53	$2,068,256	14.26%	19.19%
ROE>15, high rel. str., All Stocks	52	$4,947,751	16.78%	27.23%
EPS up 5 yrs in a row, best rel. str., All Stocks	51	$5,091,746	16.86%	28.69%
Pbook<1.5, yield>mean, PE<mean, lowest PCfl, All Stocks	51	$3,047,216	15.37%	23.38%
Low Pbook, Large Stocks	51	$1,887,298	14.00%	19.79%
Market leaders, low PE	50	$1,909,245	14.03%	20.21%
Low PCfl, Large Stocks	50	$1,928,230	14.06%	20.11%
High yield, Large Stocks	49	$1,203,091	12.72%	16.99%
1-yr EPS ch>25%, high rel. str., All Stocks	48	$3,866,729	16.06%	29.04%
Low PSR, All Stocks	48	$3,099,258	15.42%	26.17%
EPS up 5 yrs in a row, high rel. str., Large Stocks	48	$1,975,520	14.13%	22.23%
5-yr EPS ch>mean, Pmargin>mean, EPS up 5 yrs in a row, best rel. str., Large Stocks	47	$1,507,533	13.36%	20.14%
High 1-yr rel. str., Large Stocks	46	$1,832,764	13.91%	22.75%
Low PSR, Large Stocks	46	$1,437,221	13.22%	20.79%
Low Pbook, All Stocks	45	$2,156,845	14.38%	25.63%
Low PE, Large Stocks	44	$1,281,467	12.90%	20.88%

Table 21-3. Summary returns for all strategies, 1954–1994, ranked by Sharpe risk-adjusted return ratio. (Higher is better.)   (*Continued*)

Strategy	Sharpe ratio	$10,000 becomes	Compound return	Standard deviation
All Stocks	*43*	*$1,091,933*	*12.45%*	*19.83%*
Low PCfl, All Stocks	42	$1,628,222	13.58%	25.53%
ROE>15, high rel. str., Large Stocks	42	$1,275,027	12.89%	22.08%
$250M<capitalization<$500M	42	$793,780	11.56%	17.53%
High 1-yr rel. str., All Stocks	41	$1,905,842	14.03%	30.28%
Large Stocks	*41*	*$643,667*	*10.97%*	*15.88%*
$100M<capitalization<$250M	39	$833,784	11.69%	20.14%
Low 1-yr EPS gain, Large Stocks	39	$715,222	11.27%	17.98%
$25M<capitalization<$100M	38	$1,010,388	12.23%	24.70%
High ROE, All Stocks	36	$968,912	12.11%	26.40%
Low 1-yr EPS gain, All Stocks	36	$789,115	11.54%	23.99%
High Pmargin, Large Stocks	36	$491,221	10.23%	15.96%
$500M<capitalization<$1bil.	35	$472,190	10.12%	16.12%
Capitalization>$1bil.	35	$442,609	9.94%	15.52%
Low PE, All Stocks	33	$693,695	11.18%	24.67%
High yield, All Stocks	33	$571,479	10.64%	21.35%
Market leaders, high PE	33	$439,913	9.92%	17.06%
High ROE, Large Stocks	32	$461,177	10.05%	19.23%
High 1-yr EPS gain, All Stocks	31	$571,829	10.65%	26.85%
High Pmargin, All Stocks	31	$476,182	10.14%	21.18%
High 5-yr EPS gain, Large Stocks	28	$371,937	9.46%	21.73%
High Pbook, Large Stocks	27	$367,914	9.43%	23.40%
High PCfl, Large Stocks	27	$369,021	9.44%	22.42%
High 5-yr EPS gain, All Stocks	26	$353,446	9.32%	27.07%
High PE, Large Stocks	26	$310,219	8.97%	20.79%
High PSR, Large Stocks	25	$296,993	8.85%	21.17%
Low 1-yr rel. str., Large Stocks	25	$294,769	8.83%	20.47%
High 1-yr EPS gain, Large Stocks	25	$277,256	8.66%	19.14%
High PE, All Stocks	23	$254,601	8.43%	27.09%
High Pbook, All Stocks	20	$178,166	7.47%	29.04%
High PCfl, All Stocks	17	$138,791	6.80%	27.76%
High PSR, All Stocks	8	$50,910	4.15%	27.63%
Low 1-yr rel. str., All Stocks	−1	$20,231	1.78%	26.76%

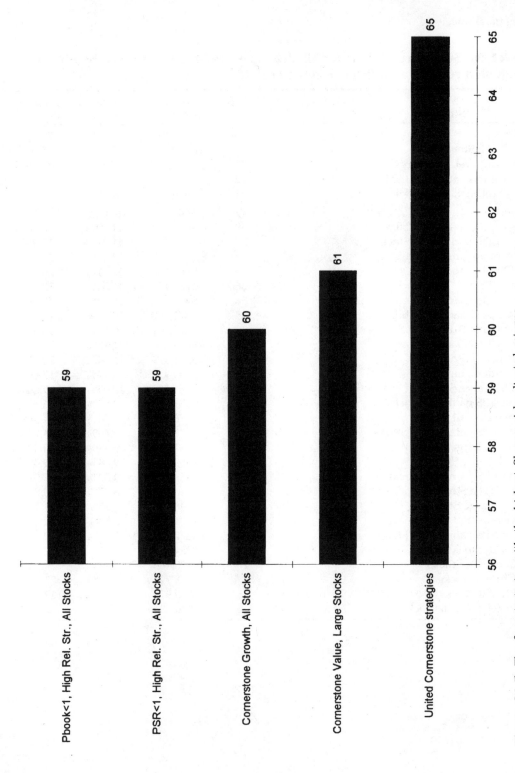

Figure 21-5. The five strategies with the highest Sharpe risk-adjusted returns, 1954–1994.

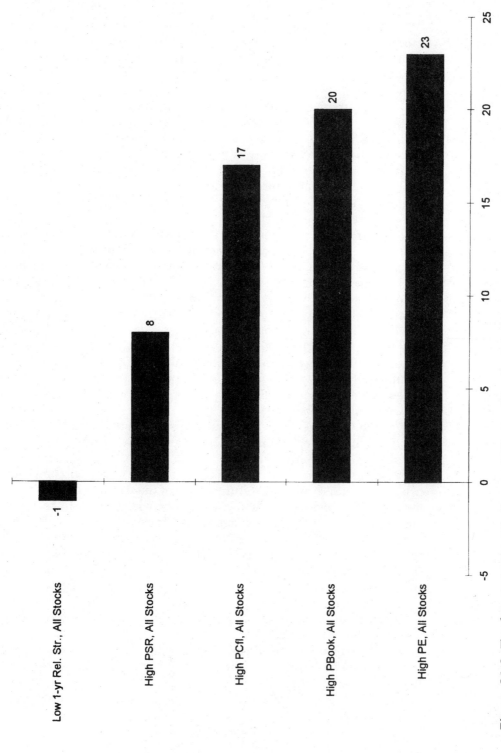

Figure 21-6. The five strategies with the worst Sharpe risk-adjusted returns, 1954–1994.

returns give you the best indication of whether a strategy is worth the inevitable hills and valleys, and teaches you how to get the most bang for your buck.

The united growth and value cornerstone strategies have the highest risk-adjusted return of all the strategies reviewed. This portfolio has a Sharpe ratio of 65, 50 percent higher than All Stocks' 43, yet the risk is the same as for the All Stocks universe. For investors with average risk tolerance, this united strategy is the best way to invest. It covers both growth and value strategies, and is an excellent way to diversify your portfolio. In second and third place are the individual value and growth cornerstone strategies. Rounding out the top five are strategies which marry relative strength to cheap stocks.

All the strategies with the best risk-adjusted returns include one or more value criteria. Value criteria act like a chaperone at a party, making sure you don't fall for some sexy stock with a great story. They may stop you from having some short-term fun, but over time they will keep you out of trouble by never letting you overpay for stocks. Except for the stocks selected by the cornerstone value strategy, most of the stocks picked by these top-performing strategies aren't household names. They choose stocks that are workhorses rather than show horses. There are plenty of buyers for stocks of companies that are continually written up in the major financial publications, and whose officers are treated like celebrities. That's what pushes their prices to levels that end up disappointing their investors. The workhorse stocks selected by most of the strategies with the highest risk-adjusted returns are non-sexy issues like Casey's General Stores. Don't look for the chairman on the cover of *Fortune* anytime soon!

You will, however, probably find magazine features on companies with the worst risk-adjusted returns. Four of the five worst-performing strategies buy stocks with the highest price-to-sales, price-to-cashflow, price-to-book, or price-to-earnings ratios. These glamour stocks command unreasonably high prices for their underlying businesses, and their investors believe that trees really *do* grow to the sky. These companies prices are based on hope, greed, or fantasies about a future that rarely comes to pass. Netscape, one of the hottest stocks of 1995, may be an excellent company, but is it worth 400 times *next year's* revenues? *It* may be, but the class of stocks with these characteristics are *not*, and investors should avoid them.

On a risk-adjusted basis, the *worst*-performing strategy is buying the 50 stocks from All Stocks with the worst 1-year price performance. The Sharpe ratio is *negative* because it fails to beat T-bills over the 40 years of our study. If you want to be a contrarian, buy stocks with low price-to-sales ratios. Avoid last year's biggest price losers at all costs—their record over the last 40 years is abysmal.

Implications

After you weigh risk, rewards, and long-term base rates, the best overall strategy is the united cornerstone growth and value portfolio. Over the 40 years studied, the strategy does nearly five times as well as All Stocks, with an annual compound return of 16.74 percent, some 4.29 percent higher than All Stocks' return of 12.45 percent a year. Yet the risk taken is virtually the same as for All Stocks. It's also extraordinarily consistent, beating All Stocks 83 percent of the time in any given year and 100 percent of the time over rolling 10-year periods.

The strategy achieves this performance with a portfolio diversified by style, with half its investments in large, market-leading stocks with high-dividend yields and half in stocks from All Stocks with persistent earnings gains, low price-to-sales ratios, and good relative strength.

If you use any of the other strategies, stick with the ones with the highest risk-adjusted returns and *always* look at the historical record if you are tempted to take a chance on a glamour stock trading at high multiples. It won't hurt to be reminded that most of those stocks crash and burn.

22

Getting the Most out of Your Equity Investments

To think is easy. To act is difficult. To act as one thinks is the most difficult of all.
—JOHANN WOLFGANG VON GOETHE

Investors can learn much from the Taoist concept of Wu Wei. Taoism is one of the three schools of Chinese philosophy that have guided thinkers for thousands of years. Literally, Wu Wei means "to act without action," but in spirit it means to let things occur as they are meant to occur. Don't try to put round pegs into square holes. Don't be more clever than you need to be, forever trying to square a circle. Understand the essence of a circle and use it as nature intended. The closest Western equivalent is Wittgenstein's maxim: "Don't look for the meaning: Look for the use!"

For investors, this means letting good strategies work. Don't second-guess them. Don't try to outsmart them. Don't abandon them because they're experiencing a rough patch. Understand the nature of what you're using and let it work. This is the hardest assignment of all. It's virtually impossible not to insert our ego into decisions, yet being dispassionate is the only way to beat the market over time. Following Ockham's Razor—which shows that most often, the simplest theory is the best—is almost impossible. We love to make the simple complex, follow the crowd, get seduced by the story about some hot stock, let our emotions dictate decisions, buy and sell on tips and hunches, and approach each investment decision on a case-by-case basis, with no underlying consistency or strategy. No wonder the S&P 500 beats 80 percent of traditionally managed mutual funds over the long term!

A Taoist story is illuminating: One day a man was standing at the edge of a pool at the bottom of a huge waterfall when he saw an old man tossed about in the turbulent water. He ran to rescue him, but by the time he got there the old man had climbed out onto the bank and was walking alone, singing to himself. The man was astonished and rushed up to the old man, questioning him about the secret of his survival. The old man said that it was nothing special. "I began to learn while very young, and grew up practicing it. Now, I'm certain of success. I go down with the water and come up with the water. I follow it and forget myself. The only reason I survive is because I don't struggle against the water's superior power."

The market is like the water, overpowering all who struggle against it and giving those who work with it a wonderful ride. But swimming lessons are in order. You can't just jump in; you need guidelines. Our study of the last 43 years suggest that to do well in the market, you must follow a prescribed course and:

Always Use Strategies

You'll get nowhere buying stocks just because they have a great story. Usually, these are the companies that have been the *worst* performers over the last 43 years. They're the stocks everyone talks about and wants to own. They often have sky-high price-to-earnings, price-to-book, and price-to-sales ratios. They're very appealing in the short term, but deadly over the long haul. You *must* avoid them. Always think in terms of overall strategies and not individual stocks. One company's data are *meaningless,* yet can be very convincing. If you can't use strategies and are inexorably drawn to the stock of the day, your returns suffer horribly in the long run. If, try as you might, you can't stick to a strategy, put the majority of your money in an index fund and treat the small amounts you put in story stocks as an entertainment expense.

Use Only Strategies Proven over the Long Term

When I started testing strategies several years ago, I thought a 10-year record was adequate to judge the effectiveness of a strategy. I was wrong. The long-term data prove that you need a minimum of 25 years when judging a strategy's effectiveness. More is even better. Buying stocks with high price-to-book ratios or high returns on equity appeared to work for as many as 15 years, but the fullness of time proves they aren't effective. Many years of data help you understand the peaks and valleys of a strategy. Attempting to use strategies that have not withstood the test of time will lead to great disappointment. Stocks change. Industries change. But the underlying reasons they are good investments remain the same. Only the fullness of time shows which are the most sound.

Invest Consistently

Consistency is the hallmark of great investors, separating them from everyone else. If you use even a mediocre strategy *consistently*, you'll beat almost all investors who jump in and out of the market, change tactics in midstream, and forever second-guess their decisions. Realistically consider your risk tolerance, plan your path, and then stick to it. You may have fewer stories to tell at parties, but you'll be among the most successful investors over the long term. Successful investing isn't alchemy; it's a simple matter of consistently using time-tested strategies and letting compounding work its magic.

Always Bet with the Base Rate

Base rates are boring, dull, and very worthwhile. Knowing how often a strategy beats the market and by how much is among the most useful information available to investors, yet few take advantage of it. You now have the numbers. Use them.

Never Use the Riskiest Strategies

There is no point in using the riskiest strategies. They will sap your will and make you abandon them, usually at their low. Given the number of highly effective strategies, always concentrate on those with the highest risk-adjusted returns.

Always Use More Than One Strategy

Unless you're near retirement and investing only in low-risk strategies, always diversify your portfolio by strategy. How much you allocate to each is a function of risk tolerance, but you should always have some growth and some value guarding you from the inevitable flow of fashion on Wall Street. Unite strategies so your portfolio can do much better than the overall market without taking more risk.

Use Multifactor Models

The single-factor models show that the market rewards certain characteristics while punishing others. Yet you're much better off using several factors to build your portfolios. Returns are higher and risk is lower. You should always make a stock pass several hurdles before investing.

Insist on Consistency

If you don't have the time to build your own portfolios and prefer investing in mutual funds, buy only those that stress consistency of style. Many fund managers follow a hit-or-miss, intuitive method of stock selection. They have no mechanism to reign in their emotions or ensure that their good ideas work. All too often their picks are based on hope rather than experience. You have no way to *really* know exactly how these funds are managing your money, or if their past performance is the result of a hot hand unguided by a coherent underlying strategy.

Don't bet with them. Buy one of the many funds on the basis of solid, rigorous strategies. If your fund doesn't clearly define its investment style, insist that it does. You should expect nothing less.

The Stock Market Is Not Random

Finally, the data prove that the stock market takes purposeful strides. Far from chaotic, random movement, the market consistently rewards specific strategies while punishing others. As Ben Graham requested, we now know the historical behavior of securities with defined characteristics. We must let history be our guide, using only those time-tested methods that have proved successful. We know what is valuable and we know what works on Wall Street. All that remains is to act upon this knowledge.

Appendix: Research Methodology

As a rule, I always look for what others ignore.
—MARSHALL McLUHAN

Data

Annual data are from Standard & Poor's Compustat database, including the research data file. The research file contains information on all companies removed from the database. Compustat PC Plus designates these files *C and *R. All data from 1950 through 1974 were uploaded to O'Shaughnessy Capital Management PCs from the Compustat mainframe. We accessed subsequent years using various Compustat PC Plus dataplates on CD.

Time Horizon

We examined the 44 years from December 31, 1950, to December 31, 1994. The use of time lags (to avoid look-ahead bias) forced us to start most tests as of December 31, 1951. Tests with 5-year inputs, such as 5-year earnings-per-share growth rates, required a starting point of December 31, 1954.

Universe

We include only stocks that could actually be purchased without a tremendous liquidity problem. We review both the "average" stock in the universe and Large Stocks in the universe. After consulting with institutional traders, we set a market capitalization of $150 million as a minimum for All Stocks. Inflation has caused a tremendous shift in nominal values since 1950, so we deflated the current value of $150 million back to 1950. We used a 5-year average of the deflated value of $150 million in each year and switched it every 5 years. Thus, these were the capitalization minimums:

December 31, 1951–December 31, 1954	$27 million
December 31, 1955–December 31, 1958	$27 million
December 31, 1959–December 31, 1963	$28 million
December 31, 1964–December 31, 1968	$31 million
December 31, 1969–December 31, 1973	$34 million
December 31, 1974–December 31, 1978	$44 million
December 31, 1979–December 31, 1983	$64 million
December 31, 1984–December 31, 1988	$97 million
December 31, 1989–December 31, 1993	$117 million

All stocks with a deflated market capitalization in excess of $150 million are included and are designated All Stocks in the book.

We also wanted to look at returns for which large stocks—the group from which many money managers select—were the universe. A simple way to achieve this was to require a stock's market capitalization to exceed the mean in any given year (Large Stocks). Generally, stocks with market capitalization in excess of the mean accounted for the upper 16 percent of the database by market capitalization, and stocks with market capitalization in excess of a deflated $150 million accounted for the upper 50 percent of the database.

Returns

Returns are calculated annually using the following formula:

$$\text{Total return} = (\text{PRCC[1y]}/\text{PRCC}) + (\text{DVPSX[1y]}/\text{PRCC})$$

where:

PRCC[1y] = year-end price of stock 1 year ahead of date of test

PRCC = price of stock at beginning of period when it qualified for inclusion in the portfolio

DVPSX[1y] = dividend actually paid in year of test

As an example, consider a stock that qualified for a low price-to-earnings screen on December 31, 1960. Total return for the period December 31, 1960, through December 31, 1961, would be calculated thus:

PRCC (price on December 31, 1960) = $10.00

PRCC[1y] (price on December 31, 1961) = $15.00

DVPSX[1y] (dividend *actually* paid in 1961) = $1.00

Thus:

$$(\$15.00/\$10.00-1) + (\$1.00/\$10.00) = 0.5 + 0.1 = 0.60$$

Or a gain of 60 percent for the year.

Returns were done on a year-by-year basis, and each year of the series was inspected for outliers. All portfolios, except in Chapter 4, contain 50 stocks. If a return for an individual stock was extreme or inconsistent with other data, it was removed. Since the dividend was not reinvested monthly, returns are slightly understated.

All stocks were equally weighted by dollar amount. Thus, if IBM was one selected stock and Terra Industries another, each would have the same amount of dollars invested (i.e., if we bought 10 stocks and invested a total of $100,000, $10,000 would be invested in each). Portfolios were not adjusted for any factor such as beta, industry, or geographical location.

Returns differ somewhat depending upon which Compustat data-plate (CD) you use. This happens because Standard & Poor's Compustat continually updates the data. A study to see if any material difference in returns occurred because of this irregularity found that over time, it was a wash.

Data Definitions

Annual data were lagged a minimum of 11 months to account for reporting delays and to avoid look-ahead bias. We used periods ranging from 11 months to 15 months because of the year-end, calendar nature of our data. This also allows the inclusion of stocks with fiscal years that are not December 31. Since we were making trading decisions only on each December 31, we had to decide what data were available *at that time.* Using several current Compustat data CDs, we studied when information became available in real-time and applied it to the historical record. Each data item's time lag is consistent with what we found examining current databases.

Here are the definitions of items, followed by time-lag information and their Compustat descriptor in parentheses.

Sales: Annual net sales, time-lagged by 15 months. (SALE[@yr(−15m)])

Common Shares Outstanding: The net number of all common shares outstanding at year-end, excluding Treasury shares and scrip. Adjusted for splits, lagged by 15 months. (CSHO[@yr(−15m)])

Common Equity Liquidating Value: The common shareholders' interest in a company in the event of liquidation of company assets.

Common equity is adjusted by the preferred stockholders' legal claims against the company. We used this as a proxy for book value. Time-lagged by 15 months. (CEQL[@yr(−15m)])

Income Before Extra Items: The income of a company after all expenses, including special items, income taxes, and minority interest but before provisions for common and/or preferred dividends. Does not reflect discontinued operations. Time-lagged in larger formulas. (IB)

Annual Dividend Per Share by Exdate: The cash dividends per share adjusted for all stock splits and stock dividends. This item excludes payments in preferred stock. All extra dividends are included. The current sources for the data are Interactive Data Service, Inc., and Standard & Poor's *Dividend Record*. Time-lagged by 15 months. (DVPSX[@yr(−11m)])

Annual Earnings Per Share, Excluding Extraordinary Items: Not restated, but adjusted by the adjustment factor for each year. Represents primary earnings per share before extraordinary items and discontinued operations. Time-lagged by 15 months. (EPSPX[@yr(−15m)])

Calendar Year Closing Price: Not lagged. (PRCC)

Pretax Income: Operating and nonoperating income before provisions for income tax and minority interest. Specifically excludes income from extraordinary items and discontinued operations. Annual figure, lagged in larger formulas. (PI)

Adjustment Factor: Ratio used to adjust all share data for splits. (AJEX)

Depreciation-Amortization: Noncash charges for obsolescence and wear and tear on property. Annual figure. (DP)

Formulas

All formulas use the above items as well as common ranking and averaging techniques. Most common formulas establish an average or rank items in descending order. Here are the definitions.

Averages are established using the @CAVG(X,SET) function. The function calculates the average value of an item or expression (X) over a set. This function returns a decimal.

For example, to obtain the average market capitalization of all the stocks in the Compustat database, the formula would be @CAVG((PRCC*CSHO[@yr(−15m)])), @SET(*C+*R,@ISVALUE((PRCC*CSHO[@yr(0m)]))). This tells the computer to calculate the average market capitalization for all items in the active (*C) and research (*R) databases that *have* a value for market capitalization—that is, it determines whether data exist for an item (@ISVALUE). The same @CAVG, @SET, and @ISVALUE formula is used to find the database average for all items, such as price-to-earnings, price-to-book, and price-to-sales.

Ranking items, such as the top 50 by dividend yield or the top 50 by sales-to-price ratio, is accomplished using Compustat's @RANK (X,SET) function. This function determines the relative rank of an entity in any item or expression (X) in a set. Entities are ranked in descending order. This function returns an integer. Thus, to get the top 50 stocks by price appreciation, the formula would read @RANK((PRCC/PRCC [−1y]), @SET(*C+*R)<51.

The @SET(base set, condition) selects entities for a set within an expression by analyzing a set (base set) according to the predetermined criterion.

Here's a *sample formula* that returns the 50 best-performing stocks from All Stocks that also have price-to-sales ratios below 1:

@IF(PSR1#AND#MK1#AND#@RANK((PRCC/PRCC[−1]),@SET(*C+*R,
PSR1#AND#MK1))<51,1.0,.0)

where:

PSR1 = (PRCC/(SALE/CSHO)[@yr(15m)])<1 establishes a price-to-sales ratio less than 1.
  MK1 = (PRCC*CSHO[@yr(−15m)])>117 establishes that all market capitalizations must exceed 117 million.

The 1.0,.0 at the end simply tells the program to include a stock if it meets all the criteria and exclude it if not. The <51 says we just want the top 50 by price appreciation.

Here are the formula definitions followed by the code written for Compustat PC Plus:

Market Capitalization: 12/31/yy price times common shares outstanding, lagged by 15 months. (PRCC*CSHO[@yr(−15m)])

Return on Equity: 100 times (IB divided by CEQL), lagged by 15 months. (100*(IB/CEQL)) used as (ROE[@yr(−15m)])

Annual Indicated Dividend Yield: DVPSX, lagged 11 months divided by PRCC. (DVPSX[@yr(−11m)]/PRCC)

Pretax Profit Margin: 100 times (PI divided by SALE), lagged by 15 months, called PPM. (PPM[@yr(−15m)])

Sales-to-Price Ratio: Annual sales per share, lagged by 15 months, divided by year-end price. ((SALE/CSHO)[@yr(−15m)]/PRCC)

Price-to-Sales Ratio: Year-end price, divided by annual sales data per share, lagged by 15 months. ((PRCC/(SALE/CSHO)[@yr(−15m)])

1-Year Earnings-Per-Share Gain: Change in earning per share compared with the year earlier figure, lagged by 15 months. (EPSPX/EPSPX[−1y])[@yr(−15m)]. Worst earnings-per-share changes were found using the inverse: (EPSPX[−1y]/EPSPX)[@yr(−15m)].

Earnings-to-Price Ratio: The inverse of the price-to-earnings ratio, with earnings lagged by 15 months. (EPSPX[@yr(−15m)]/PRCC)

Price-to-Earnings Ratio: (PRCC/EPSPX[@yr(−15m)])

Book-to-Price Ratio: The inverse of the price-to-book ratio, with book value lagged by 15 months. A simple book value was calculated by dividing common equity liquidating value (CEQL) by common shares outstanding. ((CEQL/CSHO)[@yr(−15m)]/PRCC)

Price-to-Book Ratio: ((PRCC/(CEQL/CSHO)[@yr(−15m)])

Cashflow: Income before extraordinary gains. CFL represents the income of a company after all expenses except provisions for common and preferred dividends plus depreciation, lagged by 15 months. (CFL = (IB + DP), CFL[@yr(−15m)])

Cashflow-to-Price Ratio: Cashflow, from above, divided by common shares outstanding, divided by price. ((CFL/CSHO)[@yr(−15m)]/PRCC)

Price-to-Cashflow Ratio: ((PRCC/(CFL/CSHO[@yr(−15m)])

1-Year Sales Gain: Change in sales compared with the year earlier figure, lagged by 15 months. (SALE/SALE[−1y])[@yr(−15m)]. Worst 1-year sales gains were obtained using (SALE[−1y]/SALE)[@yr(−15m)].

5-Year Compound Growth Rate for Earnings Per Share: Uses a Compustat function—@CGR—to calculate the 5-year compound growth rate for earnings per share. The function returns a percent. The first and last observations must be positive. ((@CGR(EPSPX,−5,0)[@yr(−15m)])

5-Year Compound Growth Rate for Sales: Uses a Compustat function—@CGR—to calculate the 5-year compound growth rate for sales. The function returns a percent. The first and last observations must be positive. ((@CGR(SALE,−5,0)[@yr(−15m)])

Annual Relative Strength: Excludes dividends and uses simple share price appreciation. (PRCC/PRCC[−1y]). Worst annual price appreciation is obtained by dividing this year's closing price by the previous year's. (PRCC[−1y]/PRCC)

Taxes, Commissions, and Market Impact Costs

These costs are not included in the data.

Bibliography

Ambachtsheer, Keith P., "The Persistence of Investment Risk," *The Journal of Portfolio Management,* Fall 1989, pp. 69–72.

Arnott, Robert D., Kelso, Charles M., Jr., Kiscadden, Stephan, and Macedo, Rosemary, "Forecasting Factor Returns: An Intriguing Possibility," *The Journal of Portfolio Management,* Fall 1990, pp. 28–35.

Banz, R., and Breen, W., "Sample-Dependent Results Using Accounting and Market Data: Some Evidence," *The Journal of Finance,* September 1986, pp. 779–793.

Barach, Roland, *Mind Traps: Mastering The Inner World of Investing,* Dow Jones-Irwin, Homewood, IL, 1988.

Basu, S., "The Relationship Between Earnings Yield, Market Value, and Return for NYSE Common Stocks: Further Evidence," *The Journal of Financial Economics,* June 1983, pp. 129–156.

Bell, David E., Raiffa, Howard, and Tversky, Amos, *Decision Making: Descriptive, Normative, and Prescriptive Interactions,* Cambridge University Press, Cambridge, England, 1988.

Bernstein, Peter L., *Capital Ideas: The Improbable Origins of Modern Wall Street,* The Free Press, New York, 1992.

Bjerring, James H., Lakonishok, Josef, and Vermaelen, Theo, "Stock Prices and Financial Analysts' Recommendations," *The Journal of Finance,* March 1983, pp. 187–204.

Blakney, R. B., *The Way of Life: A New Translation of Tao Te Ching,* New American Library, New York, 1983.

Bogle, John C., *Bogle on Mutual Funds: New Perspectives for the Intelligent Investor,* Irwin Professional Publishing, New York, 1994.

Brandes, Charles H., *Value Investing Today,* Dow Jones-Irwin, Homewood, IL, 1989.

Brealey, Richard A., *An Introduction to Risk and Return from Common Stocks,* 2d ed, MIT Press, Cambridge, MA, 1993.

Brealey, Richard A., "Portfolio Theory Versus Portfolio Practice," *The Journal of Portfolio Management,* Summer 1990, pp. 6–10.

Brock, William, Lakonishok, Josef, and LeBaron, Blake, "Simple Technical Trading Rules and the Stochastic Properties of Stock Returns," *The Journal of Finance,* December 1992, pp. 1731–1764.

Brown, John Dennis, *101 Years on Wall Street: An Investor's Almanac,* Prentice Hall, Englewood Cliffs, NJ, 1991.

Brown, Stephen J. and Kritzman, Mark P., CFA, *Quantitative Methods for Financial Analysis*, Dow Jones-Irwin, Homewood, IL, 1987.

Brown, Stephen J., Leonard Stear School of Business, NYU; and Goetzmann, William N., Yale School of Management, "Performance Persistence," *The Journal of Finance*, 1995. First Draft: November 1992, Current Draft: September 30, 1994.

Brush, John S., and Boles, Keith E., "The Predictive Power in Relative Strength and CAPM," *The Journal of Portfolio Management*, Summer 1983, pp. 20–23.

Brush, John S., "Eight Relative Strength Models Compared," *The Journal of Portfolio Management*, Fall 1986, pp. 21–28.

Casti, John L., *COMPLEX-ification, Explaining a Paradoxical World Through the Science of Surprise*, HarperCollins Publishers, New York, 1994.

Chan, Louis K., Hamao, Yasushi, and Lakonishok, Josef, "Fundamentals and Stock Returns in Japan," *The Journal of Finance*, December 1991, pp. 1739–1764.

Chan, Louis K. C., and Lakonishok, Josef, "Are the Reports of Beta's Death Premature?" *The Journal of Portfolio Management*, Summer 1993, pp. 51–62.

Chopra, Navin, Lakonishok, Josef, and Ritter, Jay R., "Measuring Abnormal Performance: Do Stocks Overreact?" *The Journal of Financial Economics*, November 1992, pp. 235–268.

Cottle, Sidney, Murray, Roger F., and Block, Frank E., *Graham and Dodd's Security Analysis*, 5th ed., McGraw-Hill, New York, 1988.

Coulson, Robert D., *The Intelligent Investor's Guide to Profiting from Stock Market Inefficiencies*, Probus Publishing, Chicago, IL, 1987.

Dawes, Robyn M., *House of Cards: Psychology and Psychotherapy Built on Myth*, The Free Press, New York, 1994.

Dewdney, A. K., *200% of Nothing: An Eye-Opening Tour Through the Twists and Turns of Math Abuse and Innumeracy*, John Wiley & Sons, New York, 1993.

Dreman, David N., *Psychology and the Stock Market*, Warner Books, New York, 1977.

Dreman, David N., *The New Contrarian Investment Strategy*, Random House, New York, 1980.

Dreman, David N., "Good-bye EMH," *Forbes Magazine*, June 20, 1994, p. 261.

Dreman, David N., "Nasty Surprises," *Forbes Magazine*, July 19, 1993, p. 246.

Dreman, David N., "Choronically Clouded Crystal Balls," *Forbes Magazine*, October 11, 1993, p. 178.

Dunn, Patricia C., and Theisen, Rolf D., "How Consistently Do Active Managers Win?" *The Journal of Portfolio Management*, Summer 1983, pp. 47–50.

Ellis, Charles D., and Vertin, James R., *Classics: An Investor's Anthology*, Dow Jones-Irwin, Homewood, IL, 1989.

Ellis, Charles D., and Vertin, James R., *Classics II: Another Investor's Anthology*, Dow Jones-Irwin, Homewood, IL, 1991.

Fabozzi, Frank J., Fogler, H. Russell, and Harrington, Diana R., *The New Stock Market, A Complete Guide to the Latest Research, Analysis and Performance*, Probus Publishing, Chicago, IL, 1990.

Fabozzi, Frank J., *Pension Fund Investment Management*, Probus Publishing, Chicago, IL, 1990.

Fabozzi, Frank J., and Zarb, Frank G., *Handbook of Financial Markets: Securities, Options, and Futures*, Dow Jones-Irwin, Homewood, IL, 1986.

Faust, David, *The Limits of Scientific Reasoning*, University of Minnesota Press, Minneapolis, MN, 1984.

Ferguson, Robert, "The Trouble with Performance Measurement," *The Journal of Portfolio Management*, Spring 1986, pp. 4–9.

Ferguson, Robert, "The Plight of the Pension Fund Officer," *Financial Analysts Journal*, May–June 1989, pp. 8–9.

Fisher, Kenneth L., *Super Stocks*, Dow Jones-Irwin, Homewood, IL, 1984.

Fogler, H. Russell, "Common Stock Management in the 1990s," *The Journal of Portfolio Management*, Winter 1990, pp. 26–34.

Freeman, John D., "Behind the Smoke and Mirrors: Gauging the Integrity of Investment Simulations," *Financial Analysts Journal*, November–December 1992, pp. 26–31.

Fridson, Martin S., *Investment Illusions*, John Wiley & Sons, New York, 1993.

Givoly, Dan, and Lakonishok, Josef, "Financial Analysts' Forecasts of Earnings: Their Value to Investors," *The Journal of Banking and Finance*, December 1979, pp. 221–233.

Gleick, James, *Chaos: Making A New Science*, Viking Penguin, New York, 1987.

Guerard, John, and Vaught, H. T., *The Handbook of Financial Modeling*, Probus Publishing, Chicago, IL, 1989.

Hackel, Kenneth S., and Livnat, Joshua, *Cash Flow and Security Analysis*, Business-One Irwin, Homewood, IL, 1992.

Hagin, Bob, "What Practitioners Need to Know About T-Tests," *Financial Analysts Journal*, May–June 1990, pp. 17–20.

Harrington, Diana R., Fabozzi, Frank J., and Fogler, H. Russell, *The New Stock Market*, Probus Publishing, Chicago, IL, 1990.

Haugen, Robert A., and Baker, Nardin L., "Dedicated Stock Portfolios," *The Journal of Portfolio Management*, Summer 1990, pp. 17–22.

Hoff, Benjamin, *The Tao of Pooh*, Penguin Books, New York, 1982.

Ibbotson Associates, *Stocks, Bonds, Bills, and Inflation 1995 Yearbook*, Ibbotson Associates, Chicago, IL, 1995.

Ibbotson, Roger G., and Brinson, Gary P., *Gaining the Performance Advantage: Investment Markets*, McGraw-Hill, New York, 1987.

Ikenberry, David, Lakonishok, Josef, and Vermaelen, Theo, "Market Under Reaction to Open Market Share Repurchases," July 1994, unpublished.

Jacobs, Bruce J., and Levy, Kenneth N., "Disentangling Equity Return Regularities: New Insights and Investment Opportunities," *Financial Analysts Journal*, May–June 1988, pp. 18–38.

Jeffrey, Robert H., "Do Clients Need So Many Portfolio Managers?" *The Journal of Portfolio Management*, Fall 1991, pp. 13–19.

Kahn, Ronald N., "What Practitioners Need to Know About Back Testing," *Financial Analysts Journal*, July–August 1990, pp. 17–20.

Keane, Simon M., "Paradox in the Current Crisis in Efficient Market Theory," *The Journal of Portfolio Management*, Winter 1991, pp. 30–34.

Keppler, A. Michael, "Further Evidence on the Predictability of International Equity Returns," *The Journal of Portfolio Management*, Fall 1991, pp. 48–53.

Keppler, A. Michael, "The Importance of Dividend Yields in Country Selection," *The Journal of Portfolio Management*, Winter 1991, pp. 24–29.

Klein, Robert A., and Lederman, Jess, *Small Cap Stocks: Investment and Portfolio Strategies for the Institutional Investor*, Probus Publishing, Chicago, IL, 1993.

Knowles, Harvey C. III, and Petty, Damon H., *The Dividend Investor*, Probus Publishing, Chicago, IL, 1992.

Kritzman, Mark, "How to Detect Skill in Management Performance," *The Journal of Portfolio Management*, Winter 1986, pp. 16–20.

Kuhn, Thomas S., *The Copernican Revolution: Planetary Astronomy in the Development of Western Thought*, Harvard University Press, Cambridge, MA, 1957.

Kuhn, Thomas S., *The Structure of Scientific Revolutions*, University of Chicago Press, Chicago, IL, 1970.

Lakonishok, Josef, Shleifer, Andrei, and Vishny, Robert W., "Contrarian Investment, Extrapolation, and Risk," Working Paper, June 1994.

Lee, Wayne Y., "Diversification and Time: Do Investment Horizons Matter?" *The Journal of Portfolio Management*, Spring 1990, pp. 21–26.

Lerner, Eugene M., and Theerathorn, Pochara, "The Returns of Different Investment Strategies," *The Journal of Portfolio Management*, Summer 1983, pp. 26–28.

Lofthouse, Stephen, *Equity Investment Mangement: How to Select Stocks and Markets*, John Wiley & Sons, Chichester, England, 1994.

Lorie, James H., Dodd, Peter, and Kimpton, Mary Hamilton, *The Stock Market: Theories and Evidence*, Dow Jones-Irwin, Homewood, IL, 1985.

Lowe, Janet, *Benjamin Graham on Value Investing: Lessons from the Dean of Wall Street*, Dearborn Financial Publishing, Chicago, IL, 1994.

Lowenstein, Louis, *What's Wrong with Wall Street*, Addison-Wesley, New York, 1988.

Maital, Shloml, *Minds, Markets, and Money: Psychological Foundation of Economic Behavior*, Basic Books, New York, 1982.

Malkiel, Burton G., "Returns from Investing in Equity Mutual Funds 1971–1991," Princeton University Press, Princeton, NJ, 1994.

Martin, Linda J., "Uncertain? How Do You Spell Relief?" *The Journal of Portfolio Management*, Spring 1985, pp. 5–8.

Marcus, Alan J., "The Magellan Fund and Market Efficiency," *The Journal of Portfolio Management*, Fall 1990, pp. 85–88.

Mattlin, Everett, "Reliability Math: Manager Selection by the Numbers," *Institutional Investor*, January 1993, pp. 141–142.

Maturi, Richard J., *Stock Picking: The 11 Best Tactics for Beating the Market*, McGraw-Hill, New York, 1993.

McElreath, Robert B., Jr., and Wiggins, C. Donald, "Using the COMPUSTAT Tapes in Financial Research: Problems and Solutions," *Financial Analysts Journal*, January–February 1984, pp. 71–76.

Melnikoff, Meyer, "Anomaly Investing," in *The Financial Analyst's Handbook*, edited by Sumner N. Levine, Dow Jones-Irwin, Homewood, IL, 1988, pp. 699–721.

Murphy, Joseph E., Jr., *Stock Market Probability*, rev. ed., Probus Publishing, Chicago, IL, 1994.

Nisbett, Richard, and Ross, Lee, *Human Inference: Strategies and Shortcomings of Social Judgment,* Prentice-Hall, Englewood Cliffs, NJ, 1980.

O'Barr, William M., and Conley, John M., *Fortune and Folly: The Wealth and Power of Institutional Investing,* Business One-Irwin, Homewood, IL, 1992.

O'Hanlon, John, and Ward, Charles W. R., "How to Lose at Winning Strategies," *The Journal of Portfolio Management,* Spring 1986.

Oppenheimer, Henry R., "A Test of Ben Graham's Stock Selection Criteria," *Financial Analysts Journal,* September–October 1984, pp. 68–74.

O'Shaughnessy, James P., "Quantitative Models as an Aid in Offsetting Systematic Errors in Decision Making," St. Paul, MN, 1988, unpublished.

O'Shaughnessy, James P., *Invest Like the Best: Using Your Computer to Unlock the Secrets of the Top Money Managers,* McGraw-Hill, New York, 1994.

Paulos, John Allen, *Innumeracy: Mathematical Illiteracy and Its Consequences,* Hill and Wang, New York, 1989.

Perritt, Gerald W., *Small Stocks, Big Profit,* Dearborn Financial Publishing, Chicago, IL, 1993.

Perritt, Gerald W., and Lavine, Alan, *Diversify Your Way to Wealth: How to Customize Your Investment Portfolio to Protect and Build Your Net Worth,* Probus Publishing, Chicago, IL, 1994.

Peter, Edgar E., *Chaos and Order in the Capital Markets: A New View of Cycles, Prices, and Market Volatility,* John Wiley & Sons, New York, 1991.

Peters, Donald J., *A Contrarian Strategy for Growth Stock Investing: Theoretical Foundations and Empirical Evidence,* Quorum Books, Westport, CT, 1993.

Pettengill, Glenn N., and Jordan, Bradford D., "The Overreaction Hypothesis, Firm Size, and Stock Market Seasonality," *The Journal of Portfolio Management,* Spring 1990, pp. 60–64.

Reinganum, M., "Misspecification of Capital Asset Pricing: Empirical Anomalies Based on Earnings' Yields and Market Values," *The Journal of Financial Economics,* March 1981, pp. 19–46.

Schwager, Jack D., *Market Wizards: Interviews with Top Traders,* Simon & Schuster, New York, 1992.

Schwager, Jack D., *The New Market Wizards,* Harper-Collins Publishers, New York, 1992.

Sharp, Robert M., *The Lore and Legends of Wall Street,* Dow Jones-Irwin, Homewood, IL, 1989.

Siegel, Jeremy J., *Stocks for the Long Run,* Irwin Professional Publishing, Burr Ridge, IL, 1994.

Siegel, Laurence B., *Stocks, Bonds, Bills, and Inflation 1994 Yearbook,* Ibbotson Associates, Chicago, IL, 1994.

Smullyan, Raymond M., *The Tao Is Silent,* Harper & Row, New York, 1977.

Speidell, Lawrence S., "The New Wave Theory," *Financial Analysts Journal,* July–August 1988, pp. 9–12.

Speidell, Lawrence S., "Embarrassment and Riches: The Discomfort of Alternative Investment Strategies," *The Journal of Portfolio Management,* Fall 1990, pp. 6–11.

Stumpp, Mark, and Scott, James, "Does Liquidity Predict Stock Returns?" *The Journal of Portfolio Management,* Winter 1991, pp. 35–40.

Thomas, Dana L., *The Plungers and the Peacocks: An Update of the Classic History of the Stock Market,* William Morrow, New York, 1989.

Tierney, David E., and Winston, Kenneth, "Using Generic Benchmarks to Present Manager Styles," *The Journal of Portfolio Management,* Summer 1991, pp. 33–36.

Train, John, *The Money Masters,* Harper & Row, New York, 1985.

Train, John, *Famous Financial Fiascos,* Clarkson N. Potter, New York, 1985.

Train, John, *The New Money Masters: Winning Investment Strategies of: Soros, Lynch, Steinhardt, Rogers, Neff, Wanger, Michaelis, Carret,* Harper & Row, New York, 1989.

Treynor, Jack L., "Information-Based Investing," *Financial Analysts Journal,* May–June 1989, pp. 6–7.

Treynor, Jack L., "The 10 Most Important Questions to Ask in Selecting a Money Manager," *Financial Analysts Journal,* May–June 1990, pp. 4–5.

Trippe, Robert R., and Lee, Jae K., *State-of-the-Art Portfolio Selection: Using Knowledge-Based Systems to Enhance Investment Performance,* Probus Publishing, Chicago, IL, 1992.

Tsetsekos, George P., and DeFusco, Richard, "Portfolio Performance, Managerial Ownership, and the Size Effect," *The Journal of Portfolio Management,* Spring 1990, pp. 33–39.

Twark, Allan, and D'Mello, James P., "Model Indexation: A Portfolio Management Tool," *The Journal of Portfolio Management,* Summer 1991, pp. 37–40.

Valentine, Jerome L., CFA, "Investment Analysis and Capital Market Theory," *The Financial Analysts,* Occasional Paper Number 1, 1975.

Valentine, Jerome L., CFA, and Mennis, Edmund A., CFA, *Quantitative Techniques for Financial Analysis,* Richard D. Irwin, Homewood, IL, 1980.

Vandell, Robert F., and Parrino, Robert, "A Purposeful Stride Down Wall Street," *The Journal of Portfolio Management,* Winter 1986, pp. 31–39.

Vince, Ralph, *The Mathematics of Money Management,* John Wiley & Sons, New York, 1992.

Vishny, Robert W., Shleifer, Andrei, and Lakonishok, Josef, "The Structure and Performance of the Money Management Industry," in the *Brookings Papers on Economic Activity, Microeconomics 1992.*

Watzlawick, Paul, *How Real Is Real? Confusion, Disinformation, Communication,* Vintage Books, New York, 1977.

Williams, John Burr, Ph.D., "Fifty Years of Investment Analysis," *The Financial Analysts Research Foundation,* 1979.

Wood, Arnold S., "Fatal Attractions for Money Managers," *Financial Analysts Journal,* May–June 1989, pp. 3–5.

Zeikel, Arthur, "Investment Management in the 1990s," *Financial Analysts Journal,* September–October 1990, pp. 6–9.

Index

Note: Page numbers followed by F indicate figures; those followed by T indicate tables.

About the Author

James P. O'Shaughnessy is founder and president of O'Shaughnessy Capital Management, Inc., a Greenwich, Connecticut, investment advisory firm and is recognized as a leading expert and pioneer in quantitative equity analysis. *Barron's* calls him a "statistical guru," and *Higher Returns* said he is "one of the most original market thinkers we've come across." *Forbes* pronounced his previous book *Invest Like the Best* "awesome" and named it one of the best financial books of the year. *Stock Trader's Almanac* called *Invest Like the Best* the "Best Investment Book of 1994." O'Shaughnessy's investment strategies have been featured in *The New York Times*, the *Financial Times*, *Barron's*, *Forbes*, *Smart Money*, *Worth*, and *Money*, as well as on CNN, Wall Street Journal TV, CNBC, New York One, PBS's "Nightly Business Report's Morning Monitor," "Inside Money," and "Financial Freedom." He lives in Greenwich, Connecticut, with his wife and three children.